Saram

The Adventures
of a soul
&
Insight into the
Male Psyche

Saram

The Adventures of a Soul

&
Insight into the
Male Psyche

Robert Elias Najemy

Holistic Harmony Publishers
PO Box 93 Markopoulo
Greece, 19003
www.HolisticHarmony.com
armoniki@holisticharmony.com

Cover image - mandala -Louitgart Huntra

Cover Layout - Litsa Cheirouveim

isbn 0-9710116-7-2

DEDICATION

This book is dedicated to all
the personas in all of us.

May you be united
so that we may all become whole.

TABLE OF CONTENTS

CHAPTER   PAGE

INTRODUCTION

I hope that this book will, in an entertaining way, give each reader insight into the functionings of his own mind, and will help him in the process of inner reconciliation allowing him or her to become one.

Each of us has parts of our personalities which we need to meet, understand, accept and reconcile.

In response to early childhood experiences, we develop various inner emotional responses in an effort to maintain a feeling of security, self worth, personal freedom and self-expression. These responses grow in their own separate ways, manifesting as **parts** of our personality that have their own personal beliefs, logic and identity. We can call these roles *personas* or *subpersonalities*.

Each persona has its own core belief which creates and sustains its existence in our larger identity. This core belief will have something to do with the need for security, pleasure, affirmation or freedom, or in a few special cases, other less common needs such as the need to be useful, or for salvation or enlightenment. In some cases, the basic needs may be distorted and in conflict with survival or growth, such as the need to harm ourselves or others.

We are often not aware of the dynamics of these subpersonalities which develop gradually within us as we seek to cope simultaneously with a world full of insecurities and our own differing needs.

The wide variety of our needs, from the basic needs to survive and have safety, to the needs for love, growth and expression, cause different parts of ourselves to sometimes come into conflict concerning what to do in certain situations, how to spend our time or how to live our lives.

The subject of how these personalities develop and sometimes conflict is covered in chapters 24 and 25.

I believe, however, that it will be useful here to reprint the same list of possible conflicts that you will find again in chapter 24, so that you can have in mind the types of conflicts we are talking about, because surely you will have at least one, if not many of them.

SOME SAMPLE CONFLICTS

Let us look at some examples of the inner conflicts which may disturb our peace.

1. One part of ourselves may feel the need to spend more time in our **professional life,** while another part may believe that we should be spending more time with our **family**.

2. On the one hand, a part of our selves may want to open up to a **conscious love** relationship, while another part **fears** being abandoned or hurt, suppressed, manipulated, or not being able to say no.

3. One part of ourselves may want to give those around us (children, spouse, friends) total **freedom** to pursue their happiness in their own ways, and another part may **fear losing control.**

4. The part of ourselves which wants to **please others**, may come into direct conflict with our **own needs**.

5. We may on the one hand, want **others to support us,** but on the other feel that they **restrict us** with their support or advice.

6. One part of our selves may **want spiritual growth**, while another may feel the need for **material security**.

7. We may on the one hand want to **help** a loved one or friend, but on the other, feel that perhaps we are doing them harm by bailing them out continuously and not letting them **solve their own problems.**

8. One part of our selves may feel a need to **protect the planet** through a simple life with very little consumption of energy and products, while another part may want to enjoy all the **comforts** of an energy consuming, pollution-producing life style.

9. We may on the one hand want to take or leave a **job** that we have, while another part of our selves wants the **opposite** for different reasons.

10. One part of ourselves may believe in **cooperating** with others, while another finds it **difficult** or unnecessary.

11. We may have a desire for various objects or situations as a source of **pleasure**. Another part of ourselves may feel, however, that this is a **sin**, or that we are **not spiritual** if we partake in such pleasures. Or it may feel that this type of pleasure seeking is a **waste of time** and **energy** considering our spiritual goals. Thus these two aspects of our own being conflict.

12. One part of ourselves may feel the need to have an **exclusive relationship**, in which our happiness and security depend on another person (usually a mate). Another part of ourselves may find this an obstacle towards its (our) need for **independence**, self-dependence, and freedom.

13. Similarly there may be a conflict between the need for **personal love** and the need to develop **universal love**.

14. The need to **forgive** may conflict with the need to hold on to **negative feelings** towards someone.

15. The need to employ various **disciplines** may conflict with the need to feel **free** to do what we want when we want to.

16. The need to **follow** our **inner voice** in some cases conflicts with the need to be **like the others** and be **accepted** by them.

17. The need to **express our feelings** as they are can conflict with our need **not to hurt anyone**.

18. The need to **express our real feelings** and thoughts might clash with our need to have the **acceptance** of those around us.

19. The need to **follow a spiritual guide** might conflict with the need to **rebel** against all types of advice or control.

20. The **need to control persons** and situations in order to feel secure and the need to **let things flow** and allow others to act freely.

21. Our need to **never show weakness** can come into conflict with our need to **share our weaknesses** with others.

22. One part may need **not to ask anything** from others while another may need to have their **help** and **support**.

23. A part of us might need a **stable routine** for our balance and growth while another might need **variety** and **change**.

24. A part of us needs to **play our familiar emotional relationship games** while another part wants to **get free** from them.

25. One part of us wants to **face and overcome our fears** and blockages while another prefers to **avoid** them and **hide** from them.

There are certainly conflicts which we haven't mentioned, but most will fall into these categories.

At the end of the book you will find two chapters concerning how we can discover, analyze and reconcile our personas or subpersonalities. Some readers may want to first read those chapters and then the story. In this way they would have a deeper psychological understanding of how the hero's subconscious is developing.

Other readers may prefer to read those chapters after reading the story.

May you be well.
(All of you)

THE MOST PAINFUL MOMENT IN HIS LIFE

THE CIRCLE OF JUDGMENT

Ran's heart was pounding. He was in pain. He had never felt worse in his life. He sat humbled and shamed before the thirty people he loved most. He knew these faces so well. He had counseled them innumerable times. Until now, they had respected and loved him. Until now, they had been so grateful for all that he offered them.

He had, in a few short hours, been transformed in their minds from their beloved friend, guide and teacher to their disgraced, betraying, two-faced enemy. Their faces now displayed none of that love or gratitude. They showed a wide variety of emotions ranging from pain and confusion to hate, but also including betrayal, despite, hurt and perhaps relief that he was not perfect.

No, he was not perfect. He never said he was. They wanted him to be. He tried to be so for them and for himself. He believed that being perfect was a prerequisite to being loved and accepted.

He wished he could turn the clock back just one day and change what had happened. He had done what he had taught that one should ever do. He had created a double relationship. He loved two women simultaneously. Although married, he was seeing another woman. He had not yet consummated the act of love with her, but their erotic play amounted to the same.

Now he sat before his wife and closest friends – many of whom who considered him their teacher – as they waited for some explanation as to how he had done this, how he had failed to live up to his own values and teachings.

He began to read to them his apology written an hour earlier. He was afraid perhaps that, in the waves of emotion, he would forget something he wanted to say. One-line phrases rushed through his mind, incongruent and often not clearly connected.

THE CONFESSION

"My head is spinning.
"So many feelings flood my mind simultaneously.
"I feel hurt and misunderstood.
"I feel sad and guilty towards all those whom I have caused to become disillusioned with the spiritual path.
"I feel weak and helpless against the forces of my subconscious mind.
"I feel horrible for the pain I have created for my wife Issabella, and for so many others.
"Yet, I feel love for all who come to my mind. I feel love as my broken heart opens.
"At last, I am humbled. Finally, (today) comes my release from the role of the teacher, and my need to be perfect, not for myself but for others.
"It was as if a part of me had gone crazy, and proceeded towards total destruction of all that I had created.
"It is as if I had decided to destroy it all, as if God has planned this moment..."

HOW DID THIS HAPPEN?

It was now time for him to leave everything that he loved so much. Everything he had spent 18 years creating.

How did Ran end up this way after so many years of effort? How could he make such a catastrophic mistake? What were these contradictory and conflicting forces working within him? How had he become so spilt within himself – two persons living in one body?

The answer lies in the fact that Ran is not one person, but rather a composite of many "personas" living in the same body. Each persona or sub-personality has developed throughout the thousands of years as his character evolved from one life to another.

In the process of evolution, we develop various roles or personas which gradually begin to separate themselves from our control and develop along their own lines. These personas separated themselves from Ran's central identity, functioning through separate, and often conflicting roles such as the child, the parent, the teacher, the victim, the unworthy one, etc. We might liken this to our believing ourselves to be separate from God and developing various characteristics which are foreign to, and temporarily independent of, their central Divine Self. Disconnected from our central nature, we are conflict with ourself. These same conflicts were occurring within Ran, as his subpersonalities had different needs, values and beliefs and were struggling for control or his time, energy and lifestyle.

Each persona, at some point in our character's evolution, seeks to separate itself from the central soul Self, becoming egocentric in an attempt to satisfy its own needs, regardless of the needs of the other personas or the spirit-centric Self.

A prerequisite to wholeness is to discover these personas and unite them, enabling them to live in harmony rather than in conflict with each other and with the soul. This is the purpose of spiritual life.

Externally, mankind's further evolution would manifest as the process of unifying all men and women as they became united under their one collective spiritual Self, God. This unification process eventually would encompass all beings, including animals, plants and insects as well as the elements of nature.

Our life purpose is to move towards unification. First, however, we pass through the awareness of separateness, of our separate identity(-ies), before we evolve to the conscious choice of unity through acceptance and love. This unification process is obviously a necessary on an external level, and must now be equally applied to our internal conflicts between personas.

RAN'S EVOLUTION

Let us follow then the evolution of Saram's (Ran's soul's name) personas throughout his lifetimes on planet Earth culminating in his incarnation as Ran on the planet Alithea, a dimension of the universe in which the personas and their inner dialogues become even more distinct.

Let us begin.

CHAPTER ONE

SARAM'S
PREVIOUS INCARNATIONS

IASOS THE FARMER

Saram watched as his parents-to-be made love. As they reached orgasm, he singled out, from his father's immeasurable selection, the particular sperm cell which offered the specific chromosomes needed to produce the body he had designed for this incarnation.

This time the body would be a rugged male body, designed for farming. A strong durable body free from weakness or illness. This body would work the hard unyielding soil on the Greek Island of Santorini.

Saram watched as the sperm cell penetrated the recently released ovum. After verifying that the operation was successful, he disengaged his awareness from the Earth plane.

During those nine months, he occasionally «peeped in» to see how the embryo was doing. He witnessed millions of years of evolution of nature take place before his eyes, as this cell multiplied, developed into a fish, reptile and eventually into mammal and a human being.

He thought, «How much we have evolved from those days of one celled beings and lower life forms. Now what took billions of years takes only nine months.»

He was not at all anxious to be once again limited in a physical body, but he knew he had no choice. Evolution had to go on. He also knew that the moment he got into that body, he would forget his previous reality and live in total ignorance of his greater being. This forgetting was most painful.

Once he forgot, everything would become meaningless, fearsome, dangerous and unjust. However, there was nothing he could do. The laws of nature and evolution were greater than he.

Iasos was his personality's name. He matured into a no-nonsense man. He had no need for a wife, nor for children. He lived with the earth. He learned self-dependency. He developed a one sided, antisocial character. Had few words for anyone. Work was his life. He worked from daybreak to sunset, ate and then slept. This was his life.

He criticized those who sat and philosophized, who built imaginary realities, or who lived in theories and words. These seemed a waste of time to him. He was a practical man; an efficient man. A man who created results from hard work. He rejected those who did not work as hard as he. It was in this incarnation that the *Efficient Worker* persona was born in him.

He did, however, occasionally communicate with his brother (his parents died when he was twelve). One day his brother managed to persuade him to take a walk up to the crater. They sat there in silence, watching smoke bellow up from under the earth, sensing the power which lay under the surface where they were perched.

They were in awe. It was the only moment in his life in which he realized that there was something else except work.

He had never thought about where he came from or what might be the purpose of his existence. Now these thoughts came to a slow simmer in his mind. They were not so much clear-cut thoughts about what is life, or "who am I". It was more like a cloud of confusion which developed as his belief system began to evaporate, without his knowing why and without it being replaced by any concrete thoughts. He experienced wonder for the first time. He wondered at what he saw and felt.

However, there was no time for further development. The mountain began to shake slowly at first and then with rapidly increasing, undulating waves. He and his brother were thrown into the volcano. His last thought as he was falling was, "I should never have stopped working".

Saram left his body while still falling. He watched his body fall into the volcano and disappear. At first he tried to race after it and save it. But in his new subtle body he had no control over matter. He hovered over the crater which was overflowing with volcanic ash. He watched on as hundreds died in the ensuing flow. He had no emotions.

He slowly began to remember his true identity. He was dazed and confused. His thought forms still had a powerful hold over him. His mind was the same even though he no longer had a physical body.

Since, however, he had no body to work with, he was in a state of limbo. He knew not what to do. A Being of Light appeared beside him. Saram hardly noticed his presence, as he had hardly noticed anyone's presence throughout his life.

The Being of Light spoke gently and assuredly, "Saram you are dead now, your body has died. It is time for you to move on. Come, let me guide you"

"My name is Iasos", he answered, "why do you call me Saram? Who are you?"

The Being had now become light without form, "I am your guardian angel. I am assigned to help you, to protect you and to guide you. "

Saram began to awaken to the truth. As he did so, his mind was flooded with images of his life just lived. He saw himself objectively, saw his mistakes, his strengths; realized that he still had much to learn.

He then became aware of his previous existences and all that he had done and learned in them. He followed the light now as *Saram*, of which "Iasos" was now only a small part.

KARAN THE ESSENE COOK

In his next incarnation, Saram was "Karan," once again male – a cook in an Essene community. There he learned to combine food essences for taste, health and spiritual awakening. He enjoyed working in the kitchen. He preferred this to working hard in the fields, or being in a position of responsibility for the others.

While cutting vegetables or sweeping the floor, he would experience the joy of creating, of offering, of serving his brothers, or serving the God in his brothers. He often chanted while working, or silently spoke with God, offering up his work, his life, and his self. Life was simple. As in his previous incarnation as Iasos, he was not a philosophical type. Nor was he very sociable. He liked to work. He enjoyed serving others. His communicated with others through the food he offered them. His food was his expression of love. In this incarnation the *Cooperating Server* persona and the *Holy Pure Monk* persona were developing as Karan found meaning and joy in serving and seeking God through prayer and a simple life.

No one paid much attention to him and he preferred it this way. He liked being the invisible servant. He enjoyed the unity which he felt when cooperating with the other brothers. He held the ants and bees as examples to be followed. This was the extent of his philosophical wanderings. As he often shared with others, "if we could only be as cooperative and as selfless as the bees and ants, who work incessantly for the good of whole, we could create paradise on earth."

He died a peaceful death, with a few brothers at his bedside. They chanted as he departed. He slipped out of his body unnoticed. They continued chanting for another hour. He remained in his spiritual body and listened to them for some time and then ascended on their melodies into the spiritual realms.

His simplicity and peaceful state of mind allowed him to recognize the Being of Light immediately. He readily examined his life and continued with his evolution.

Saram

SHALA THE EROTIC DANCER

Saram's next incarnation was as Shala who was a full-grown woman at the time of Christ's march into Jerusalem. Shala was a dancer, a woman of questionable repute. She loved lifting others' spirits through her often erotically expressive dancing. She danced without thinking. She never bothered with technique, but depended on her inner instinct and inspiration. She would become lost in the ecstasy of movement, becoming one with the music. She had developed into an organ for the transmutation of music into form.

Her endless variety of flowing motions and gestures made the music visible to the audience. This form permeated their minds, loosening them, relaxing them, helping them release their tensions and experience joy, even if only for a short period of time. This was her offering; her way of helping. In this incarnation, the *Erotic Dancer* persona became a member of Saram's persona complex.

Many, especially the other women, condemned her as unethical, and it was true that she would make love to men when she felt close to them. She didn't seem to be obstructed when, in some cases, the men were married. If she perceived them as unhappy, and felt a connection with them, she would make love to them. She never took money for this. She saw it as her service to those who were unhappy or lonely.

When Christ arrived in Jerusalem, she decided to go and see this miracle man they were all talking about. She fell in love with Him immediately, not with His body, but with His gentleness, His freedom, His love for all, His ability to help others, and most of all for His teachings.

A simple person, who could never understand the complicated teachings of the priests of the time, and who rejected their pompousness and hypocrisy, she was swept away by Jesus' simple teachings. She loved Him for teaching love. She loved Him for putting this above all other laws.

She loved Him for not condemning anyone (except for hypocrites).

She loved Him for his selflessness. She loved Him for His fearlessness and His strength in facing powers apparently so much greater than He. She loved Him most for his ability to forgive in every case – even those who persecuted Him.

She cried deeply at His crucifixion. When her tears paused for a moment, she avowed to serve Him. To serve Him by loving and serving others, by forgiving others, by gradually becoming like Him. She vowed that she would never condemn others as she had been condemned and as He had been condemned. She would always return hate with love. She would be strong and serve others selflessly.

She was eventually able to manifest this promise, to a modest degree, during the last few years of her life. She approached His disciples, confessed and asked for forgiveness. She gave up her previous way of life and lived in one of the first Christian communities.

Those living in these communities came together and under the apostles' guidance, sold their fortunes and possessions and lived a humble communal life together, trying to put into practice Jesus' commandment to them to love, share and serve each other as He loved them.

Shala spent the rest of her years cooking for the community, a skill which she had abhorred until now, but which strangely came very easily to her.

She felt the need to dance occasionally but would do so by herself, imagining that she was dancing for Him. At the moment of death, this was the image she held as she left her body – dancing with Him.

As Saram disengaged from Shala's personality, he realized his larger self again, and passed through his examinations, realizing the weaknesses and strengths manifested in that incarnation. He had some guilt about her sexual promiscuity, but was left with no choice but to accept it as a learning experience.

BABU THE PRANKSTER INDIAN MONK

Saram was now called "Babu" – an elderly ascetic wandering the villages of India. He had renounced the pleasures of life. He never touched a woman in that life. He walked from village to village sleeping anywhere. The earth was his bed and the sky his roof and all humanity his family. His only belongings were a bowl to eat and drink from, and a cloth which he used alternatively as a shawl, a bed sheet, cover, towel and head cover.

He never spent more than three days in any village at one time. He would, however, occasionally return to that village later. His hours were spent mostly in meditation while sitting in nature, by a river if one was available.

A few hours a day would be dedicated to answering the villagers' questions and listening to their problems. He would seldom answer them in a straightforward manner, but would ask them questions. Their search for the answer to his questions would help them discover the answers that were within them. He was often vague and left them without answers. He was also a prankster who enjoyed joking with them and even fooling them. He would occasionally leave them with false impressions and confusion.

He sometimes felt guilty about his joking with them in this way, but the prankster in him was uncontrollable at times. He realized that he was creating karma (he believed in reincarnation in this life), and that one day he would be paid back in some way, perhaps by future students. But this was his only source of recreation, his only game.

He was like a little child with an insatiable appetite for play. Nothing was sacred for him. Realizing that all were expressions of the one universal life consciousness, he laughed at the social norms and games created by importance given to position, social customs and even to religious ceremonies. In spite of his childish pranks, and frequent blunt lack of respect for social laws and customs, he was loved by most, but not all, who came into contact with him.

His last years were spent alone in a cave struggling with his mind, as he attempted to break through the veil of ignorance, which still covered his mental body. He made progress, but the mind was still heavily weighted down by attachment and unlearned lessons. He was never actually totally satisfied with the degree of detachment and freedom he had achieved. He had declared war on his thoughts and this obstructed his ability to perceive the Divine there, in his own thoughts.

He saw the Divine everywhere except in his own mind. He perceived his thoughts as something against the Divine, against the truth. It was at this point in his evolutionary process that the personas called the *Disciplined Meditator* and *Seeker of Enlightenment* became an integral part of his developing character.

He relaxed only a few days before leaving his body. He accepted his defeat. A defeat which 99% of other earthlings would have considered a major victory over the senses and mind. But Babu was beset by spiritual greed and impatience for enlightenment. He overcame all desires except the desire for enlightenment itself.

As he left his body he realized this, but it was too late.

RUPERT THE IMPRISONED GERMAN GENERAL

Rupert (the shining one) was Saram's next life of lessons. As a male German body in the middle ages, he became a general. A man who fought for what he believed. He had very strong beliefs about what was right and was ready to protect "rightness" by fighting for it.

One day, however, while passing a tent in which his soldiers were sitting, he overheard them talking about the next day's offensive.

"We will easily sack this town and after we do we will ransack their homes and take whatever we want."

"Keep away from that tower clock, it is mine."
"Who cares about a silly clock, all I want is to make love to a few of those young women. You know what they say about how lively their

women are, especially the peasants."

Rupert was shocked, "Is this why they are fighting? They haven't understood anything. They are not fighting for principles. They are murderers!"

He felt unbearable disappointment, as he was suddenly assaulted by a stream of realizations that the whole war itself was based on selfish motives and not on the principles which he thought he was fighting for. He did not go in. He was in total confusion as his whole belief system was in an uproar. His whole sense of values was turned upside down in a few minutes. He was totally confused. Such a rapid change of perception seldom occurred in the evolutionary process.

He walked out into the forest. He could fight no longer. Yet neither was it possible to explain his realizations to anyone else. He was deeply confused and could think of no solutions and thus just continued walking for about thirty straight hours.

Tired and hungry he knocked on the door of an isolated house. A woman in her thirties answered. Karen, a war widow, was alone and afraid. She hesitated to open the door, but seeing how exhausted and apparently depressed he was, she eventually let him in.

He ate and fell asleep in the same chair. She felt compassion and covered him, but did not feel safe enough to sleep. She sat up all night long watching him. Her fear however gradually dissipated as compassion and interest grew from within.

The next day he offered to help her with the house which was in shambles. She accepted. They began to come closer. After a few days they made love. He stayed for about two weeks, but something was eating him. He was not at peace with himself. He did not know what to do. He had no purpose. Until now, he had always had a purpose. He had learned to live for a purpose, to fight for a purpose and, as much as he found this woman to his liking, she was not a purpose for him.

He had a responsibility complex. He felt responsible for the world, as if there was no God to take care of it. He had to make the world right. If he could not, he was a failure.

He wandered, a lost man. He was totally disappointed with people and with life. No one understood him. He felt painfully alone, that no one understood what was important in life.

A few months after the end of the war, one of his officers recognized him and reported him to the authorities. He was arrested, accused of desertion and thrown into a damp, dirty prison cell with only a sliver of light coming through a tiny slit high up on the wall.

He spent the rest of his years in this prison cell. Although, on the one hand, he understood how they perceived him and their obvious condemnation of his desertion, on the other, he also felt injustice, loneliness, betrayal by God, and totally misunderstood by man, as he was unable to convey to them the deeper truths which had caused him to see through the false justifications for war. He felt disappointed in himself for having failed to inspire others. His disappointment in life and in others was overwhelming. He became claustrophobic and obsessed with the idea of freedom.

He never allowed himself to cry. He hid his pain. It was at this point that some other personas were developed. For example, the *Unemotional Stoic* who wanted to appear to be able to cope with anything. Inside, however, he was crying, screaming with the pain of loneliness and feelings of injustice. The *Anxious Worrier* learned to fear and expect the worse. The *Sacrificing Hero* felt that, although he had deserted the war, he had sacrificed his freedom and life for a higher cause. The *Unjustly Persecuted* learned to expect injustice and persecution. The *Righteous Rebel* became obsessed with freedom and the fight for higher ideals. The *Poor Unloved Child* felt that no one understood him, that no one loved him. He felt very lonely.

Something which he never learned was that he had left Karen, the woman in that house, pregnant. She brought up his child without ever seeing its father again.

Upon death, he left his body, and immediately passed through the prison walls thirsty for light and freedom. Having no other emotional connections, this woman came to his mind. He traveled to her in his spiritual body and immediately understood what had happened. He vowed to meet her again to be with that child which he never saw.

He looked at his life, and saw his obsession with being right, his disappointment with himself and others, his fear of restriction, his overly zealous sense of responsibility for all and everyone and hia mania for freedom and realized that these would need to be worked on in the future.

HANS THE DISAPPOINTED GERMAN DOCTOR

Saram returned to Germany in his next incarnation now as doctor Hans. Hans shared Rupert's sense of responsibility for others, but now he would save others through medicine. He was actually a continuation of Rupert. The strong Stoic dedicated type, beyond feelings and needs. He was married to his work more than to his wife.

He became a capable and dedicated doctor. He fought illnesses with the same enthusiasm and dedication. But Hans too fought a losing battle. After about ten years of trying to solve people's health problems, he was forced to realize that if the ill themselves do not take responsibility for their health, he could do nothing.

One part of him believed in science and its power to find solutions to heal all illnesses. On the other hand, he noticed that new illnesses kept cropping up and also that if people didn't change the way they thought and lived, their therapy would fail or be only short lived.

He shared Rupert's disappointment, both in himself as a doctor and in his fellow beings who were so short-sighted and sought superficial, effortless solutions for health problems they themselves were creating through their ways of living and thinking.
He tried to help them see that they must take responsibility for their

health, but, as he himself was not entirely free from the "thoughtform" that he the doctor was responsible for their health, he failed to convince any significant number of them. He too, felt deeply responsible for others and often became angry at them, when they would not cooperate.

His relationship with his wife was negligible. She was there to have his food ready and clean clothes so that he could return to work. In the evenings, he would write his thoughts, which he hoped to someday publish. His life continued in this way, until he himself eventually contracted a contagious illness from one of his patients and died at the age of forty.

Upon leaving his body, Saram perceived Hans's lack of contact with his wife. In general his relationship with the opposite sex would have to be worked out in some future life. He noticed again his pattern of an overwhelming feeling of responsibility for others and his nagging feeling of disappointment both in himself, as a doctor, and in others who did not understand. The persona called the *Disappointed One* was further developed in this life.

FRANZ - A MONK IN CONFLICT WITH HIMSELF

His next incarnation was as a monk in a European monastery. This felt familiar to him. Here he found the community life which he had loved as Karan with the *Essences*, and as "Shala" in the first Christian communities. Familiar also were the principles of detachment from material objects and pleasures of the flesh which he knew from his life as Babu in India. He was, however, not happy. Franz was a man in conflict with himself.

One part of him loved Christ deeply and wanted to be devoted to Him only. He enjoyed the hours of prayer and even more the moments of contemplation on His teachings. He loved to search for deeper and deeper meanings in Christ's parables and examples. He wrote them down carefully and enumerated them. He could discover as many as thirty interpretations for one parable. His mind developed extensively in this way.
He enjoyed chanting and felt his heart open as experienced a

pulsing heat in the center of his chest when he completed his chants. He would then imagine that Christ had come into his chest, and would enjoy this divine rapture.

On the other hand, his mind was ravaged by thoughts of lust. It had been so many incarnations since he had worked on the sexual aspect of his being, that he had made the woman into this mysterious powerful goddess. He gave her much power. He was afraid of her rejection and yet obsessed with the pleasures of uniting with her. These pleasures had not to do with her body only, but also with the feeling of being in contact with the mother, being breast-fed, and being loved. He desired to become lost in the feminine, the flow, the heart which would help balance his sterile mental existence.

One would have expected that one aspect would diminish the other. This, however, was not true. His desire for a woman and love for God coexisted, side by side, simply occupying his mind and heart at other hours. He was not bothered by thoughts of being with a woman when he was praying or contemplating. Neither was he obstructed from his erotic longing by his spiritual contemplations of the previous hour.

Nothing else was missing from his life. He cared not for money, nor for fame, nor for luxuries nor travel. His only unfulfilled need was to be embraced and to be lost in that embrace.

These two parts seldom but occasionally met, when strangely he felt himself as a woman who was opening herself up to be penetrated by God, to be taken by Him whom she loved. He imagined that he surrendered himself physically, emotionally and spiritually to God, his loved one, his everything.

Of course, his case was by no means the exception; it was the norm for that monastery and for most monasteries of the time and of all times. Monasteries have been the theater for this battle between these two aspects of man, ever since their creation.

In his last years, he realized that this sexual part of himself would some day need to be faced, to be integrated. It could not be ignored, nor conquered by force. He would have to accept it, work with it, play with it, become one with it and transcend it. But it was too late.

He passed away, while on a walk in nature. His brother monks found him and prayed for his salvation.

PHANTOM HEALER - THE INDIAN MEDICINE MAN

Saram's next incarnation was in the New World. Phantom Healer was his American Indian name. He was the Medicine Man of the area. We use the word area rather than tribe, because he refused to be limited to any particular tribal group. He lived by the river; in a small hut alone most of his adult years, with the exception of about three months which he shared with a woman named Autumn Leaf.

Nature was his source of power and guidance. He learned from all beings in the forest. But his greatest teacher was the river on whose banks he resided. This river was a live being for him. They talked. They loved and fought just like any couple. He was, however, usually submissive and humble before this great teacher.

He learned the power which lay in the flow of submission, in the feminine power. In this life Saram was coming into contact with the feminine through it's most powerful manifestation, Nature. It was easier for him in this way. He would get lost in Her embrace without facing the often confusing issues created by sex and personality.

This relationship between man and nature was as erotic as any human relationship. He became ever more absorbed in his rapture with the elements and beings of nature. It was as if he were surrounded by one being with many forms. He saw this one being in its myriad forms and spoke to it through all of them. It was at this time that the *Fascinated Wonderer* persona became a full-fledged member of his persona complex.

He had become well known to the animals of the area. Wolves, bears, squirrels, chipmunks, even the fish in the river came to visit and play with him, to receive his attention and love.

He went into the villages only when asked. There he would administer herbs, roots, barks and leaves which he collected and had learned to prepare.

His real power, however, was in distracting the person from the psychology of his illness. He saw the One Great Spirit in that ill person, who was for him a being of nature, for he could not separate man from nature. Man was to him like all the other beings – a manifestation of the One.

He would chant syllables which only he understood, whose intent was to awaken the inner healing power in that individual. He would call forth the One Universal Power, the Only Healing Power in the universe from the depths of that being. He knew that health was hidden within each being, that the essence of nature was that individual's real being, and that health was his natural state. He called forth in powerful and sometimes frightening-to-the-ill-person incantations.

One who knew not what he chanted, might imagine that he was threatening or driving out the evil spirits which had entered this ill person. But Phantom Healer believed not in evil spirits. For him there was only one Universal being who was in all and everything. There was no space in his universe for evil beings. He understood that people lived in a way which buried their power, and caused them to lose their connection with their all-powerful center. When this happened, they became confused and ill.

His chants called that center up to the surface so that it might heal. He focused on calling forth the forces of Goodness and Harmony rather than focusing on some – non-existent for him anyway – evil powers.

He was, as were most of his ancestors in Saram's list of previous incarnations, what one might call "antisocial." He would enter the village, pay his respects to the chief, ask how he might be of use, go on to do his work, give a few suggestions to the ill and their families, and return back to his power base, to where he felt comfortable – at home, with his river.

One late afternoon he was called to attend to Autumn Leaf who was ill, not so much physically but of emotional pain and disappointment. She had lost all interest in life. She was emotionally devastated, having lost her husband to a rattlesnake. Since then she had been feeling dizzy, losing awareness, fainting and having nightmares.

Phantom Healer was struck by her beauty and touched by her suffering, something he seldom allowed himself to feel. He felt her pain and wanted to help. At the same time was enamored by her beauty. Thirdly, he was challenged by her case. He wanted her to be well.

As her symptoms did not subside after a few months, he suggested that she come and live with him, so that he could attend to her on a more intensive basis. He was becoming attached to her and enjoyed being with her. She would forget her suffering when near him, but when he was gone, she would again move into her depression and dizziness.

He became ever more infatuated with her. He began to show her affection. This led to erotic play. This play was liberating and healing for both of them.

After about sixty days, Autumn Leaf was feeling much better. As she opened to life again, it became apparent that here needs differend from his. Her destiny was not to live in this hut next to this river. Neither of them wanted to see this at first. They had become quite attached.

The idea of separating was unbearable for both of them. And as usual when two people are together but their destiny is elsewhere, they began to find unconscious reasons to argue and conflict, so that supposedly they separated because they did not match together. The truth was simply that they had separate destinies.
He continued alone in Nature. He was relieved because he was now

free from his inner conflicts concerning how he should live. These inner conflicts had become outer ones. Now he was at peace again. He died alone, unless you consider some of the animals who were present at his departure.

SARAM'S DILEMMA AND SOLUTION

As Saram detached himself from Phantom Healer and remembered all his previous incarnations, only a few of which have been related here, he realized that he wasn't making much progress with his incarnations on the Earth. His problem was that he was unable to compromise in a harmonious way the various personas, or subpersonalities, which had developed throughout his various incarnational experiences.

He had developed two camps of personas, the materially, sensually-oriented group and the evolutionary, spiritually, service-oriented group. He had a highly developed spiritual self, without having dealt with some of the basic material lessons such as his sensual nature. He had tried to ignore or suppress this aspect of his being in a succession of lifetimes. He was at a stalemate – neither group was willing to give in.

PREPARING FOR INCARNATION ON ALITHEA

He was counseled by a Being of Light to try an incarnation on the planet *Alithea*, in hope of uniting this array of personalities in some way. Alithea is an exact replica of the planet Earth in *Virtual Reality*. It is as material and real as the Earth but in another dimension. Everything is the same there. The same laws of nature, the same continents, same countries and languages, races and religions.

Although other names are used there, the names of beings beyond the reincarnational cycle are the same there as their presence permeates all dimensions. Thus the name Christ here refers to the same Christ known on Earth.

There is one other difference. On Alithea, there are no individuals.

Each Alithean incarnation is a group of personas which share the same body. These personas are subpersonalities which have developed over a series of incarnations. Souls incarnate on Alithea when they have come to an impasse in attempting to unify their various subpersonalities.

On Alithea each persona gradually manifests more distinctly with age. The body and mind become a mind-body that these personas share. This at first creates greater confusion and intensifies inner conflicts, but it also facilitates the eventual assimilation, reunification and transcendence process.

Actually, the same process takes place on earth. On Alithea it is simply accentuated.

AN INCARNATIONAL BRIEFING

The Being of Light read to Saram a briefing of what to expect as he incarnated on Alithea:

"1. All personas will all share one mobile compartment.

It will have two legs, two hands, one head, one brain and various other organs and systems necessary for you to perceive and function on the material plane.

a. No persona will be able to leave it individually.

b. No persona will ever be able to go anywhere alone, you always travel together.

"2. You will all share one energy system

a. Thus each uses the energy which belongs to all of you.

b. What each does with this energy affects all of you.

"3. You will share one consciousness

a. Although you will each have your own beliefs and thoughts, you have only one screen of consciousness on which to project them.

b. These thoughts, however, can be projected in succeeding order with such rapidity, that it may seem to you that they exist simultaneously.

c. The thoughts projected by each, will in many ways limit the others' mental freedom.

4. The lines which separate you, and give you the feeling of individuality, are imaginary, mutable and often disappearing.

"5. You must find happiness together, or not at all.

You will never be able to find happiness:

a. by fighting each other .

b. by suppressing one another or

c. by ignoring one another.

 "6. Your source is one and your separate identities are illusion.

"7. You will all evolve together.

The balance of powers and strengths between you will be dynamic and ever-changing.

"8. Each of you, and the nature of your relationships with each other will be continuously reflected in the world and

events around you, especially by others' reactions to you.

"9. Your have three powers with which to become free to be happy.

a. love - acceptance

 b. truth

c. awareness

"10. You will forget all this.

You will believe that you are one,
until the day you fall apart
and realize that you are many
and then really become one."

The Being of Light finished reading the instructions read to all before incarnation on Alithea, and left Saram with a thought to think about.

"Remember one more thing.

The pieces of a broken vase can be glued together again to form the appearance of a vase,
but it is not actually whole.

The parts remain separate although appearing united.

They can never re-emerge totally unless they are actually

melted down and loose their form, their identity.

Only then can the unbroken vase be reformed. "

CHAPTER TWO

Ran's Beginnings

BORN IN ALAND

Saram was born as Ran on Alithea in the country called Aland which was one of the most technologically progressive countries offering a wide variety of experiences. He chose this period knowing that there would be a revival of interest in spiritual and psychological growth, resulting from a general disillusionment with the possibilities of happiness through material affluence.

He was the first born to a middle class Alander family, whose ancestral roots were to be found in the Land of Moor, a less developed area, 7000 kilometers to the east. His parents knew Moorish, but never taught it to him or his siblings. Thus, he was never actually able to communicate, to a satisfying degree, with his four grandparents, who spoke only Moorish, and never learned Alandish although they lived in Aland for over 70 years.

His father was a strong, intelligent person, who seemed to be always at ease and in control. He became imprinted in Ran's subconscious as the personas we will call the Efficient Worker, the Unemotional Stoic, the Understanding Listener, and the Responsible for Everyone. His mother was very warm and emotionally expressive, but had many fears and doubts about herself. She imprinted herself in Ran's subconscious as the *Poor Unloved Child*, the *Good Obedient Child*, the *Anxious Worrier* and the *Unjustly Persecuted* personas.

DANCE CLASS

Ran was off to dance class, which he both liked and disliked. He didn't like it because except for one other boy, all the rest were girls. He felt silly wearing that special costume and became bored with learning specific movements. However, he did like to dance, to move with rhythm to the music.

At church outings he would dance when the orchestra would play Moorish music. Little did he know that he was being instinctually guided by his previous incarnation as Shala who danced to these rhythms two thousand years earlier. People threw money (collected for the church), as was the custom, and laughed at this three-year-old child who could mimic so perfectly the adult dancers. This *Erotic Female Dancer* persona passed quickly into his subconscious, and would be given very few future chances for expression in this incarnation.

A TRAUMATIC EXPERIENCE

Ran, the four-year-old, was standing in the neighbor's kitchen watching as his playmate was having her clothes changed by her mother. Suddenly her mother turned around, and shouted at him, "get out of here you nasty little boy, what are you looking at."

He ran out of the house confused. He wasn't able to make much sense of this woman's accusations. His childhood logic came to three conclusions. One was that he was not supposed to look at girls being dressed; that was evil. Secondly, he concluded that he himself was evil.

Thirdly, he concluded that other people do not understand him, as he had no evil intentions; he just happened to be there, when her mother decided to change her. He became programmed to believe that he would be misunderstood.

The Bad Unworthy Child persona learned to feel guilty while the Poor Unloved Child developed feelings of being unloved, rejected and misunderstood.

MOVING TO BROWPORT

He was sitting in the sandbox with three other five-year-olds.

"We are moving next week to Browport. That is very far away," he proudly announced to his friends. He felt simultaneously proud and apprehensive, as to what he would find in this new place 400 kilometers away.

This was the first of many separations Ran would experience as his family, and then he himself, moved from one place to another. These repeated separations gave birth the Unemotional Stoic persona, who could "handle" those losses.

THE DEVIL IN HIS MIND

Six year old Ran listened to his friend talking about the devil.

«My mother says the devil wants to get into your head and make your thoughts evil.»

Upon hearing this Ran darted home shaking his head wildly so that the devil could not get in. He told his mother about what his friend said and what he was doing to keep the devil out. His mother assured him that he was not in danger.

He believed her but the seeds of fear of demons and the fear of evil within were planted.

MONSTER MOVIES

On Saturday afternoons he would take his brothers to the Merron cinema. He was nine and his brothers, seven and six. Mostly they saw cartoons, but there were also monster movies. At night, after watching these movies, when Ran would turn off the lights at night to sleep, he would see these monsters coming out of the closet or through the windows. He would mistake a jacket hanging on a chair to be some type of monster which was after him. He would pull the blankets up over his head. He had this strange concept that if they could not see him under the covers, they would not hurt him. This was also true of the snakes which he dreamt were under his bed. Strange because he liked snakes and would play with them. But at night they were after him. He feared the dark.

DREAMS

He would often have the following dream: It was night and he was in his pajamas. He would look out his bedroom window and, although it was night, the sun would be shining brightly, more orange than usual. He would fly down to the other children. They would play, flying to various heights, until he flew back up to his room. When he would wake up from these dreams, it seemed so natural to him that he could fly. In disbelief and disappointment he found that he actually could not fly with his physical body. It made him sad that he could not fly.

Such flying dreams were a frequent nighttime activity. He enjoyed the freedom that flying gave him. He wanted to be this free always. In some dreams he would "show off" to the others what he could perform in the air. But this always ended up in disaster, the least of which was that no one would pay any attention to him.

He would also have other dreams, such as falling from a balcony, usually his grandmother's. His worst dream, however, was realizing that for some reason he was naked on the school grounds and that the others were laughing at him.

He would also have dreams that he was being chased and could not run. His legs were made of lead – they just would not move and those chasing him were coming closer. But he always woke up before they caught him, except for one time after many years, in which he turned to them and said, "Okay kill me if you want to." They did and he felt a deep inner peace in his surrender to death.

DEMANDING HIS RIGHTS

The family was gathered for the evening meal. Ran, the ten year old, his two brothers, eight and seven, and his two-year-old sister. Ran had been studying about human rights in school. At the table he had a difference in opinion with his father. Remembering his studies of the previous day, he stood up and said to his father, "I demand my rights".

His father answered him half angrily and half-amused, "You want your rights, here take your right."

And he gave him the back of his right hand, which knocked Ran off his chair, humiliated, and onto the floor.

It was a joke — his siblings laughed and joked about it many times in later years, goading him to "ask for your rights Ran, ask for your rights."

He too realized it was a joke. But it was also an opportunity for «General Rupert's» (his previous life) pain and disappointment to come forth from the subconscious, causing the *Righteous Rebel* persona manifest again in this incarnation. The *Poor Unloved Child* found still another opportunity to feel rejected and unloved. These personas believed that they were unloved, misunderstood, and alone in a world that did not understand them.

PROJECTS

Ran was frequently instigating projects. Even at ten years of age, he would be inspired to create something and would manage to get others interested in helping out, if only for a short period of time. He inevitably ended up finishing these projects alone, often feeling disappointed at the others' lack of dedication. But it was his idea and need, not theirs.

This time it was a "dug out" for the home team at their make-shift baseball field. They (mostly he) dug it out, and placed various boards for shelter and for sitting. It took two days. No one ever used it, as there was never anyone who was actually playing. His *Joyful Creator* persona, however, was getting practice in the joy of creativity, while the *Efficient Organizer* persona exercised its organizational abilities.

Another time he instigated the building of an Eskimo igloo, which consisted of a huge mound of snow, in which they dug a hole from the side and then hollowed from within. Once hollowed out it became an igloo which held three children. They all had colds for a week.

RAN THE HUNTER

A friend had given him an air gun to play with. It shot small pellets. He felt power as he held it, power over other beings whom he could shoot, affect or control through one squeeze of the trigger. He aimed at a frog, and instinctively pulled the trigger. It was dead. He was horrified. What had he done? It could not be undone.

He walked on to another pond where his friends had been playing with air guns. As he approached, he saw about twenty dead frogs floating on the surface of the water. He never used a gun of any type again. But this small experience showed him how man's need to feel powerful could easily lead to such a disaster – or much worse.

THE SNAKE TRAINER

He would gather a large variety of reptiles in large basins in his back yard. Frogs, and their eggs (which hatch into tadpoles and develop into tiny frogs) lizards, salamanders, snakes and turtles. All of these to his mother's «delight». The yard was crawling with various reptiles seeking their freedom from captivity.

He once "tamed" a snake which he would have crawl around his neck and body. He put on a "circus show" for the other children. The only way he could control the snake's movements on the ground was to stomp his foot just in front of the snake's head.

About the fourth time he stomped to again change the direction of the snake's movement, there was mutual miscalculation by both Ran and the snake, which resulted in his stomping on the snake's head. It died instantly and Ran felt a fool. Not, of course, for the last time.

Saram

SNAKE CATCHING TECHNIQUES

His father told him that he didn't need to capture the snakes with two sticks as was his procedure until now (one stick on the body, and then one on the head, so that he could pick it up by the neck without getting bitten).

"Just go ahead and pick up with your hands" he told him, showing that, once again, he knew more than Ran.

Ran was eager to try out his new technique and did just that the next morning. The snake turned around and bit him a number of times on his fingers. He let go of it and the snake took off into the swamp. Ran was determined, and jumped into the swamp, and chased after it. Amazing he actually cornered it and caught it in the murky, muddy swamp water.

He returned with his catch in a bottle. Seeing the blood from the snakebites, his mother went into "high-gear fear" and anxiety. His father was called home and Ran was rushed off to the hospital with the snake in the jar.

He kept explaining that the snake was not poisonous; something he could tell by the shape of its head. The doctor verified that it was not poisonous, but gave him a tetanus shot, as his hand had been in a swamp with innumerable organisms.

Ran returned to his old hunting technique.

This became a lesson in believing in his own instinct and logic. The "Intelligent Problem Solver" persona gained the confidence to follow his own solutions rather than others'.

A number of years later, he picked up a wild kitten which also bit him a number of times. The doctor feared that it might be rabid and Ran had to have ten rabies shot into his abdomen. It was a horrible experience to feel the needle moving through the layers of muscles into his abdomen.

None of these experiences, however, diminished his love for nature and all her creatures.

LEARNING TO COMPETE

Ran was a good athlete. He enjoyed the adventure of competing; the excitement of making the effort, and the affirmation he received because he was capable. He played hard, giving all of himself. When playing any ball game, he was the type who would dive for the ball and give every bit of his energy.

Through these activities the *Cooperating Server* persona learned to collaborate with other teammates. The *Sacrificing Hero* persona sought self-verification imagining himself the hero of the game as was often the case. He would also fantasize himself winning games at the last moment and being admired by all.

RAN THE "SQUARE"

Ran had very little contact with girls. Until puberty, he simply wasn't interested. Sports and the forest were much more interesting. Moving into puberty, he was very shy. He began to become interested, but was sure that no girl would ever be interested in him. He was afraid of being rejected.

Once, when eleven years old, he heard that some classmates had a party and that they were kissing. He asked his mother what this meant, and she told him that it was something dirty, and for him not to associate with them. He didn't.

The stage was being set for various personas, some of which developed a need for a woman, and gave her the power to determine his self-worth. Others saw sex as evil and not spiritual, while others still, saw relationships as a type of dependency caused by weakness and a lack of self-sufficiency. These three groups of personas would be continually interacting and conflicting throughout his life. The balance of power between them would alter at various stages of his development.

CHAPTER THREE

MATURING

CROSSING THE OCEAN

Ran's *Fascinated Wonderer* persona gazed in amazement at the powerful, pulsating ocean. They were five days out to sea and wouldn't see land for another five days. The immensity of it was beyond his comprehension. He tried to imagine what infinity would be like. He was only twelve years old and was on his way from Aland to Moor to live where his father had been offered a professorship at a University there.

ARRIVING IN MOOR

The clouds were colored reddish-pink by the warm red sun which would soon appear on the eastern horizon. The houses were low and roofed with red ceramic tiles. This was Moor, the land his grandparents had left fifty years ago. And now his parents were completing that return journey to a land they had never seen, and to which their parents had never returned. Ran's grandfather left Moor to die in Aland. And now his father was leaving Aland to die in Moor.

On his first walk down a Moorish street, Ran saw an army tank coming towards him. He was not afraid but thought that it would be best to change direction. Moor was just recovering from a civil war.

A few weeks later he had made some Moorish friends. They were setting off firecrackers. Within minutes the police had arrived and were ready to take them down to the station. Ran was now afraid.

Suddenly his mother appeared. She was normally a very shy, inhibited person, who had difficulty expressing herself freely. Now she had become a powerhouse of words. She really let into those policemen, in Moorish, a language she feared she could not speak well.

The police left defeated, and Ran realized how much power and resourcefulness we hide in ourselves, and also, how that power springs forth from within when something is important enough to us.

UNANSWERABLE QUESTIONS

The approaching sunset had become an orange glow on the brilliant blue-green sea. Ran sat on the rocks, mesmerized into a semi-trance by the rhythmic, ever changing lapping of the waves. Although only 13 years of age, his thoughts were ancient.

"Why? Why am I here and not somewhere else? Why was I born in Aland and not elsewhere? Why did we then move here to Moor and not to some other country? Why was I born on this planet and not on some other, like the planet Earth? If I were born there on Earth, what would I have been like?

"Look – what are those things which we call hands? Why only two and not three or four or even only one? Why two eyes and not more or less? How strange these hands; look – are they mine? It is as if I am seeing them for the first time, as if they do not belong to me."

His mind raced in confusion – "why do I exist at all? How can I know the answers to these questions? Will I ever know? No one else seems interested at all. No one talks about any of this. Neither do I. I don't want to seem strange. I want to be like the others."

Then an interesting possibility passed through his mind: "But maybe they are like me and think these thoughts but do not talk about them because they are afraid, like me, to be different... No, I am not going to risk it."

His awareness came back to the sun setting into the darkening sea. He could no longer see the fish and various other life forms. These creatures were his teachers. He would watch them for hours, observing and learning from them. He learned from the way they moved, the ways in which they protected themselves and survived. He learned as much from them as from his teachers at school.

He had, as yet, no recollection of his previous incarnation as Phantom Healer which now manifested in him as the *Fascinated Wonderer* persona.

It was getting dark and his mother would begin to worry. That was her specialty – to worry. It was not her fault. She had learned it from her mother, and her mother from hers. This way of seeing life, and fearing the worst in every situation; seeing everything as dangerous was ingrained in his race from the beginning of its appearance on this planet. It was the same on the Earth.

RAN THE STUDENT

When he arrived home, dinner was ready. He wolfed it down, drowning with it all the questions and wonderings which previously preoccupied his mind. After stuffing himself, like a hungry prisoner given only minimal amounts of food, he went to his room to study.

He was a "good" student. This means that he had enough anxiety about being accepted by his parents and others, that he managed to suppress himself sufficiently to study even the things he was not interested in, and thus get "good grades." It never passed through his mind that he had a choice to study or not. It was simply "what he must do." He would sit there with his head nodding out of boredom and force himself to learn. He was always first or second in his class.

But what he really enjoyed were sports, contact with nature, and his recently growing interest in girls. He found it difficult to believe that any girl might ever be interested in him.

He had invested all his self-worth on these three points; his grades, his athletic performance, and girls. Peer pressure supported these needs and his interest in nature gradually diminished as did his weekend camping trips to the mountains.

He was shy. He had a poor self-image and was sure that others, especially girls, did not really notice him. He needed other people to verify his worth. He received this verification through friendship.

His thoughts were overly sophisticated and mature for his age level, but he would try to hide that and act like the others, often outdoing their silliness and immature behavior.

He was also a rebel. He had passed into the stage of adolescent idealism. He was reacting against all that he saw as hypocritical, wrong and unjust in society.

He also had a mania about freedom. At the age of thirteen, he wanted to establish his freedom to do whatever he wanted. This manifested as frequent arguments with his father, and occasionally, his stomping out of the house to stay elsewhere until "his family saw that he was right and apologized." He would sleep out on the roof of a friend's house or in some park.

He would inevitably return out of his own need for security. His family put up with this and his father called his bluff on this matter considerable times. This obsession with the idea of freedom remained with him until late in his life, often causing problems for himself and others.

On the other hand his need to be really free became a motivating force which drove him towards deeper self-knowledge. He gradually realized that he was not free from his needs, his fears, his weaknesses, his insecurity, and his attachments, and thus began a rebellion even against these inner obstacles to his freedom.

But we are getting ahead of ourselves.

Saram

THE DIFFERENCE BETWEEN EARTH AND ALITHEA

He rose his hand and asked his teacher, Mr. Torand, "How is life different on the planet Earth?"

Mr. Torand was surprised by the question which was out of context, but having recognized Ran's obsession with such matters, decided to answer.

"Ran, there is no difference. Life on both planets is exactly alike. The natural and physical laws are the same. The constitution of the planets are exactly the same and we Alitheans are exactly like the human beings, as they are called, who live there. We and they have similar bodies, emotions and thought processes. There is no difference. You might as well be born on the one planet or the other."

Then he looked reflectively inward and added hesitantly, as if he was about to say something which simultaneously would be very difficult for these children to understand and also was against school policy to discuss. It fell in the jurisdiction of religion and spirituality, something which, due to the freedom of religion act, was prohibited to be discussed in school. But something caused Mr. Torand to ignore all this (we all have these moments occasionally).

He continued, "Actually, Ran there is one small difference. It has to do with the soul and incarnation. On earth it is believed that one soul creates one personality. Here, on our planet Alithea, we evolve in a slightly different way. You see we have realized that just as the cell divides and becomes many, that the personality as it expresses itself on our planet, begins gradually throughout the years to divide into various personas which are like subpersonalities. Just as the one cell differentiates and develops into various specialized cells in order to perform specialized functions for your survival and growth, the same happens with your personality."

The children stared without understanding what he was saying. Not even Ran could comprehend the meaning of all this. They were, however, interested without knowing why, or even understanding the words or concepts being expressed. It was as if a seed were being planted in the depths of their minds. A seed which would grow and gradually become apparent as a full seedling and fruit-bearing plant at some point in the future. For most students, in the very far future.

Mr. Torand continued, oblivious to the fact that the children were obviously not comprehending, "On Alithea we are born with one basic character just as on the Earth. But, as we develop into adults, various environmental forces and experiences cause our personality to split into various personas or subpersonalities, each of which then develops by itself, becomes autonomous, and continues its own evolutionary path, independent of our central identity."

By now they were completely tuned out and looking at each other, and making various signs to each other indicating that Mr. Torand was strange, if not completely crazy.

But he, in his enthusiasm, was totally out of contact with what was going on with them. This was his subject, his quest – the most important thing in his life. He was obsessed with observing, analyzing and unifying these personas or "masks" as he had now understood them to be.

"Actually it is the same on the Earth, but they have simply not understood this very fine point. They think that they are one person. But this person they think they are has no consistency. It is so incongruent. They want to do something, but they also do not want to do the same thing. They make a promise and then they do not keep it. They love something and hate it also. They need something and fear it at the same time. They are so confused and discrepant, and yet they have not realized that their personalities have split and that they are many subpersonalities or personas living in the same body."

"They have not realized that the purpose of their lives is to recognize these various subpersonalities and love them and reunite them. This, my children, is the purpose of our lives."

Although his eyes were open all the time, as he explained all this, it was as if he had just now opened them to see a classroom of children who were paying no attention to him, not even Ran. Some had their heads down. Others were communicating softly. He was jolted into reality.

"I guess I got carried away. Sorry."

He looked at his watch. The bell was about to ring. He remembered the world he was living in – the school rules – the social laws. It was forbidden to discuss such subjects and especially with children. His *fear personas* came into action and pumped adrenaline through his system.

"Forget all that we said about those personas. The answer to Ran's question is that there is no difference whatsoever between life on Alithea and Earth. Be sure not to discuss what I said with your parents."

The bell rang. The classroom emptied and Mr. Torand was left with self-created anxiety and insecurities, even though no one had even heard him, let alone understand him and be able to repeat what he said. He didn't sleep well that night, but by the next morning he had managed to explain to his fear personas that there was no danger and they could relax. For the remainder of the next day they would activate at hourly intervals, but he would be able to quickly persuade them that all was okay. They gradually withdrew until the next triggering mechanism.

SPORTS

Ran went on to basketball practice. He was not thinking consciously about what Mr. Torand had said. Actually he was not thinking of anything. His mind was blank. Although he had not clearly understood Mr. Torand's explanation about the persona, these words had passed deeply into him and had put him into the same state that he had experienced with the sea and sun the previous afternoon.

He mechanically put on his gym outfit, in the smelly and noisy locker room. Soon, however, he was wholeheartedly connected to passing, dribbling, shooting baskets and working on the game plans.

He was a team man, a cooperator. He lived by the rules. The coach wanted team play and this was what he did. He did as he was told. And this was why he was captain of the team. Not because he was the best player or scorer. But because he did what the coach taught them. He was smart and could remember the plays and the numbers and could guide the others through them.

He liked unity, cooperation, teamwork and becoming one with the others. This was one of the first areas where his *Cooperating Server* persona manifested.

This persona could sacrifice its needs for the sake of the whole. The *Cooperator* loved to watch those movies where everyone in the town got together and built a barn together in synchronicity and harmony. He felt a deep sense of joy, when he perceived unity and harmony with the others around him. He often cried out of joy in such situations, but of course as long as no one saw him.

That perfect cooperation, that perfect unity connected with a deeply ingrained archetype. There were no thoughts such as "this is what he must just do." There was simply a nonintellectual recognition of truth. His connection with the selflessness which he saw in these movies was beyond thoughts. It was *nature touching nature*.

But the *Cooperator* did not live alone in this body. When the other personas were convinced of the worthiness of the goal and usefulness of cooperation, they would participate fully. When, however, the *Rebel* or some other persona felt some danger (such as loss of freedom or self worth) in this cooperation, then there was internal and often external conflict. There would be internal turmoil.

The *Righteous Rebel* felt suppressed and reacted towards any type of external restraint. Whenever the Rebel declared that he would not cooperate, the *Cooperator* would feel guilty that he was not performing his function, and suppressed what he was not able to do, or that which he really believed in and wanted to do.

The *Rebel* also conflicted with the *Good Obedient Boy* as they had conflicting needs and fears. The *Rebel* wanted freedom and the *Good Obedient Boy* needed affirmation. Who would win? Who would reign? Who would govern the actions of this one body that they were destined to share? Who would decide what to do with the hands, the legs, the tongue, let alone the mind. Eventually there would be forty personas living in one body, each having his own needs and beliefs. Each would have its own survival mechanisms which, at times, conflicted with the others'.

The Earthlings who were oblivious to all this, and being unaware of this multitude of inner subpersonalities, unconsciously acted out most of their dramas with others. Being unable to work out their differences internally, they were forced to work them out through contact with others. On Earth, others took on the roles of the conflicting personas and thus dramas were acted out between individuals, allowing each to solve his or her differences through external conflict rather than internal conflict as was the main way here on Alithea.

However, the young and less evolved on Alithea proceeded similar to those on the Earth. They first became aware of their internal conflicts through external conflicts. This was one of the basic natural laws on Alithea as it is also on the Earth. Internal conflicts became external ones. We learn through facing others, until we are ready, or aware enough, to face ourselves. Then the internal conflicts are worked out internally, without the need for others to play out the personas which we could not yet see in our selves.

FANTASIES

Ran loved basketball and all sports. He enjoyed the exhilaration of competing and cooperating. He enjoyed the sense of peace which came with physical exhaustion. As in his younger years, he often imagined himself as a hero who saved the game. This persona began to play an important part in his adolescent years – the *Hero*. As mentioned, he loved to fantasize that he would save the game and that all would admire him. The *Hero* also liked to imagine himself being severely hurt or persecuted (he had this in common with the *Unjustly Persecuted* persona). He would be done injustice to. He would be misunderstood and persecuted by society only to be admired by those who knew the truth.

Such fantasies were most common before sleep. Remembering real, or imaginary, moments of saving the game or being the hero who risks his own welfare for the sake of the whole, and being admired by all, put him into a state of inner peace and sleep. In later years such fantasies shared time with erotic ones focusing on the girls who attracted his interest.

Thus these personas the *Hero*, the *Persecuted One*, and the *Enjoyer of the Senses,* who imagined erotic fantasies, would often overtake the mental field before sleep or occasionally during "non-action" hours, such as riding in a bus, boat or airplane. These three personas seldom had use of the "mind - time" during the waking and more active hours.

THE EMOTIONAL STOIC

Ran was walking ahead of his friend Direg who had one girl under each arm. Ran looked out at the sea as if extremely interested in the waves and his inner philosophical world. The reality was that he was very hurt that Direg was getting attention from two girls and he from none. The *Poor Unloved Child* persona felt hurt, rejected, undesirable and unloved. The *Unemotional Stoic,* however, refused to allow him to show what he was feeling.

Ran was afraid of girls. He was afraid of rejection. He was programmed that he would be rejected. He felt himself as unattractive, overweight and basically what they called a "square" or a "nerd." He was not "cool" like the other guys of his age. He was very serious.

He was the proverbial "wall flower" at parties, standing near the wall, watching. He tried to appear indifferent and self-sufficient. The truth was that he very much wanted to have a personal relationship with a girl. He was sure, however, that he would be rejected.

On the other hand, he was able to develop deep friendships with girls who were more intellectually and psychologically oriented. They would talk about the psychology of relationships, sex, and the way both boys and girls acted. But he would never have thought of having a relationship with these girls.

RELATIONSHIPS

From the age of fifteen to forty seven Ran passed through eight serious relationships, each lasting from two to twelve years, in addition to a number of shorter relationships in-between. He obviously had much to learn from this aspect of his life. He noticed that he quickly lost interest in being with someone. He was torn between his love for these women combined with his need to be loved by them, and his obsession with freedom and independence. This was a major conflict in his life; he, on the one hand, needed to love and be loved and, on the other, to be free from obligations and limitations.

The *Poor Unloved Child* persona continued to survive many years, even though Ran received frequent and abundant affirmation from the opposite sex from the age of fifteen on, throughout his life. Occasionally this *Poor Unloved Child* would, although infrequently, arise from the "dead."

No persona ever dies completely until it is destroyed in the *great fire of truth* by the intense energy created by the awakening of the *central being*. Then the central being, free from identification with all personas, acts spontaneously through each persona without, however, being controlled by them.

Thus, although the *Poor Unloved Child* "died" around the age of twenty one, he would reincarnate at various intervals, seeking affirmation of his self worth and worthiness of love; usually through affection from the opposite sex. He wanted everyone to love him. When awakened, this child was insatiable. He wanted everyone's love, every one's acceptance.

The child was for the most part, however, suppressed by the other personas who had other needs and interests. He was allowed very little freedom for large periods of time, sometimes for 15 or more years. Then he would awaken and seek to gain some "Mind- and body-time" from the other personas. Even then it was not easy as they had divided time between them in a very rigid way and were not very willing to share their time slots with him.

In addition to seeking affirmation through affection every decade or so, the child would also seek affirmation by being accepted by others in other ways. He would occasionally use other personas' talents and strengths in order to attract the affirmation he needed to feel secure and worthy. We will see how he did this as our story unfolds.

DID MAN MAKE GOD?

"What do you believe God is? Is your belief the same as that of your parents?" Ran was interviewing one of his fellow students. He had created a questionnaire and was completing his survey on what his fellow classmates believed about God at the age of seventeen, and whether those beliefs were conscious or simply programmings which they had inherited from their parents.

Ran then handed in his forty-page term paper on how <u>Man Has Created God, and not God man</u>. His conclusion was that man, out of his fear of death and inability to explain the phenomena of the universe around him, sought refuge in the idea of God. Science would explain everything and religion would disappear.

Ran was not sure what was motivating him to think and write along these lines, but at the end of the paper he noted, "Although I have in this paper found much evidence to lead the conclusion that man has created the idea of God, I personally still tend to believe that God exists." Ran's *Philosopher* and *Scientist* personas were coming into action.

UNIVERSITY YEARS

His university years were years of extremes. He started out as the *Good Obedient Boy* and was on the honor role for two years. The *Rebel* came into gear in the third year and he spent most of his time drinking and partying. He went through a series of short contacts with various women until his third year in which he committed himself to a four-year relationship.

In addition to the loans he took, he also worked at various jobs in order to cover his living and tuition expenses. He washed cars, sold books, worked for the city road department, polished floors at a nearby hospital, served food in the university kitchen, cooked at a nearby restaurant, and worked in the university library. None of these jobs fulfilled him. He performed them in order to get the money he needed to continue his education.

During this time he understood how important it was to him to like his work and to find meaning in it. It was at this time, that he began to doubt that he wanted to be a scientist. But he already had four years behind him and he decided to finish.

A NIGHT IN JAIL

It was three in the morning as the police car pulled up to their left-hand side and motioned for them to pull over to the side of the road. They were three young men on a four thousand-kilometer drive to the other coast of Aland. They were told to get out of their car. They were frisked and put into jail. Their belongings were taken. They would never see them again. Ran lay on metal grating which was supposed to be his cell bed. He was going crazy.

His *Rebel* persona and his previous incarnation as Rupert the General were mad with fear and anger. Fear that they might be in there forever, anger that they had not even told them why they had picked them up and put them in jail.

In the morning, he was led to the common room, where all the prisoners spent the day. There were two metallic tables and benches. There was a toilet with no walls in full view of the tables. A slot was opened and food passed through on rusty metallic plates. It was Sunday and they were not forced to work on the Sheriff's farm, as on other days.

Every time the slot was opened, Ran began to shout and swear and warn them that his father was a correspondent for an international magazine and this injustice would appear to all the world. He was lying of course, but it seems that they took him seriously, because at about five in the evening they came and let them out, and told them to get out of the state, without giving them back their belongings.

They were so happy to get out, they didn't even mention their belongings, but drove as fast as they could to get out of that area.

As they drove away, and for many years after, one thing remained in Ran's mind. While he was going crazy and shouting, there was a young man of his own age in the corner sitting in a cross-legged position with his eyes closed. He exuded peace and composure. When he opened his eyes, he simply asked for books to read, which they brought him.

That young man stuck in Ran's mind as an example of how it was possible to maintain one's inner peace even in difficult external situations. Later Ran learned that what that man was doing was called meditation.

CHAPTER FOUR

THE GREAT DISILLUSIONMENT

A MEANINGLESS WORLD

Ran, the successful college graduate, working for a successful international company, living as a successful manager-potential member of society, was watching TV. He had money, a car, an apartment with a pool, and a steady relationship. He had everything society said he needed to have in order to be happy and yet he was not. He was free to do what he wanted, but he did not know what he wanted.

He was not happy. His life had no meaning. He had rejected religion in order to find the truth about the universe through science. In science, however, he had found no meaningful answers.

On the TV, the news broadcasters presented one horror after another. The news might as well have been a documentary on <u>Man's Irrational Harming of Himself and Others Without Reason</u>, or <u>Man's Injustice to Man</u>, or <u>Man's Insane Self-Destruction</u>, or simply, <u>Man's Insanity</u>. These insane events of man's violence to others and nature repeatedly presented on TV triggered a rush of powerfully emotional thoughts.

He thought, "Why live? Why go to work? Why do anything? Why be a good person? Why abide by the law? Since there was no God, no afterlife, nothing but this material existence which might last from two to eighty years... why not end it now? I do not want to live in this world, if this is all it has to offer. I do not want live in an irrational world without meaning. I prefer to commit suicide." He had come to a dead end. He did not want to live anymore.

He had never felt so lonely and misunderstood. The *Poor Unloved Child* persona had full control over his mind-space, especially after his father's visit last week. There was nothing on which they could agree. The *Righteous Rebel* found all of his father's beliefs and perspectives totally unacceptable. After leaving his father off at the airport, he was filled with deep loneliness and sorrow. His father did not understand him. No one would ever understand him.

As he drove, he thought, " I was born alone. I will die alone. In all my life there will never be anyone who will be able to understand me totally or love me exactly as I am. Each will perceive things somewhat differently than I do. No one will ever be able to experience or perceive things exactly as I do. I am alone, and always will be. I will always be alone!"

These thoughts created a general panic in all of his personas. Each persona, in his or her own way, wanted to be loved, to be accepted, or at least to be understood. Realizing this impossibility created a group persona-panic.

He felt horrible, as if he had fallen into a deep dark abyss, with no light, no hope of getting out.

After about ten minutes, a voice, which did not belong to any of the presently known personas, suddenly proposed a rather radical, and until then unthought-of, possibility.

"Why don't you just accept that?"

"Silence....!"

"What did he say?" they chorused in unison, "to accept that we will never be understood, never totally loved and approved of as we are? Accept that we will always be alone?"

"Yes," – that is what he said (and they knew not even who he was nor where he had come from), "accept it!"

It was such a simple solution to such an insolvable problem.

Peace ensued.

"Okay, let's just live with that fact," was the group response. It was one of the few times they agreed. In general, they agreed only when there was no other choice, when the external forces were too overwhelming to allow any other possibility than unity, or as in this case, *submission.*

This same phenomenon was also true on a national level. Many of the countries on Alithea and Earth experience continual inner conflict until external threats force them to unite. Then when the danger has passed, they once again resume inner conflict.

Peace, however, had been declared on this issue only – of never being understood, and of accepting that there would never be anyone who would love unconditionally all of his personas. Many years later, he realized that this was a natural reflection of the fact that his personas themselves did not accept and love *each other* unconditionally. However at this age, he had not yet realized that these personas existed. He was still like those on the Earth who believe that as personalities, they are individuals.

ALTERING PERCEPTION

This inner turmoil caused him to seek an illusory, externally-induced peace by drinking various Alithean "time-drinks." The Alitheans had realized that desire, when experienced in our normal sense of time, created anxiety as the desire was slow in being fulfilled. As they were unable to remove desire, they tried to find ways to stop time. When their sense of time stopped, desire and anxiety became greatly diminished.

He would imbibe these drinks upon arriving home after work. His mind would cease racing into the past and future and would focus in the present. He would become totally absorbed in listening to music or drawing various designs which would spontaneously flow through his hands onto the paper without his mind participating. He became the witness who would watch in wonder the various patterns of colors or notes which were passing before it.

These time-altered states reminded him of those days as a youth sitting in the forest or by the lake, just watching and wondering, just soaking up the unutterable wisdom which was manifest in all of the forms which surrounded him.

Another activity that stopped time and reduced anxiety was his program of exercises which he enjoyed every evening. He had bought a book about Yoga exercises. He would sit in these various positions for long periods of time, feeling the energies moving and rearranging themselves in his psycho-energetic system. He enjoyed those moments.

Despite his deep loneliness, he was, in this way developing a relationship with himself, listening to music, exercising and drawing.

These drinks, however, were obviously not the solution to his problem. On the one hand, they opened his overly analytical scientific mind and unfeeling brain to deeper sensual and emotional experiences. But they also numbed his mental clarity and weakened his will power. He realized that his mind was becoming clouded. He was losing his ability to discriminate, to make simple decisions, as all seemed vague and meaningless. He had no point of reference, no absolutes upon which to base his decisions or choices.

ATTEMPTING SUICIDE

Then one day he could not bear his office anymore. It had become a prison. The *Rebel* persona had become claustrophobic. The *Rebel* wanted out of this suffocating position, out of this sleeping society which lived a meaningless existence. Most others around him had either put their Rebel persona in perspective by this age or had become anarchists or dropouts. His other personas would not allow the latter two options. The *Good Obedient Child*, and the *Poor Unloved Child* who wanted to be loved, would not allow him to drop out of society and be so radically different. Thus he was left with only one solution: suicide.

Although it was only twelve noon, he left his office and drove in random directions, without destination. As the main roads turned into country roads, he moved on in semi-trance, with thousands of "dead end" thoughts; thoughts which left no way out, no solutions; a river of thoughts in a frozen mind.

He drove totally unconsciously. Then his right foot pressed on the brakes. He got out of the car. He sat down on the earth covered with wild grass. As he raised his head to see where he was, there was a lake a few meters in front of him. He stared.

He stared as he did when he was a young boy watching the creatures of nature. The fish, frogs, snakes, turtles, tadpoles, ants, bees and plants bursting forth from the ground, the leaves high above playing with the sunlight, the ripple patterns on the water and the air massaging his face.

The *Wonderer* persona began to stir from its slumber. As time passed the *Wonderer* awakened all the more as the *Rebel* began to subside, defeated by the no-win possibilities of his thought processes. The Wonderer had no thoughts – just silence and an empty watching.

Then a snake appeared in front of him. He had not noticed it approaching. The snake was a few feet in front of him, between him and the lake. He was too tired to react. No persona was active enough at this point to react in any way. He looked with childlike wonder, even with love. There was a strange sense of meeting an old friend he had not seen for many years. He remembered how he used to play intimately with snakes as a child allowing them to slither around his neck and arms to impress the other children. He loved all such creatures which he found in the forest, and felt very comfortable with them.

Ran and the snake stared at each other for about ten minutes. Neither moved. Ran's mind was empty. All personas were on temporary hold.

The snake disconnected from this visual lock and continued on his way disappearing as mystically as he appeared.

Ran was changed. His mind still empty, there was a sliver of hope in his cloud of desperation. He had no idea what this hope might be. This was not a thought, but a positive, thoughtless condition. He was being guided now. He drove with determination, without knowing where he was going or why. He was at peace with himself, without knowing why.

He drove into town, parked his car at a bookstore, walked in, went directly to a shelf, picked up a title by an author of which he had never heard, paid for it, got in the car, drove home, lay down on his bed and started reading.

He was not reading a book. He was not reading and comprehending someone else's thoughts. He was connecting with deeply buried truths which had not yet been revealed in this life, but which were so apparent when uncovered that he was amazed at how they had remained buried within him all these twenty one years.

As he read, he realized that he had been living an illusion for so many years, that there is much more to life than he had realized, or than society in general had realized. He did not know yet what it was, but he now sensed life was more than working eight hours, coming home to the family, eating, drinking and watching the TV for eighty years and then dying; and that was it.

He knew now that there was more, but didn't know what it was.

He put the book down and gazed at the ceiling. There was a pause in his mind-space.

Saram

He just looked without thinking.

Then that non-persona voice, which spoke to him in the car telling him to accept, appeared again, now saying:

"You don't have to spend your life doing what you spent so much time training to do."

It was as if he had been struck by lightening. He had never thought of this possibility. He had even chosen suicide, because such a possibility had never even passed through his mind. He *didn't have to stay* in this profession if it did not interest him.

Some personas reacted weakly – "Not be the scientist I was trained to be, which I spent so much money to become, and for which I still owe so much for the loans which I had taken?"

But these reactions were weak and without real support from any persona. How they could all agree to such a radical change in life style was unexplainable. This *unknown* voice, although it spoke quite infrequently and usually in moments of crisis, had a peculiar control over them all.

It was as if this powerfully wise voice, which had the answers all along, would allow the personas to learn through their often unsuccessful attempts to cope with their survival and growth needs together as a group, and then would intervene only when there was no other solution. Now that they were ready to commit suicide, it spoke and receded.

HIS RESIGNATION

The next day Ran handed in his resignation. He had no answers for his superiors as to why. No, he did not want a higher position, nor an increase in salary nor a transfer to another location. No, he had no complaints. No, he had no idea what he was going to do.

HIS LAST FISHING TRIP

Before leaving, he went on a fishing trip with a friend. The object was not so much to catch fish, but to experience nature. A fish did, however, attach itself to his hook. He pulled it in. He removed the hook from its mouth and held it in his hands studying it. The fish looked directly into his eyes opening and closing its mouth as if pleading to be allowed to live.

Although as a child, he had brought many fish to their end, he was somehow shocked by what he was about to do. He threw the fish into the water and never ate fish again for the rest of that incarnation.

Saram

CHAPTER FIVE

THE SEARCH FOR MEANING

ON THE ROAD

An exhilarating sense of freedom filled his chest as Ran drove with everything he owned packed into, and on top of, his miniature sized vehicle. He had no idea where he was going or what he was going to do. This did not seem to bother any of his personas.

He wanted to leave his belongings somewhere and then set out to find a meaning to life. He was giving himself one year to find a reason worth living for, otherwise he would reconsider suicide again.

His journey took him to one of the largest cities of the planet. He stopped to ask for directions from an Alithean of the darker race. Her name was Sonna and she told him that she was going that way and got in with him. This was strange for both of them. As neither of them was very forward or bold, but some strange destiny had caused him to stop and her to respond in this way (neither of them was aware of the fact that Sonna was Karen the village woman who had put him up during his life as Rupert the general. He had left her pregnant then without knowing. Now she would help him learn many lessons about love).

They talked incessantly, laughing all the way. They enjoyed each other's presence immensely. He was always attracted to the black race. They embodied a spontaneity and freedom of physical and emotional expression which he was severely lacking. He let Sonna off at her home and continued on his way. But they had agreed to get together again in the near future.

A week later, he called her and they met again in the big city. They had been together only a half-hour when, while walking through a park, two young men stopped them with knives held at their backs, demanding all their money. He wanted adventure and he was getting it.

Ran, although afraid of violence, had the resources to explain to them that he was from out of town, and that they should at least give him a small amount back so that he could make a telephone call in order to get help. What caused them to respond positively he will never understand. They gave him some money back.

Ran and Sonna set off to find a way to get money for him to return home. He remembered an old friend, who lived in this city, and they walked to his house to find him. He was not there and they decided to wait on the doorsteps for him to return. His adventures, however had not ended for the evening.

After ten minutes of waiting, the building door opened and as five burly men rushed through the doors, gunfire passed over their heads to and from these men. The police were sitting behind them waiting for the men to come out. Bullets whizzed over their heads in both directions. Ran and Sonna bolted down the street, not bothering to look back to see what was going on.

This was a strange welcome to the world of "freedom and search for meaning."

Eventually they decided to stay at another friend's house. They made love there for the first time. It was not gentle love, but it manifested all of the evening's tension. But it did bond them into a relationship which lasted three years and was played out on two continents.

REDISCOVERING MEDITATION

He established himself in another city, large but more intellectually oriented. There were more than 80 universities and colleges packed into the larger city area. It was the learning capital of Alithea.

He had not yet discovered the meaning of life nor of the existence of his various personas. He was still seeking answers. One day he saw an advertisement in an underground newspaper about a lecture on a technique called "meditation." This technique, also employed on Earth and throughout the various galaxies, was taught by various groups in slightly different ways.

Listening to the lecture was like reading that book he read a few months earlier. He was hearing what he knew to be true but had forgotten. As they listened, once again his personas were overcome by a strange submissiveness, as they accepted concepts and changes in their life style, which were clearly not always in alignment with their more external needs. They agreed to make changes, without much resistance. They agreed to meditate twice daily, everyday.

He never thought much about this. For many years he thought that his other needs had simply died, but much later, he discovered that they had simply become temporarily dormant so that these changes in lifestyle could take place.

The idea of meditation seemed so clear and logical. It was based on the concept that we are manifestations of something much greater than we can perceive consciously. That we are in a process of evolution. The word "evolution" brought back memories of his eight-grade teacher Mr. Torand, without his remembering exactly what he had said.

He listened to the lecturer. "Meditation is a process in which we simply turn our minds inwardly by focusing on an object of concentration. This allows the mind to sink into the depths of our being, from which flows all creativity, wisdom, inner guidance, health, harmony etc." The lecturer went on and on and, although the *Rebel* persona rejected his style and condescending manner, some new persona was being born. In fact many personas were awakened that evening. Some became apparent immediately and others gradually.

The first persona appeared the next day – the *Disciplined Meditator*. This was the first of a series of "spiritual personas" which were to develop over the years. For many years Ran believed these to be his true self, or his "higher self" but eventually realized that these, too, were personas who participated in the evolutionary process. He, however, was still oblivious to all this.

He tried out this meditation technique the very next day and experienced a rush of energy through his mind and body, similar to the effect created by the Alithean time-drinks he had used until now to relax his mind-body system. He was elated. He had found the way out of this addiction to the time-drinks. He could relax his body and mind by simply focusing inwardly on the mind itself. Watching the mind, in some magical way, stopped the mind. He was not always successful, but he always felt clearer, more energized, more positive and optimistic after sitting in this way for twenty to thirty minutes.

This was his first clue in his search for a meaningful life. For the first time in his life, he was introduced to the possibility of changing who he was, of improving himself. This appealed to his scientific mind and to his *Intelligent Problem Solver*. He had addressed himself until now to solving practical material problems, and now he was challenged to solve the problem of his own personal harmony and self-improvement. He now had a goal, a reason to live for – *evolution* and *self-improvement*.

The *Good Obedient Child* helped him be regular in his meditation, though the truth was that all the personas enjoyed the feeling of peace and eventual clarity and revitalization which ensued.

He had, by that time, connected with old friends, alumni from the same university, living in the area to which he had recently moved. They too, in spite of their scientific education, opened immediately to the idea, and started meditating daily.

Sonna moved up from the Big City to live with him. She brought her three-year-old son Arand from her broken marriage (this was the child which Ran gave her in those few weeks he spent with her in his life as the German general). The three of them shared a large three story apartment with two other men, an engineer from the same university and an eye doctor at a nearby hospital.

Life was full. There were so many things to learn and to do. Every day was an opening to a new aspect of life. Ran accompanied the doctor to classes for hypnotism for doctors at the hospital. He learned astrology from a well-known and respected astrologer. He read more books which simply verified what he already knew but had never thought consciously. It was as if these books were pulling up the answers which were buried within him.

A NEW CONCEPT OF GOD

He made his living in strange and innovative ways. He hypnotized women who wanted to lose weight. He made candles and sold them on the street. He collected unemployment checks. He worked as a cook in restaurants. He wrote term papers for university students who were unable to.

One of these term papers opened him up to another world of possibilities. He was asked to write a term paper on *Orism*. He had never heard of this religion, or philosophy, depending on how you look at it.

It opened him up to two important avenues in his growth. One was a newly found respect for the feminine attributes of receptivity and the power of acceptance, as exemplified by the powerful, but always succumbing, yet always conquering, flow of water. Water always wins. It always gets where it wants to go, by succumbing, by being fluid and receptive.

This was a new concept for Ran. He had gotten a hint of this from the voice in the car which suggested simply accepting not being loved or understood. This power of acceptance is a theme which would repeat itself throughout his life, and even more so many years later.

The second concept was that there were other religions than the one into which he was born, and which he had rejected at the age of nineteen, because of the hypocrisy and injustice which it seemed to embody. The truths offered him by the religion of his birth did not agree with what his senses and logic told him.

He remembered the 40-page term paper he wrote at the age of seventeen, explaining how man had created the idea of God, out of his need to feel secure and to establish his immortality. Ran had expected that science would explain all mysteries of life. Thus according to him, the Alitheans had created God and not God the Alitheans. Throughout the years, however, he had found no real answers in science.

It was this rejection of any absolute, and his fascination with the relativity of all things which lead him to his existential crisis and desire to commit suicide. He still had a problem with the word "God." For him, God was until now a super person with various feelings like love, anger, and revenge who would punish or reward according to whether one lived as He commanded or not. Ran could not accept this, especially his *Righteous Rebel* who could not accept injustice, especially to the underdog.

He thought "Did we Alitheans ask to be created? Did we go to this God and say, 'please create us'? This was His idea. He created us as we are: weak, fearful, and full of faults. He created us this way and now He condemns us for being this way. Now He is going to punish us for being the way He created us ??? This is ridiculous. I cannot accept this kind of God. He asks us to love even our enemies and He doesn't even have enough love for those who try but are weak, and He is going to send them to eternal damnation?"

These thoughts caused him to reject this God as He had been presented in his childhood. His instincts told him that God could be only love and nothing else. He saw this in nature, in the rivers, the sea, the clouds, the rising and setting sun. He felt God more in nature than in the various buildings of worship. He was a *Rebel* and his God was the God of the universe, not simply of man. For him God was manifest in every flower and small insect, in every atom of existence.

Now for the first time, as he was studying to write this "mercenary" term paper, he was reading about such a God. He was reading about a God who resided in all beings and all things, even in all events.

He was enthusiastic. "Yes, this is a God I can relate to," he thought.

As time passed, he experienced this God more as a formless energy, a universal consciousness which was all pervading. He began to perceive a creative intelligence which manifests itself as all the universe and all the beings in it. This consciousness simultaneously lives in, and expresses itself through, all beings throughout their lives. This way of perceiving God appealed to various personas. Later on, however, he made two important discoveries. The first, after a few years, was that there were personas who still had the need to worship God as a person. It took time, but he was eventually able to return to the religion of his birth, however, with a totally different perspective of God. God for him now could be both a person and a universal consciousness. Worshiping the person, did not blind him to God's universal presence.

The second revelation, which came even later, was that those who really understood the religion of his birth also perceived God in this way. He had simply been misinformed about what God was by those in his religion who had not dug deeply enough into its theology.

CHAPTER SIX

DISCOVERING "CREACTIVITY"

CANDLE MAKING

Ran was dipping candles. Music was blaring and he was simultaneously dancing with the ecstasy of creativity. At the age of 23 he was rediscovering creativity or, as one author friend of his coined it, "Creactivity" for creative activity. Meditation had opened the faucet of creativity which had been closed and locked for years.

Producing candles was a playful game. Each candle was completely a different creation. However, he was not nearly as good at selling. He found it difficult to accept money. There was a part of him which always felt that selling was not a pure thing. He always had difficulty accepting money for any act or object. This attitude belonged to the very old persona from previous lives, the *Holy Pure Monk*, who had learned to live free from worldly attachments and needs or desires.

The truth is that none of his personas gave much importance to money. Perhaps they had worked out that lesson in previous lives. Without ever seeking to make money, there was always enough to survive. He was never interested in more than enough to survive and thus that was all that he ever had. He created what interested him.

DANCING

One evening he walked into a large hall, where people were dancing freely, most alone, some in pairs, others in threes, fours and more. There were no "dance steps." There were people dancing, each in his own unique way.

He knew no one there. He was not sure why he was there. He felt very self-conscious. He walked out onto the dance floor. No one noticed him, as all were lost in their dancing.

He stood alone, closed his eyes, and focused inwardly. He hadn't danced in years. He decided to start humbly. He started to move one finger. Just one finger to rhythm of the music. The one finger dragged along another and soon the whole hand was moving. The hand pulled the arm into the act. The other hand and arm came in to balance things. His head began moving, his eyes still closed. His waist started rocking with the rhythm. Now his legs joined in, and his body was lost in the ecstasy of dance.

He had no thoughts whatsoever. Each persona took turns expressing itself through movements. The *Rebel*, the *Poor Unloved Child*, the *Fascinated Wonderer*, the *Sacrificing Hero*, the *Playful Prankster*, the *Macho Man* and even the *Erotic Woman Dancer* who was awakened from his incarnation as Shala the dancer in the time of Christ.

Just as they shared the mind for thoughts, they now shared the body for physical expression, each dancing in his or her own unique way. They all enjoyed it immensely, and decided unanimously to do this at least once a week.

One day, some years later, while camping alone, Ran was feeling depressed for no apparent reason. He closed his eyes, went inward and asked his subconscious what it needed. The answer came in the form of an image of himself dancing. He had neglected to take his personas for their weekly creative expression for some time and they were complaining. His depression passed immediately.

Dancing became a metaphor for him. He learned much about himself while dancing. He came into contact with various parts of himself who could express themselves only through dance. He learned how to connect with others while dancing by simulating the others' movement and touching their psychological state. At other times he would then gradually take them with him into his ecstasy of movement as he gradually guided them to move in his freer way.

Occasionally, while dancing with some persons, he experienced the joy of total oneness, similar to that of making love, but usually without erotic overtones. He learned from this that *if you want to help someone experience what you are experiencing, you first have to get in touch with their experience and then move together with them to your experience.* He realized that this was a basic truth of all teaching. He learned this from dancing.

He was simultaneously also self-initiated into the world of creating music. He found himself "playing with" various organs. We use the words playing "with" and not "playing," because he actually never learned to play any musical instrument, but literally played with them in his own crude way, discovering for himself sounds and rhythms just as a small child would.

In the same way, he learned to connect with others as they made music together. He learned the lesson of being simultaneously in contact with his creative source while also being in contact with what the others were creating. Having experienced the loss of both contacts at times, he realized the importance of both in life. This too became a metaphor for how to live and cooperate with others.

He needed on the one hand to be in touch with his own creative source, his own ideas and ideals, or else all would be dead and boring and superficial. On the other hand, he needed to be in touch with what the others are saying, feeling and expressing, so that there could be harmony in their co-creative process. This was an important lesson which he learned from making music with others and which he would try to apply in all his efforts of cooperation with others.

ASTROLOGY

During this same period of his life he was introduced to Astrology. He learned how to draw up charts of the positions of the heavenly bodies at the moment of birth for his various friends, and later on what others would call clients. He, himself, could never perceive them as clients as he was unable to view them as sources of money.

He loved to consult the various "ephemeredes" (as they were called) with the positions of the planets of the Alithean solar system at each hour according the various locations on Alithea. He would map out their positions on a circular diagram and then make connecting lines showing angular relationships between the various planets. He then asked for inner guidance and began to notice the positions of the planets, their clusters, their oppositions and other angles, thus determining the character, life goals, and important dates for that particular Alithean to watch for.

It was great fun for many of the personas who participated – the *Scientist*, the *Joyful Creator*, the *Loving Friend*, the *Intelligent Problem Solver*, the *Fascinated Wonderer*, and a new persona which began to emerge with this very activity, the *Counselor* who eventually evolved into the *Savior-Teacher*.

Twelve years and hundreds of charts later, he gave up this activity, realizing that most Alitheans were only interested in knowing if and when they would get married or what to do about their business. For him Astrology was a tool for self-knowledge and self-transformation; not for seeing the future.

Thus he eventually directed his energies towards helping himself and others be prepared for whatever might happen and learn from it, rather than try to peep ahead to see what might happen.

Another reason he eventually gave up astrology was that people would frequently project, and thus create, that which they were told might happen. He was struck by the example of a friend of his who went to an astrologer who told her that her husband would leave her for another woman in seven years. The woman become so panic stricken that she began to follow her husband around, never letting him out of her sight, and making herself very unpleasant every time he looked at another woman for more than two seconds, or was late coming home from work. She literally began to suffocate and alienate her husband so that he left after only two years, proving the astrologer wrong about the seven years. This was a classic example how *we create exactly what we fear.*

He did not want to do this to anyone by telling them that something might happen in their lives, and thus be responsible for their creating exactly what they believe will happen. He preferred not to interfere in their future creations in that way. He had by now realized that, just as it is on Earth, *our thoughts create our reality.*

On Alithea those who have searched below the surface of their external personality have realized that their personal reality is the group persona creation. On the Earth, however, they cannot find the source of their conflicts, because they are not yet aware of the subpersonalities which make up each individual. Thus the Earthlings are, in a way, handicapped in their attempts to find solutions.

Ran, however, was not yet aware of his personas, he was simply experiencing their effect upon his life. He often wondered where his various differing perceptions, emotions and needs were coming from. His friends were often confused by his changing beliefs and needs. He seemed like a chameleon to them, who could change perspectives instantly. This was an obstacle to making decisions, or deciding on a specific plan of action, as he always saw many differing possibilities, which were presented by his various personas.

This condition, however, blessed him with the ability to understand just about everyone, as he would have at least one persona who would have the same problem or needs as that person. Another positive aspect was that he had greater possibilities of creativity and effective problem solving, as one of his personas would come up with solution when need.

Some Alitheans saw him as fickle, always changing, not stable, not true to his image. But what image? There was no one image which he could possibly present, which would encompass all his personas.

It is true that like all Alitheans (and also Earthlings) he did occasionally hide some personas which he feared would not be accepted by certain other Alitheans or in specific environments. At each stage of his life, he hid certain personas for various reasons. In all cases, however, it was because some personas felt that the personas which they wanted to suppress or hide would not be acceptable to others. In the later years, he did this mostly because he himself or more accurately, his *Spiritually Righteous* personas, could not accept some of the personas they were ashamed of and believed were "not spiritually appropriate".

He was controlled, to a great extent, for almost thirty years of his life, by these "Spiritual" personas whom he believed to be his "real" or "higher self." For their sake, he suppressed various other personas, denying their existence both to himself and others.

The truth is that these rejected personas were actually seldom to be heard from, and were not an important force in his personality as they were actually dormant for the most part of those years until they eventually staged a revolution when he was about 46, in his "second adolescence" as it is called on Alithea.

WRITING

Writing also became a creative outlet for some of the personas. They kept a dream journal for years, filling up over three hundred pages of remembered dreams. This helped to bridge the gap between their dream and waking selves.

At first they would write poems. Much later they began to write "How To" books about physical, emotional, mental and spiritual health and harmony.

Writing eventually became not only one of Ran's major forms of creative expression – it became simultaneously an important

Saram

means of communication with others. When he wrote, he had others in his mind and imagined that he was writing to them. This helped him to feel connected with all those around him.

COOKING

Yet another creative experiment was with cooking. It was the eye doctor's idea that they put an advertisement in a local newspaper, announcing that they would be having an Ethnic Food Evening at their apartment. Ran was elected to cook. He liked the cooking part, but not sitting with people and trying to think up things to talk about. He was never good at this.

Ever since adolescence, he had little to say in a social setting. He would be able to communicate fine in a person-to-person, deep confessional type of exchange. He could listen patiently for hours as long as the other was sharing something important about himself. He also enjoyed opening up and sharing about himself in such moments.

But in situations where people talked about subjects which were not vital to their happiness, survival or evolution, he just blanked out. He had nothing to say. He had no opinions. He often wondered throughout the years, whether this was a positive or negative trait. On the one hand, he never wasted time on "social" contact. He eventually discontinued all social contact. He stopped accepting invitations to people's homes to eat or to talk. He would, however, receive them at any hour, if there was "some problem to solve" or if there was some "work to be organized."

None of his personas found much joy in "hanging out," in socializing. Some personas such as the *Savior-Teacher* would create guilt saying, "we have too much work to do to be sitting, wasting our time." The *Joyful Creator* would complain, "This is not real communication. No one is talking about his real feelings and needs – they are just killing time. I would rather be at home, creating." The *Seeker of Enlightenment* would most often feel that he would rather be at home meditating. When, however, leaving would be very difficult, he tried to focus on the inner spiritual nature of each Alithean there.

He had the same problem after viewing performances of any type. He had no opinions immediately after any performance. He could never conceptualize and analyze a movie, theater, or even dance performance for at least days. He was still "wearing the experience" and thus unable to evaluate it; still sitting too deeply among the trees, and thus unable to see the forest. He was still digesting and absorbing.

Coming back to our dinner, he enjoyed preparing and cooking for these events, but let the doctor "create" the conversations. He would limit himself to "would you like some more of this or that," like a very proper hostess from one of those Alithean countries, where women are there to be seen, but not heard. He had no trouble with this role.

This fact may seem strange to many who met him many years later where he spoke in public about 25 hours a week. But this, however, was no contradiction for him. There was a purpose in this lecturing. Ever since he began meditating, the "purpose" became a screening mechanism for just about everything he did. We say "just about," because there were some short laps in that screening mechanism when the revolt of the "childhood personas" took place in his late forties.

PERCEIVING MEAT IN ANOTHER WAY

One evening he had set a large piece of steak on the kitchen counter. He had used a tenderizer so that it would be more tender and tastier later on.

He went down to meditate. He experienced an unusually deep meditation. When he returned to prepare his evening meal, he was shocked at what he saw. On the counter was a piece of flesh, the muscle of a cow, a living being. He was revolted. He offered it to the others to eat. He never ate meat in this form again. For a year or so, he would occasionally eat some minced meat "camouflaged" in other dishes. After a year he stopped eating any type of meat, fish or poultry. A few years later he gave up eggs. Although he did experience some lack of energy the first months, after that he felt great. His blood was rich and he would donate blood regularly.

This experience and the following years of not eating meat taught him two lessons.

The first was that he need not force changes intellectually. That his body would instinctively guide him through any changes which were necessary in his life. Thus, it was not necessary to stop eating meat because some book or teacher said to. He could just allow his *instinct* to guide him.

Later he did make up his own philosophy about eating. It was simple. *Eat what you can feel good about procuring with your own hands.* He could uproot a carrot, or pluck an apple, or gather rice, or milk a cow. But he could not cut a cow's throat, or a chicken's neck or kill a fish. Thus, these were not suitable foods for him.

It was fine then for others, who felt comfortable killing those animals to eat them. In this way, the problem was solved personally for each. Perhaps if Ran had nothing else to eat, he might be able to kill. But as he did have plenty to eat, there was no need to do otherwise.

The second lesson that he learned was that modern science and medicine do not have all the answers. They maintained that a body could not thrive without animal flesh of some type, and yet he and millions of others, who abstained from meat for various reasons, were healthy and thriving. He was free from the medical myths and was now able to experiment with what really creates health.

This, in conjunction with his lives as Hans the doctor and the Phantom Healer, started him on a journey in search for methods of creating and maintaining health.

CHAPTER SEVEN

RAN'S RELATIONSHIPS

MAKING LOVE

Ran and Sonna were making love. They were looking directly into each other eyes, moving slowly, rhythmically, consciously, lovingly. They were offering immense joy to each other. They felt their separate existences melting away. Their faces were glowing with joy, love and unity. Each experienced the other's divinity and beauty in those moments.

It was not always like this for Ran. He had few such moments in his life. Not all his personas were in agreement with the matter of sexual union. Some felt it to be something evil, sinful. Others felt that it was waste of time and energy, which could be better placed elsewhere. The *Poor Unloved Boy* needed this contact not for the sexual act, but because of the *affection* that he received and gave. The *Playful Prankster* and the *Rebel* often experienced erotic play (not necessarily the sexual act itself) as an expression of freedom. They felt freedom in doing "what they were not supposed to do." The *Loving Friend* enjoyed these opportunities to express love and affection. The *Joyful Creator* took this opportunity to be creative in this playful atmosphere. The *Fascinated Wonderer* admired the opposite sex, as it admired the other creations of Nature, the flowers, and the sea. The *Macho Man* needed to prove his manliness by making the woman loose control and become ecstatic.

On the other hand, the *Holy-Pure-Monk*, the *Savior-Teacher*, the *Seeker of Enlightenment*, the *Bad Unworthy Child*, the *Disciplined Meditator*, the *Righteous Critic*, each for his own reasons did not like losing time in this "lower," "evil," "energy wasting," or "non-spiritual" activity.

These two opposing groups of personas conflicted frequently on this subject. Finally the *Body Maintainer* got the final word as he reported that the energy level was too low after orgasm, and thus sexual activity was gradually phased out as the years passed.

This all happened, however, before some group personas were ready. After 18 years of almost no erotic contact, this group of personas broke to the surface and demanded that their needs be recognized.

IN THE MOUNTAINS

One night while camping with Sonna in the mountains of Moor, they walked down by the river. They talked for a while, embraced and then made love. But there was something strange about the orgasm which they felt. It was physical but not emotional, not spiritual. They discussed this and could not explain it.

Meanwhile, Ran had spent the whole day engaged in his *Fascinated Wonderer* persona, observing all of God's creatures along the river that flowed down between the two mountains. For hours he remained fascinated by the various tiny life forms in and around the river. At one point he saw a pure white butterfly posed on an equally white laurel flower. He approached. It did not fly away. He reached out and dared to gently touch it. It fell to the ground, exposing a pure white spider, which was living in that white flower, eating that white butterfly. His mind was full of such images from the day's walk.

Later, while sitting on opposite sides of the fire, Sonna and Ran began silently looking into each others' eyes. It was not something which they decided to do. It happened spontaneously. As they looked more and more deeply into each other's eyes, they began communicating without words. They began to feel rushes of energy flowing up through them. They then had that previously missing emotional - spiritual orgasm sitting there a few meters apart, looking into each others' eyes. They experienced unity, oneness.

Ran closed his eyes, and began to travel up into the universe, into space. He began to experience that he was one with all, with the flowers, the insects, the spiders, the sun, the earth, all Alitheans, the Earthlings, all beings.

As he was experiencing this expansion of his personal self, he suddenly feared that his personal existence was ready to disappear altogether. He feared nonexistence. If he went further he would stop existing as he knew himself.

He fell back on the ground shivering. He was not ready. He was not ready to move into such an unfamiliar existence, with no identity, no separate existence. Sonna came over and held him as he shivered in fear. A hot tea boiled on the campfire gradually brought him to. There were times later in his life where he regretted that he did not have the faith to stay with the experience and let go.

HIS PARENTS OR SONNA?

During their year in Moor, Ran taught at the Junior High School he attended as an adolescent. Sonna worked as a model and sold her paintings. Arand, now four, went to a day care center. Ran's main lesson that year was to accept being unable to lessen his parents' pain and shame that he was in a relationship with a black woman.

They had brought him up to see all beings equal. But now that he had brought this black woman to live with them, they suffered deeply. They were afraid of what repercussions it might have on his father's position in the community. His father by now had been appointed President of the Aland University in Moor. He was a very respected member of society; and remained so. No one thought less of him because his son was dating a black woman.

Ran experienced the pain of seeing his parents cry in front of him, without being able to do anything about it. Some personas occasionally felt responsible for his parents' pain, but he had been analyzing himself enough to realize that we each create our own pain through our beliefs and interpretations. He wanted to remove their pain. But they were in pain because he loved someone whom they did not accept on a racial basis. Was it right to stop loving to comply with another's prejudice?

He was caught between two worlds. Sonna was angry that he did not reject his parents. His parents were angry that he was with Sonna. He explained as well as he could to all of them, but none of them was not in a position to listen.

This situation became a point of reference for Ran for the rest of his life. He saw that it was important *to be able to do what one believes is right even when others around him create suffering for themselves through that*. This was not always easy or possible, but it was one of the lessons he needed to learn.

His *Bad Unworthy Child* and *Responsible for Everyone* personas, always perceived that they were to blame for other people's dissatisfaction. They easily felt guilty for others' unhappiness. The *Seeker of Truth* and *Universal Philosopher* personas were able, however, to perceive the truth, that his loving Sonna was not the cause of his parents pain, and also, that his inability to reject his parents was not the cause of Sonna's pain. He also was able to perceive that their anger at him was not the cause of his pain. He managed to take responsibility for his reality and let the others do the same.

Eventually Ran thought that the best solution would be for Sonna to return to Aland and for him to continue on to Bharat, a country even further east than Moor. He hoped to get help with his spiritual effort there. Bharat was materially impoverished but spiritually rich.

Sonna returned to Aland with Arand, and Ran prepared for Bharat. But as he received letters from Sonna, he began to miss her, and decided to return to be with her again in Aland.

DYING

One evening before leaving for Aland, Ran was lying on the roof of the apartment building. He was doing a deep relaxation. He withdrew deeper and deeper into himself, until his breath stopped. There was a total sensation of activity in his being. No thoughts, no breath, no heartbeat that he could be aware of.

He thought, "I am dying." Most personas panicked. In seconds, all that he was about to loose through dying passed through his mind. His family, friends, activities, plans, the planet Alithea itself.

Then that nonpersona voice, or perhaps it was the *Child of the Universe*, whispered, "Accept it."

These simple, and yet so powerful words, again changed the nature of his reality. He experienced bliss. The bliss of "being" rather than of trying or becoming. The *bliss of existence*.

It lasted only minutes before he started to return to his normal waking state.

The experience was short lived, but became a frame of reference for how he could eventually feel and for what his true self was like.

It repeated itself a few more times throughout the years, giving him courage to continue his search for his Real Self.

RAN, A CONFUSING PARTNER

Ran was not easy to be with in a relationship. Sonna suffered from his ever-changing flow of personas. One moment the *Playful Prankster* would be joyfully playing and the next the *Unemotional Stoic* would remind her and him that they must not become dependent on each other. That they must be independent. He had a mania with independence and feared being restricted in a relationship from his very first relationships, even at the age of fifteen.

The *Poor Unloved Boy* wanted to be in a relationship to give and take. The *Fascinated Wonderer* wanted someone to share his wonder. The *Joyful Creator* found inspiration in the right balance of playful loving contact and time alone to create. The *Loving Friend* enjoyed caring for another person, supporting him or her physically, emotionally, spiritually. The *Cooperating Server* perceived his spouse as a being to serve and connect with in an efficient and mutually productive way.

However, the other camp of personas made him move away. This was confusing for Sonna and every other unfortunate woman who came into his life. He loved them and wanted them to be happy, but he always gradually became more distant. The *Holy-Pure-Monk* made for rather dull company, there were so many joys forbidden for him. The *Unemotional Stoic* was not allowed to express his love and enthusiasm overtly. His actions would give hints of his affection, but seldom his words.

Ran would go camping by himself frequently. He would listen to music with headphones and read when they had visitors. He was becoming increasingly antisocial. He would prefer to read or be alone than engage in what he considered "superficial conversation."

He would travel up to the mountains alone and sit and look out below for hours. He would pray, meditate, or chant and sing. The villagers must have taken him for a madman. He would sit immobile for hours as he passed through various inner states. He was a loner in a relationship.

The *Bad Unworthy Child* occasionally feared that he was not good, not loved, that his partner would seek someone better than him. The *Savior Teacher* believed that a relationship was possible only if it served the overall goal of helping others. For that reason after at the age of 28, all of his relationships were with persons who would share the work with him.

The *Seeker of Enlightenment* was imprisoned in a prototype of enlightenment for bachelors only and thus was totally against having relationships. The *Bad Unworthy Boy,* on the other hand, experienced every expression of displeasure or unhappiness on the other's part to be "his fault," and became hurt and defensive.

Of course, throughout the years each of these personas grew more mature. They learned mostly through suffering. Although they had ample opportunities to learn through teachings and techniques, both of which they employed as much as possible, their final and lasting lessons were learned by making mistakes and suffering.

He had a knack for wanting what he didn't have and then not wanting it when he had it. This was because one set of personas would want it and, once he had manifested it, the other set felt guilty, bored or trapped, or some persona would have some other complaint.

So you can see why it was difficult for any Alithean to come very close to him, let alone live with him. From afar he seemed the perfect mate. All those traits which appeared from afar were true, but there were also other aspects which were not visible from afar. Eventually, through his mistakes, he learned much and with the "spiritual personas" much humbled, he might become a suitable loving mate, for a woman who would have the patience to live with a rather widely mixed group of personas.

EXCLUSIVITY AND PAIN

After moving back to Aland, Ran and Sonna decided that they each needed space. As they were having frequent arguments and conflicts, they agreed that each would have his own room and that they would be free to have other relationships simultaneously. This idea was very appealing to Ran intellectually. He believed that real love had nothing to do with limiting the other, or bargaining for the exclusivity of his love.

He was ready intellectually, but not emotionally. After a few weeks Sonna brought her first male friend home and entertained him in her room, which was adjacent to Ran's. When he saw and heard them, he felt a tightening in his solar plexus, a knot in his throat, together with intense emotional pain. He immediately regressed to the *Poor Unloved Child* who was not loved, not cared for, and misunderstood. He was in deep emotional pain. The *Bad Unworthy Child* was resurrected again as he had invested his self-worth in the other's attention, especially his relationship partners. He believed that if someone so close to him didn't recognize his worthiness to be loved exclusively, then he was logically not worthy.

The *Unemotional Stoic, however,* would not let him show his pain or need. In the following days he nagged and criticized Sonna for various reasons, many reasons except for his real pain, which he could not admit. He made himself unpleasant. And since he was unpleasant, she naturally preferred to be with this new man, as all fresh connections are interesting and exciting.

A few nights later, in his room, while lost in the creation of an acrylic mandalic circular design, he heard sounds of them making love in the other room. This was the woman he had shared his life with for the last three years on two continents. They were raising her son Arand together. How could she do this to him? The sound of her feeling erotically ecstatic with another man was driving him crazy.

He was at an impasse. He tried to continue his painting. The *Unemotional Stoic*, the *Sacrificing Hero* and the *Poor Unloved Child* wanted to continue drawing. He continued for about an hour after the sounds of their lovemaking had abated. He was feeling horrible. His stomach and neck were like iron.

Suddenly, that non-persona voice, which appeared in crisis, whispered "Why not love them both. Get to know him. If you love them both, you will be happy that they are happy together."

It was then that the *Seeker of Truth* realized that his pain had nothing to do with love. His pain was the result of his lack of self-acceptance, his need for security and affirmation.

He knocked on their door, with a tray of herb tea and nuts and raisins. They sat around sharing for about two hours. He got to know and like this other man. He made friends with him, and felt much better. This lesson was deeply imprinted in his mind; that love is always the solution.

But he was not completely free from the pain. It was not only the pain of the present situation, but the pain of many previous experiences in this and other lives. It had settled in like a coat of armor in his abdominal - chest - throat area.

There was a three-day meditation intensive taking place the next weekend. He found himself in a wood cabin with one of his old university buddies who had also been taken up with meditation. Each meditation was a process of disentangling his mind from the web of this emotional suit of armor which was restricting his physical-emotional-spiritual being. During each meditation, he felt this energy field begin to lighten, to move, to shake. He would experience freedom from it temporarily and then, coming out of meditation, it would be there again.

He was meditating five to seven times a day, performing yoga exercises and breathing techniques before each meditation. On the third day, in his last meditation, he felt this energy field begin to shake and move upward. As it passed through his head, he feared losing consciousness. It was an unfamiliar state of consciousness. It moved up and out. It was gone. The tightness, the pain, all the emotions were gone. He was free from his attachment. What he knew intellectually had now been experienced by his emotional and energy bodies. He was whole without Sonna. He could love her without needing her. His *Seeker of Truth* persona and *Loving Friend* personas were strengthened by this experience.

Upon returning, he shared his experience with Sonna, and told her how he wanted her to be happy in any way which she could, with or without him. Being released in this way, Sonna lost interest in this other man, with whom it seems she was already having conflicts.

Ran, however, had also seen that they had different needs, different goals in life and proposed that they continue to support each other as friends. But this was not to be the last lesson in love that he was to learn with Sonna's help.

LEARNING FROM CHILDREN

Ran had a very loving relationship with Sonna's son Arand. Ran played the role of father for him from the age of two and a half until he was five and a half. Then, even when Ran and Sonna separated, Arand would come and stay with Ran occasionally on the weekends to play, be together and go on various excursions.

At that time, Ran was working at the day care center which Arand was attending. He was the only white person and the only male adult in the center. All of the sixty children from 2 to 6 were black except for three white children.

Ran loved his work. It was totally exhausting, but his contact with the children was very healing and educating for him. He learned to give and received affection, to be totally honest, to be simple, to play, to create more freely, to have patience, to express his emotions, and to have plenty of energy and imagination.

At around one thirty after their meal, it was time for their short nap. This was a real challenge, to get twenty children of this age to sleep in the same room (there were three rooms). He would attend to the more anxious ones, rub their stomachs or simply place his hand on their solar plexus, and pass peaceful vibrations into that area until they slept. This system worked well and was adopted by the other workers.

One morning he overheard the following discussion among the older boys (5 and 6 years old). Theodore bragged to his friends, "Went with my mother's boy friend to a meeting last night. You know, all white people are evil."

Arand and the others looked at him, because Ran was only a few feet away.

"But Ran is white," they chorused back to him.
He looked at Ran, and was in total confusion. They loved each other, and yet he was now being told that Ran was the enemy.

The only solution he could find for his dilemma was to answer, "No he's not."

He was not afraid of what Ran thought. He simply could not reconcile these two very important contradictory realities, that he loved Ran and that Ran was evil. Thus he chose to ignore the truth that Ran was white. He never seemed bothered about this point after that day.

This was a very clear lesson to Ran as to how we all ignore and deny whatever threatens our belief system. It was a process he would witness in himself and others frequently.

Another day a young boy asked Ran to read a book with the title "<u>CURIOUS GEORGE</u>" about a playful monkey. Ran asked him before they started, "Do you know what the word 'Curious' means?"

The boy answered with total confidence, "it means when you get in trouble."

This too was a very revealing discovery for Ran. He realized that the educational system was educating people to memorize facts but not to think, to be curious, to research, to analyze, to organize, to discriminate, to evaluate, to judge or make decisions. They were manufacturing robots with no ability to think.

This, along with the fact that he believed that each child was a seed which had its own knowledge of what it should be in life, caused Ran to leave this day care center and to start his own at home.

He rented a six-room apartment for very little money, made one room into his bedroom, one into a living room and the rest was a Home Day Care Center. He had one room for creative activities, one for playing theater, a closet with rabbits and guinea pigs, and the kitchen and pantry.

Between 6 and 7 am each morning six children including Arand would arrive. He would be alone with these children until five to seven in the evening. He allowed the children to guide the activities.

He tried to find that balance of flowing with their rhythms and interests and guiding them towards learning what was essential to their growth. Having the latter in mind, he would usually seize upon opportunities which appeared spontaneously in their flow of events. This balance was difficult, and not always successful, but very rewarding and exhilarating when it was. This was real learning; learning from life itself.

When they shopped together, he had to have them empty their pockets at the cash register, as they had the habit of stuffing them with things they liked. They would cook together, eat together, but doing the dishes was left up to him. There are some things which children just do not enjoy. Unless, of course, you don't mind finding a kitchen full of soapsuds and broken plates.

Those days passed quickly and he was more than totally exhausted when the children left. He was in the habit of lying down immediately after the last one left. The *Discipline Meditator* would not, however, let him sleep. He must do his exercises and meditation.

Lying on his back, he had only enough energy to twist his body into the lying torsion. After falling asleep on the one side for about twenty minutes, he managed to get over on to the other side. He felt his energy shifting, moving again. The tiredness and tensions were flowing out of his system.

This newly flowing energy allowed him to continue his postures. He rested in the various yoga postures called the shoulder stand, the plough, the fish, the forward stretch, the cobra, the bow and the yoga mudra. He moved through them slowly; it took from 45 minutes to an hour and a half depending on how much time he had, for there were evening activities waiting. These postures were his source of rejuvenation. He felt much gratitude for them.

Even later, after thirty years of employing them, he remained in wonder at their efficiency in the transforming his physical, emotional, mental and spiritual state. He was grateful. This was a manifestation of another of his predominant personas, the *Chooser of Goodness.* This was a big crybaby who would feel grateful for the smallest and silliest things. He would also cry regularly when he saw people being kind and loving to each other. Gratitude was his main emotion.

Upon completing the exercises, he would sit in meditation for 20 to 30 minutes and then would be off on his bicycle to one of his various evening activities. "Dance Free" was Wednesdays and Saturdays. Monday was Sufi dancing. Tuesday was astrology class. Friday was for the spiritual group meetings with a beautiful elderly woman teacher with much wisdom and the power to transmit it.

That left Thursday and Sunday to read and work on astrological charts. He had little social contact outside of these groups.

EGO HUMILIATION

He and Sonna had separated for about six months. He had no desire to be with her, but he loved her and wanted to make her a surprise for her birthday in a week's time. He decided to invite her to a concert, and secretly paint her a mandala and bake her a cake. It was agreed. He picked her up for the concert. She knew nothing about the cake and mandala. He was going to surprise her with those when they arrived back at his place after the concert.

As they were walking out, after two hours of inspiring and exhilarating music, he noticed Sonna speaking with an unknown gentleman who was walking next to them along with the crowd's motion towards the exit. When they arrived at the exit, she nonchalantly informed Ran that she would be going with the gentleman for a drink.

He was totally shocked and so caught by surprise, that he completely lost any ability to say anything. He walked home devastated. He had spent over ten hours preparing this Mandala, not to mention the cake. He had passed so many times through his mind, how pleased she would be when she received them and felt his love and caring. He kept running the scene through his mind.

He was unable to comprehend how someone could do this. She acted as if it was totally natural to go out with someone to a concert and then connect with a total stranger, and spend the rest of the evening with him.

Each persona went through its own emotions. The *Poor Unloved Child* once again found proof that he was not loved. He felt rejected, lonely, and misunderstood. The *Righteous Rebel* was outraged at this injustice. The *Righteous Critic* found her behavior unacceptable. He was immersed in a cloud of suffering, self-pity and disappointment, and did not sleep all night.

His meditator friend called in the morning to see if he was ready to go to the homecoming football game at their old university. Ran explained what had happened and that he didn't feel like going. His friend persuaded him, and Ran went along. Meeting old friends and sharing with them gradually dispersed the cloud. He drank and danced and shared.

As he was returning home he thought, "why was I so unhappy?" His *Child of the Universe* persona started clarifying his mental field. "Your feelings had nothing to do with love or wanting to give. You wanted recognition for what you were giving. You were giving in order to receive admiration, gratitude and attention. You were also giving because you wanted to give happiness. You did love and want to give love. But these were not the motives which made you feel so unhappy."

For the first time, but certainly not for the last, Ran realized that he and probably most other Alitheans, function out of simultaneous motives, some sincerely altruistic and others ego-centered. He realized that, although his motives were real love and caring, there was also simultaneously a part that was seeking recognition.

Although he himself was not yet aware of his personas, we can see that some of his needy personas were using various activities started out by more altruistic personas for their own needs. Thus it is not always so easy to clearly determine whether an action is altruistically or egocentrically motivated. It is often both.

The next day he passed by Sonna's and gave her the mandala and birthday cake. He had learned another important lesson about love. He was grateful. How did she enjoy her time with that gentleman? "Not at all, he was on a big ego trip." They both learned from this.

PAST LIFE REGRESSIONS

Before separating, Ran and Sonna performed various regressions into past lives on each other. They then discovered various "continuations" of their relationship such as that of the German General Rupert and the widow woman Karen.

Ran realized that this technique had many possibilities and started to employ it where necessary on those who came for "astrological" guidance. He learned much from guiding over 250 persons into past life memories. He saw the intricate relationship between lives and how the soul carried over from one life to another its belief systems, needs, and motives. He saw how our character in this life was simply a continuation of the last. Just as our personality does not change with sleep, our character does not change in the longer "sleep" between lives.

He learned about the beauty of the death process. He would be amazed that, while in regression, Alitheans sweating and writhing in pain, as they were experiencing a violent death, such as being hacked to pieces by an angry mob, would suddenly fall into total relaxation and deep peace once they had left their bodies in that death process of the previous life.

In one such case, a young woman, after writhing on the floor, screaming as she was being hacked to death, suddenly went limp and totally relaxed as she explained that she had just left the body. Then she began laughing as she reported, "They are still hacking at my body – they think that I am in there. How stupid they are – they don't realize that I am here above them."
As he guided hundreds of people through such experiences, even his *Scientist* persona became convinced that these were, in 90 % of the cases, not imagination. There was continuity, congruency and so many details in their descriptions, that to believe that their

imagination was creating all this was even more implausible than that they were remembering past lives.

He began to see a pattern of evolution, the law of *cause and result*. The reasons for unexplained fears, unexplained guilt, or self-rejection, were quite clear in the perspective of past life experiences.

As he guided persons through their death in previous lives, he was able to construct a pattern of after-death states which he found later verified by many other sources. He found this information so useful and interesting, that he eventually wrote a book about it, so that others too might benefit from this clear and, for his *Scientist* persona, "logical enough" information.

CHAPTER EIGHT

RAN'S FURTHER "EDUCATION"

HIS CONTINUING EDUCATION

Sitting in the university classroom, Ran felt surprise and disappointment as he listened to the professor of Western Philosophy explain what Ran considered to be a very weak cosmology of Alithean existence. He had expected a deeper understanding of the levels of consciousness beyond the mind and its limited thinking processes. The *Universal Philosopher* persona demanded a more all-encompassing perception of the universe.

During this period of his life he managed to fill most evenings with some kind of learning. He didn't bother to sign up for this course in Western Philosophy. The professor soon realized that he was not registered, but was flattered that someone was interested enough to follow without needing the credits for that class. He allowed him to stay, and they would occasionally exchange thoughts after class.

A course he did register for was Open Classroom education. He was now very interested in children and their formative years.

He had by now gradually begun to suspect the existence of the personas, and had realized that they are mostly formed in the childhood years, and that those which are developed in those formative years are the most difficult to educate and evolve.

His "education" was also furthered through a series of various jobs, such as dish washer, waiter, cook, book salesman, floor polisher in a hospital, plastics cutter, road maintenance, high school science and mathematics teacher, astrologer, hypnotist, instrument development engineer, taxi cab driver, day care center worker, counselor, author....

From each work environment, he learned more about himself. His various personas had opportunities to develop and express themselves through these varied experiences.

ROBBED AT GUN POINT

Another form of education came through two robberies at gunpoint and his participation in the *Cosmic Mass* orchestrated by a famous Sufi master, all of which occurred in the same week.

As the Sufi master looked deeply into Ran's eyes, he conveyed his evaluation to his casting director, "Third Level Angel of Fire." Ran had no idea what this meant but felt an inner warmth and faith in those eyes.

Rehearsals for the Cosmic Mass, which would present to the audience the unity of all religions, required little work on learning to play parts. The participants were trained to tune into the vibration of their roles, through movement exercises, dancing, personality loosening interactions and mantras (sounds with vibrational power and meaning) for each role.

Ran was chosen to be one of the Third Level Fire Angels. His mantra was a forceful one, which expressed the dynamic externalization of inner spiritual power. He would much have preferred one of the other levels and mantras which were all very sweet and peaceful. He thought that these were more aligned with his peaceful character. His *Holy-Pure-Monk* and *Seeker of Enlightenment* personas had an invested interest in keeping up a peaceful appearance. But he did have confidence in the Sufi master and worked on his mantra and the other techniques regularly.

A few days before the performance it was New Year's Eve. He decided to spend three days in silence and fasting, while performing many meditation cycles each day. Each cycle consisted of exercises, breathing techniques, meditation and deep relaxation. Late at night on the second day, he heard his doorbell ring. There was a man who was asking for a woman named "Emily." Ran explained to him that no such person lived here. The man insisted that he was given this address. Ran asked if he had the telephone number of the woman and would like to come in and call her. The man said no and left.

Ran took a hot bath and was completely relaxed and ready for bed when the bell rang again and Ran opened the door. It was the same man. Ran smiled at him as if he was now an old friend. The man put a pistol to Ran's head and forced him into the house. Another man with a rifle came in behind him. Ran was confused and dazed. His nervous system was extremely sensitive after so many hours of meditating and silence. This was a very intense and violent intrusion into his "peace."

They began tying his hands and feet. They tied his hands with electrical wire and his feet with a scarf, shoved him face down on his bed, and covered his head with a pillow. His various personas were in a state of shock. The *Intelligent Problem Solver* and *Unemotional Stoic* personas assured the thieves that they were "welcome to take anything that they wanted – no problem, just don't kill me."

They told him to shut up, and he did. After about ten minutes of futilely searching for something worthwhile to steal, they were getting really angry. They were sure that he must have something valuable. They had unfortunately chosen probably the poorest person on the block.

They threatened him. "If you do not tell us where your money is, we are going to kill you." Ran was cooperative – all personas agreed that cooperation was in order here. He indicated where there was some money hidden in his wallet. That money was about enough to buy a very cheap radio. But at least they had saved face, and were not made fools of.

They took the money and the phonograph player, which Ran had salvaged from the junk piles a few weeks earlier. Alanders threw away useful things in their garbage.

They left him tied with his pillow on his head and left. Ran was able to get his feet free from the scarf. His hands were well tied. He walked out into the hallway and pressed the bell to his landlady's apartment above. She came down wondering who it could be at this time of night. She was shocked when she saw his hands tied. She loosened the knots and asked what she could do.

The *Unemotional Stoic* and *Sacrificing Hero* personas assured her that all would be fine. After drinking a cup of tea with her, he went back down to his apartment and sat in meditation. He hadn't planned it. It came naturally. He started sending light to the thieves. He forgave them and sent them love and light. This surprised most of his personas, but it seems that, as usual in a crisis, some other powers come into control.

After sending light he began meditating on the question, "Why did I create this event? What do I have to learn from this event which I have created?"

Ran had by now become convinced that he was the sole creator of this reality. He believed that he had manifested these robbers and this event in order to learn something. He did entertain the possibility that he could be "paying for past evil deeds," but such an answer did not satisfy his evolving cosmology of life. He could not accept the idea of punishment. It did not serve evolution. Evolution was the law and all events had to succumb to that law, so even if there was return of past actions, it could not be for punishment but only for *learning and transformation.*

Ran could, however, find no answer to the question, "Why have I created this?" He continued to send light and love to his friends who had acted out this drama with him while he searched inwardly for the lesson.

At the Cosmic Mass, the participants saw an enactment of creation and then the unification of Christianity, Islam, Hinduism,

Buddhism and Judaism. It ended with all of the actors and participants dancing together around the huge altar chanting "Alleluia." Ran was filled with joy and love. He was so happy. His *Chooser of Goodness* persona was so ecstatic that he cried. This is what he wanted; a world in which all Alitheans would live in unity, peace and joyful creativity regardless of religious beliefs. Whenever he saw what he wanted very much, he cried. He would do so at just about every touching scene in every movie, but the *Unemotional Stoic* would never let those tears show.

He left the actors' party just after midnight, as he had to make the last train to his area. It was a cold winter night; snow covered the ground. While walking from the station, he realized that he was hunching forward, resisting the cold. He decided to try out his theory that relaxation would bring greater circulation and better heating of the body. He straightened up and walked with a relaxed body. Immediately his body felt warmer.

After about 2 kilometers, he heard steps approaching from behind. Looking back he saw a man approaching him at a rapid pace. Ran felt fear. His *Anxious Worrier* was sure that this guy was coming to rob him. His experience of a few nights back was still running through his veins. Ran walked more quickly, but his *Unemotional Stoic* persona would not let him just outright run.

The man kept approaching. When he was a few steps behind him, Ran turned around and looked at him. The man kept walking and passed him. Ran's personas experienced a thousand emotions simultaneously as they registered the information that they were wrong; this man was not coming to rob them.

After moving forward a few steps the man turned around with a pistol aimed at Ran.

"Give me all your money," he said, as he indicated that Ran should throw his bag on the ground in front of them. All of this happened in a few seconds.
"He is coming to rob us."

Ran' s Further "Education"

"No he is not."

And now, "Oh yes he is."

Ran threw his bag before him, explaining to the robber that there was nothing of value in it. It was a leather bag which he had put together himself a few weeks ago by uniting scrap strips he had obtained from the children's museum recycled resource warehouse. It was worthless. It contained a bag of three-day-old alfalfa sprouts, and enough money to buy a piece of gum.

These robbers were simply not getting their money's worth for all their effort.

The robber walked off with the bag, unaware of how worthless it was.

Ran was sorry to have his first leather creation disappear in such a short time. He walked home in a daze, all personas in shock.

Again he sat and sent light, now to his three robbers. Then he asked the question, "Why have I again created this event? What do I have to learn?"

No answer came. He continued his work for about a month more. He noticed, however, that he was fearful when returning home after dark on his bicycle. His fear became a problem. He no longer felt comfortable. He was the only white person living in the area and he was obviously considered a stranger. He had become accustomed to being a stranger, never being able to communicate with his grandparents, living in Moor from the age of 12 to 18, where he did not know the language. Even when he returned to Aland to attend university, he felt as if he was from Moor, having missed out on the Alander enculturation process during high school. Thus he was always a stranger.

One message he did receive in answer to his question, "what am I supposed to learn" was, "move away from here!" He closed his Home Day Care center, said goodbye to Sonna, Arand, and all his friends, and returned to Moor where he had arranged for a job teaching chemistry and mathematics in the same high school which he had attend as an adolescent.

A RIVER LESSON

In the six-month period before leaving, he stayed with various friends and traveled around. He made a long trip to the Western part of Aland, where he stood in wonder before the beauty of nature all the way. There he hiked through the mountains, ecstatic with the exquisiteness of what he saw.

At one point he sat by a river of ice-cold crystal-clear water. He noticed a body of hair-like water grasses that were rooted to a rock, dancing as the water flowed over and through them. He became mesmerized by their endlessly mutating formations. He watched them for over an hour, as they never repeated themselves.

The *Universal Philosopher* persona flashed with a realization that this is how Ran should live his life. On the one hand he had to be rooted. If these plants were not rooted firmly to the rock, they would be swept away and destroyed in the current. On the other hand, if they did not have zero resistance, total surrender and flexibility, they would have been broken by the force of the current. He had before him a perfect example of the balance between discipline and flow.

His rooting would be his daily exercises, breathing techniques and meditation, as well as his faith in God and the spiritual truths, and most of all his life purpose. Beyond this rooting, he would then have to develop enough faith in the flow of life to be able to surrender to the movement of events in his life. It this way, his life would be as enchanting a dance as those water grasses in the river.

PSYCHIC PHENOMENA

On this trip, he met a woman with whom he connected for only a few months. He learned from her to feel the energy flow between them. They had very little actual sexual contact, but would hold each other for hours as they felt the energies passing through and between them. They would do deep relaxations with their hands united and experience a total rejuvenation of their energy patterns.

Through her, he met a group of people seeking to develop their healing abilities and psychic powers. He met with them on a weekly basis for a few months. The leader, a woman with the psychic ability to see previous lives and interpret the aura, for some reason asked him to take charge of organizing a weekend retreat where they could work more intensively.

He had never organized anything in his life that had to do with other people. It came naturally, however. He found the place, rented it, and made a program. A number of personas were born in the process. The *Capable Organizer* and the *Efficient Worker* personas were strengthened, while the seeds were sown for the *Responsible for Everyone* and the *Savior-Teacher* personas.

A few weeks later he visited another psychic, a farmer in the countryside. This man would go into trance and allow "the spirit of deceased doctor" speak through him. The farmer went totally limp, and then when he jerked up, there was a totally different personality speaking through him. This old "doctor" spoke to Ran through this farmer's body.

He told him of his previous lives, and that in this life he would become a spiritual teacher who would help many. The spirit stopped after about forty-five minutes and the body dropped limp again. After a few minutes the farmer came to in his own personality and had no idea what we had said. He was actually quite indifferent and perhaps even annoyed that he had to perform this function for the spirit of this deceased old doctor.

As Ran drove back, his mind was trying to comprehend what all this meant. He could not possibly believe that he would be a *Spiritual Teacher* some day, and thus did not mention this to anyone.

CHAPTER NINE

BACK IN MOOR

The first image he perceived upon arriving were masses of people shouting slogans. They were also burning Aland's national flag. A bystander explained to him that Aland was responsible for the invasion of a nearby island. Then the man clarified that it was not Aland which had invaded, but which had made it possible for it to be invaded by this other neighboring country.

Ran was rather apolitical. He didn't have much contact with these matters. He stayed in his room for most of the time until it was over. One thought that did come into his mind was, "these people are not taking responsibility for the reality they are creating. I wonder if they will ever solve their problems, by blaming them on other countries or burning their flags?"

Once again he was confronted with violence. "Why?"

ANOTHER LESSON IN VIOLENCE

Upon arriving in Moor, Ran was introduced to one of his father's students who had come to be close to the family. This young man was also a teacher of karate. Ran asked him to be taught.

His lessons consisted of Ran's standing there as the "teacher" used him for a punching bag, to see how much punching he could take.

Ran got a bit bored after a few months, and gave up.

However, his question, about why he was confronting aggression and violence, became clear.

He was to learn two lessons. One was that his body was not as fragile as he thought, that he could survive aggression to his body. He had been intimidated by knives and guns, and now by the hands and feet of his karate teacher, and yet he was not hurt in any way. His lesson was not to fear.

The second lesson was to learn to express his own aggressive feelings, something which he was, as yet, incapable of. His own aggressive energy which was not being expressed was being reflected back to him from life through these events.

RAN THE HIGH SCHOOL TEACHER

Ran worked again at the same high school, this time teaching Chemistry and Mathematics. At twenty-six years of age and being one of the younger faculty members, he soon became the connecting link between the students and administration, especially concerning some of the more troublesome students. His previous lifetimes as General Rupert and Shala the dancer had sensitized him to those who are rejected and misunderstood by society.

He spent considerable time trying to help these students with their emotional difficulties so that they might gain greater clarity and concentration. The *Understanding Listener* got much exercise during these days. In addition to the students, complete strangers would open up to him and telling him their problems. They would at some point become self-conscious and say something like, "what am I doing? Why am I telling you all this?"

Ran found this phenomenon natural as he had become accustomed to it by now. But this was the first time in his life that he was taking on such a role, consciously and perhaps officially, although he had no academic training in this field.

He got on well with the other faculty members. Although he never accepted any of their invitations for dinners or parties, they did not take offense, as this behavior was in context with his lifestyle. Some asked him to teach them meditation.

Here the *Savior-Teacher* persona had begun sprouting. He also began to write small pamphlets to aid his explanations and the *Writer* came into existence more officially.

These personas were being nurtured by the fact that in Moor there was no other source than him for such information. He was forced to become a *source*, rather than a receiver. He had to learn to receive from within through his meditations and then give outwardly in the various ways which were being requested.

He was not always popular for everything he thought and did, however. At one faculty - administration meeting, in which the administration described the school's very difficult financial position, he suggested that all faculty members take a cut in pay.

He was ridiculously naive at times. He was actually serious. He assumed that all felt a dedication to what they were doing, and would gladly receive a little less in order for the cause to be advanced.

Even the administrators laughed when he suggested it. Only a few held this against him. He was obviously not normal. Actually at some point Ran began to realize the benefits of others perceiving him as crazy, or not normal. They would then allow him much more freedom to be who he wanted to be. He found that in his simplicity, and naiveté he was allowed to be different without being rejected.

At least they never rejected him to his face. Later in the country of Yunan, he would find that some would smile to his face but gossip about him behind his back. He learned to accept and understand them for this. They were helping him to learn real love and understanding, both of which were possible only through his own self-acceptance.

MALE BONDING

That year in Moor was also a time of deep male bonding. Ran found that, in this incarnation, although he definitely needed female companionship, affection and affirmation, his most profound and lasting bonds were with men.

During that year he met and created relationships of the deep-felt love and mutual respect (without there being the slightest hint of erotic attraction) with three men; a Bharatian yoga teacher named Haron, another Alander named Melonas and a Moorish gentleman named Monat.

He loved and respected these men and was able to share his innermost feelings and thoughts with them. They communicated on the same wavelengths. They were all investigating life's purpose. They enjoyed creativity and serving. After that year, he saw them about once every five to fifteen years, but the strength of their connection was never diminished.

Ran then realized that missing someone was not a matter of how much you loved them, but of how accustomed or addicted you were to his or her presence. We miss someone not because we love them, but because we need them. He did not need these souls, but he loved them deeply.

Ran observed that, although he needed a female partner to share his life with and that he felt lonely without one, his male bonding lasted much longer and was steadier than his many relationships with females throughout the years. One reason was that there were more expectations, attachments and demands on both sides in these relationships with women.

LEARNING YOGA

Haron the Bharati taught him many more details about the science of Yoga. Ran had been practicing out of a book for about five years now, but Haron helped him perfect these techniques, especially breathing control, for which they would make special twenty-minute walks to the sea to perform.

Haron talked Ran into participating in a teachers' training program so as to learn to teach these techniques to others. Ran was not at all interested in teaching, but wanted to learn more. They would spend weekends in the mountains with four other men, focusing on the details of this science of human energy.

Ran was actually more interested in the psychological and philosophical aspects of human harmony. He would make charts for simplifying the concepts he wanted to communicate concerning the laws of harmony governing the body, mind and soul. He began to produce pamphlets explaining how our psychological reality is created by our beliefs, emotions and expectations.

He was asked to speak at the two yoga centers in the city. His first lectures were very intellectual and boring, as well as incomprehensible. As he relaxed, he learned to speak more simply and from the heart. Then, he and Haron began to discuss the possibility of cooperating to create a retreat center in the mountains.

One afternoon while in the mountains, Ran decided to create a thought form for his dream center, where people could live together in harmony and rejuvenate themselves.

He meditated and brought this idea clearly in his mind. He began to will it. Spontaneously, he began to chant a mantra designed for manifesting whatever one holds in his mind. He chanted for about a half an hour. This was the first and last time he used this mantra for manifesting his will. For soon after, he took another approach to life, that of letting God's will, and not his own, chose the events.

After this chanting, Ran had an idea. They would have a "Creactivity Fair." Ran's *Effective Organizer* persona assumed responsibility to organize it. Forty artists participated by exhibiting and selling their creations, on the peaceful scenic grounds of the Aland University of Moor, where Ran's father was still President. Music played throughout the day and vegetarian food and healthful drinks were sold.

The "Creactivity Fair" was a big success for the about 800 people who attended. It did not, however, manage to make enough money to pay even for a few windows of the retreat center they wanted to manifest.

A few days later the Minister of Tourism for Youth called him to his home. Ran was surprised and curious as to what he could want. The minister was a lively and practical man, who wanted very much to help society in anyway he could. He was especially interested in the youth and in creativity. He had attended the "Creactivity Fair" and was impressed.

He asked Ran what his goals were. Ran explained about the retreat center he wanted to create.

The minister then declared to Ran that he was in control of various government buildings which were at his disposal for his work. There was a large building in the mountains which was seldom used. It had room for 60 persons to sleep, a large kitchen and an impressive hall for eating and for gatherings, complete with a theatrical stage. He offered this building to Ran to create his dream.

Ran gathered up those who were interested in cooperating in this creation. They went up to paint the building and prepare it for the next fall. Twelve persons from eleven nationalities were involved in the start up. The work began. He was reminded of those movies he saw as child where everyone was cooperating and helping each other. He was so happy.

As the weeks passed, Ran experienced his first disappointments as few people were dedicated enough to help for an extended period of time. The *Disappointed One* was reawakened from his lives as Rupert the General and Hans the doctor. But he did not stop. He would even work alone when necessary to prepare the building.

When it was finished, he spent a five-day silent retreat there, fasting and meditating for inner guidance. He made such retreats regularly at this stage of his life. They gave him clarity and inspiration. He developed a relationship with himself and with God.

THE BLACK CURTAIN OF MATTER

One evening, while lying out under the stars, Ran was amazed by how many lights he saw in the sky. A strange thought appeared in his mind. "These lights are holes in the sky which is an enormous black curtain and there is a light shining behind that curtain which appears through these holes to us."

The *Scientist* persona immediately rejected this idea. The *Universal Philosopher*, however, saw that there were some interesting correlations with reality here. The light behind the curtain was the Universal Creative Power of the universe. The stars, as bodies of intense light, were actually "holes" in the curtain of matter, through which tremendous quantities of this spiritual power passed through into the physical realm as light energy.

Then Ran realized that all the plants and animals were also "holes" in the curtain of matter and that each was, in its own unique way, expressing this one universal consciousness which was behind the "curtain of matter."

Ran proceeded to conceive that each Alithean, and for that matter, every being in the universe in all dimensions, was a "hole in the curtain of matter" which expressed the same infinite potential in its own unique way.

Then the importance of creativity in every being's life became obvious to Ran. It became clear that creativity was not a luxury but the *basic purpose for existence*. We are all co-creators with that one Universal Consciousness.

This was an important lesson for all Ran's personas. Through this experience, Ran realized his position in the universe. He was a small humble "hole in the curtain of matter." In order to be an effective "hole," through which bountiful divine light could flow into his dimension, he had just one duty. To be *empty*.

LOVE & CREATIVITY

Towards the spring, Ran became attracted to a woman who was working with him on this project. Ellma was a gentle, graceful, fragile creator. This was Ran's first experience in connecting personally with someone he was also interested in helping psychologically. He was not in anyway a counselor yet, but their relationship was based on both love and emotional support.

He was attracted to her tenderness and vulnerability, something which was missing from his own character. Something that the *Unemotional Stoic* forbade.

They rented a house in the mountains together, and would spend a few weekends each month there. Ran would try to find time to walk in nature. He found an old empty water tank that he would lower himself into. There he would play the flute or chant with abandon. These were experiences in letting go and allowing creativity to flow from its source, beyond the mind and beyond his conscious control. He had already experienced this with dance. Now he was experiencing it with the flute and with his own voice. For his usually intellectual, controlled self, these moments of free flowing expression were precious and rejuvenating.

ANOTHER LESSON IN LOVE

Ellma's need for sexual contact was greater than Ran's. He would exhaust himself with his various projects, leaving little energy or time for erotic play. His *Efficient Worker* would let him stop working only late at night.

One evening he experienced a repeat of those painful events with Sonna. There was a group of friends at the house. They were joking and playing music. Ran would play the drums and occasionally a long six-stringed instrument common in Moor and surrounding countries. He played "at" these; he never bothered learning to play actual music.

They were really enjoying themselves. Then Ran realized that Ellma was missing. After about a half an hour, he opened the door to her room and found her making love to a friend of his.

His *Unemotional Stoic* did not let him say or do anything. He returned to the others and drummed with an intensity that only he could explain. His friends left after an hour and Ran went to his room but could not sleep.

In the morning, he decided that the only solution was the one he already had learned. He made tea and toast, and brought it to them and they sat together and shared. He was not totally freed from his pain, but he felt much better, and much larger, much more loving, much freer. But his *Bad Unworthy Child* and *Poor Unloved Child* still needed a lot of help.

Ellma had helped him see that he was still needy in his loving. That his love was not yet pure.

MENTAL AND PHYSICAL CONTROL

The voice on the telephone was both strong and at the same time desperate. It was a Yogi from Bharat (not Haron) who was traveling through Moor. He was working at nightclubs displaying his incredible ability to twist his body out of shape. He was a man of opposites.

He could turn his ankle completely around. He could remove his shoulder blade from its position and replace it. Ran (now accustomed to organizing) arranged for him to do a show at the Aland University of Moor. He kept the crowd well entertained. They were pleased.

In the past he had remained lying on his back without any movement (with a catheter to empty his urine) with a kernel of corn sprouting on his forehead, for ten days. He had stood with a holy book in his right hand over his head for three days. They had to massage his hand for hours to get it down. He had made a wager with doctors that if they cut the nerves to his abdominal muscles, in three months he would have total control over these muscles, making churning movements which very few people can make. The doctors took the bet, cut his nerves, and they lost the bet. He was a man of control.

But his life was out of control. He couldn't gather students to teach. He asked Ran to gather together some students for him, as he was a "certified guru." He was totally and emotionally controlled by his wife and children. He was always on the move trying to find a place to live, a way to survive.

This man was an example for Ran. He realized that having a persona who had control over the body and mind did not insure having personas which could create harmony in the remaining aspects of one's life. Spiritual techniques are the means toward the goal but *not the goal*. Spiritual disciplines are not to be limited to controlling the body, but to all aspects of human harmony.

A PRAYER FOR AN OPEN HEART

Ran looked out from the high mountains. There was a sadness. He thought, "I have wisdom. I am capable. I am intelligent. But something is missing. My heart is closed. I need someone to open my heart. I know, but I do not feel. I need a spiritual teacher to whom I can surrender in love, so that my heart and mind may be united." He prayed for a spiritual teacher and the opening of his heart.

CHAPTER TEN

A SHORT STAY IN ALAND

FRIENDSHIP

The Minister of Tourism arranged for a stipend for Ran to take with him on a short trip to Aland, where he would purchase books, cassettes and films for the center library. In Aland, Ran stayed with his good friend Peron. There he passed the days making contacts and choosing the materials he would purchase and take back to Moor.

He was grateful to Peron, who was always there for him. In Aland, Peron, Daron and Foxor were his male bonding friends. He saw them infrequently, but when they would occasionally meet it was as if they had spent much time together just the previous day. There was no trying to prove themselves, no ego games. They shared deep and honest communication without the need for various ego games.

TEN DAYS OF SILENCE

Ran attended a ten-day silent meditation retreat. It was intense. As a group they would take a mental oath three times to sit for one hour without moving at all. In the remaining hours, he would meditate another three to five hours. By the third day his abdomen, back and legs were on fire. Everything hurt. He had never experienced such excruciating pain. His *Disciplined Meditator,*

Holy Pure Monk and *Seeker of Enlightenment* personas would not let him stop, but his body and other personas were "screaming with pain."

When he could stand it no longer he shouted mentally to God, "You got me into this. Do something!!!"

Within seconds, he was out of the body. The pain was still there, but it was not his. He was in a spiritual bubble. All was the same in the body, but none of it had anything to do with him. He had become the witness or his body and mind.

The remaining seven days were painless, although he sat the same number of hours.

Ran will never forget those moments. For him, they will always be proof that consciousness is separate from the body and mind. He could feel wonderful independence from what was going on in his body. This awareness then became a tool with which he was able to relax more deeply in his yoga postures. He would take a position, and allow his awareness to pass through the body, just observing what was going on there. As the awareness would pass, it would penetrate deeper on each succeeding sweep through his body. He would "sweep" through the muscles, then through the nerves, then through the energy body, through the emotional body, and then through the mental body.

He was able to perfect postures in weeks that he had been struggling with for years. Later, when he would teach these postures to others, he would do it in this way, with ever-deepening, sweeping non-judgmental awareness. This was yet another important lesson concerning the process of change. Until now he was "trying" to relax. His efforts to relax, was an exercise in opposites. There cannot be effort and relaxation simultaneously.

This method of sweeping awareness did not try to change any state, it did not try to relax; it just observed whatever there was and accepted it. This process of acknowledging and accepting whatever there was, resulted naturally in relaxation and harmony.

Later, Ran would learn this lesson in relation to his personas. As long as he tried to change his personas, he was not accepting them and they would fight him and usually win. When, after many years, he realized that this was not working, he started accepting them. Then they were free to evolve.

A child grows through acceptance and nurturing, not through rejection. Most of his personas were still children and needed this acceptance in order to feel safe enough to change. This was an important realization, that acceptance is a prerequisite to change.

HEART OPENING EXPERIENCES

Although he had never collected soybeans before, his *Efficient Worker* persona had his hands moving with high productivity. This was always his goal, – high productivity – a carry over from his farmer life in Greece. No talk, all work.

War had broken out in Moor and Ran could not yet return, so he was spending his time with friends on this farming community. His *Cooperative Server* persona felt right at home on this small community of five persons. They shared various chores throughout the day, and meditated and chanted together in the evenings.

It was here that he met the brothers Pontor and Daron who became his lifelong friends. They were seekers learning the same lessons following different paths. They seldom came together, but when they did, they gained much.

After the evening meditation, a few members of the community were talking about their experiences with an elderly spiritual teacher named Hildma in the Big City which was an eight hour drive from there. The meetings were on Fridays.

Ran attended the next meeting. The room was packed. Except for a lucky few who had arrived early enough to take the chairs lining the perimeter of the room, all the rest were sitting on the floor, packed like sardines.

Hildma was vibrant. She exuded vitality, strength, and love. She was sure of herself. She taught a strange mixture of philosophy and devotion. She and her followers worshiped forms from all religions – Christ, Krishna, Rama, ancient Gods and Goddesses, as well as Bharatian saints including one presently living in Bharat named Premababa.

Hildma saw all these beings as expressions of the one Universal Power. For her, each was another channel of that one unmanifest being we call God. The meeting ended with very spirited chanting accompanied by live instruments. He was inspired by Hildma's powerful manner and the whole group's dedicated chanting. It opened his heart. His prayers for something which would open his heart were being answered.

After the meeting, Ran approached Hildma and explained his situation, that he had come from Moor, where they were starting a retreat center, and that he couldn't return because of the war. He wanted to work on his heart center and how could this be done? Hildma called one of her close followers and instructed him to put Ran up for the night and to take him to Shaktma's meeting the next day.

The room was even more packed and Shaktma was even more intense than Hildma. She was power incarnated. She was ruthless in her demand for truth and detachment. All had taken a vow of celibacy. Towards the end of the session she called Ran up before the others and asked him to talk about the Divine Mother. Ran knew none of these people and was not yet accustomed to speaking in front of crowds. He faltered, speaking intellectually about the symbolism of the mother.

After a few minutes Shaktma put one hand in the center of his chest and the other on his back behind his heart. She commanded him to cry out to the mother. He began crying out, quickly losing control of his voice which emerged with power and agony. He had lost all sense of where he was, and what was happening. A part of himself felt foolish, but the feelings of pain welling up within him were stronger and he heard himself calling out desperately for the Divine

Mother.

Shaktma named him "Moor" and said that he should live in house number nine in a suburb of the Big City. All was changing so quickly. Yesterday he was living with five persons on a secluded farm and today he was now living in a community of twelve in a three-story house in the Big City.

He had expected the war in Moor to end quickly but it carried on. He had no money, no job and was now living, in the largest, harshest city of Alithea, with a group of people who had known each other for some time. He felt like a lonely outsider, much as he had some years ago when he wanted to commit suicide.

He got a job driving a taxi at night. His shift was from four in the afternoon to four in the morning. Then there would be the dangerous one-hour subway ride back to his area and a fifteen-minute walk in the snow and cold to the house.

There were cases of murders on the subway and also taxi drivers being harmed or killed in the areas where he drove. In response to his fear of being harmed, he would every evening before setting off, sit in his cab and visualize it surrounded by light. He would visualize himself, driving in all areas, protected by a white light. He would visualize himself arriving safely again home. He would then go off to the most dangerous areas, as there were less taxis and more opportunities for customers there.

The only incident in the four months that he drove was an elderly woman who refused to pay. When he protested, she warned him to "shut up or I will turn you into a frog!" She walked away, without paying. He was amused by her technique for getting around without paying, and let her go.

The meetings with Shaktma were fierce and demanding. They sat like sardines pressed one next to another. Just when Ran would find a reasonably comfortable position for his cramped and paining legs, another person would arrive and his space would shrink even more.

Shaktma's teachings were not very clear. He learned not so much from what she said, but from the situations which were created around her. Ran became aware of his own lack of self-acceptance and self-confidence. He needed people to affirm him and he was not getting that here. He felt like a rejected outsider. These feelings were of course of his own creation. He intellectually knew that, but his *Poor Unloved Child* and *Bad Unworthy Child* were in full-blown control of the situation.

For the first two weeks, there was no room for him and he had to sleep in the living room, without privacy until late at night when all would vacate the living room and retire to their rooms. This was also an opportunity for him to see how much he needed to have his own space in order to regain his energies.

Once he got his own room, he set up an altar and placed various icons of Christ, mother Mary and other saints who inspired him. Someone gave him a picture of Premababa, who Ran did not know much about, but he liked the picture and placed it on his altar. He would sit there for hours praying and meditating. His prayers had been heard. His heart was opening, not only through prayer, chanting and meditation but also through pain and re-experiencing his vulnerable childlike nature.

A MEETING WITH DEATH

Shortly after moving to the Big City, Ran received news of his grandmother's death. This was the first death of a close person he experienced as an adult. He took the bus up to his hometown and attended the funeral. He kneeled before her body and prayed. While praying, he felt her presence very clearly, and communicated freely with her. He was lost in this communication for some time, it appears, as one of his aunts came and tapped him on the shoulder that he would have to get up from the stool where he was kneeling so that others could pay their respects.

Upon standing he was in a very sensitive state. He felt like crying, but the atmosphere in the room was very externally and socially oriented. It was difficult for him to communicate with anyone in his present state. He left and walked to his grandmother's home where he would spend the night. The ground was covered with snow and ice. There was a full moon with three circles around it. He cried and laughed and sang and cried *again* all the way home. He sensitivity was increasing. He was allowing himself to cry and to feel.

PREMABABA

He began to become more interested in Premababa. He attended a gathering for Premababa's birthday at which a movie was shown about his miracles and teachings. A few weeks later, he was invited to a home in the Big City where sacred ash was miraculously forming spontaneously on pictures not only of Premababa, but also of Christ and Mother Mary. This sacred ash was collected daily and given out to those in need of physical, emotional or spiritual help. This ash was supposedly appearing through Premababa's power from 10,000 kilometers away. Ran was impressed.

HIS FATHER'S ASSASSINATION

This was a trying time for Ran. He learned much through his suffering. He became stronger each day, as he became aware that he would have to love and accept himself as he was, independently of other people's behaviors and attitudes. He made progress at this but had a long road ahead of him.

One day he was inexplicably feeling lonely and reflective. He took a long walk, sat on a bridge, and watched the river flowing below. Noticing a plane passing over, he wondered when he would be returning to Moor. When would he be able to get on with his project? He thought of his family, and especially of his father with whom he had been trying to heal his relationship.

Ran had never felt that his father accepted him. His *Righteous Rebel* had developed a competitive and antagonistic relationship with his father from the age of ten. During his last stay in Moor, Ran made attempts to get closer to his father. He gave him a massage and tried to share with him some of his concepts. His father was open but had other perceptions of reality. He never obstructed

Ran's rapid life changes, mainly because he could not. Ran never felt, however, that he had his father's approval.

On the other hand he knew that his father loved him, and that he loved his father. His last letters to his father were very mushy expressing his love and gratitude so much so that his father wondered, in one of his answers to Ran's letters, why he was expressing his love so much. Although his father did not feel very comfortable with emotions (it was from him that Ran inherited the *Unemotional Stoic* persona), he considered that their mutual love was an established fact that did not need expression or verification.

The next day he was called to the telephone. He heard his brother Torman.

"Have you heard the news on the radio?"

"No, What do you mean?"

"Dad has been shot and killed."

"No, it must be some mistake."

"No, they reported his name and that he was the president of the Aland University of Moor."

"I'm sure it is a mistake, I will call the office here in the Big city to see what they know."

"It's no mistake. I'm leaving from here now, coming up by car. Wait if you want, but you had better leave immediately. Ma will need you."

As Torman was 2000 kilometers away and would be coming by car, Ran got started.

He had no money and was forced to borrow from one of the members of the community. He packed up his few belongings and placed them in the basement. Within two hours he was at the airport.

He was numb. He was in denial and did not want to believe that this was happening until he picked up a newspaper at the airport and saw it clearly stated. His father had been shot and killed instantly by a student. The student walked into the office of another professor shot him, and then into his father's office and shot him in the throat. His father had spoken only one word in Moorish: "WHY?" and the student shot again and he was dead instantly.

Later they discovered that his father was the only administrative member who was trying to help this psychologically ill student. The student didn't get the grades he wanted from the other professor and killed both of them. Ran had always admired his father for his fearlessness. He would walk into violent student riots to speak with and mediate with the students. No other administrator dared. The irony now was that he had safely survived of all these riots, only to be killed in the "safety" of his office.

CHAPTER ELEVEN

LIVING IN WAR

THE FUNERAL

Sitting on the planes and in the airports he thought only of his mother. He found it difficult to believe that she would be able to survive this event. She, until then, had no life other than her husband and children. Now her children were all grown and living on three different continents, and now her husband killed in a senseless (to his perception) incident.

He arrived at the airport in Moor after about 18 hours and found his sister Melini and brother Jorak also arriving at the same time, each from different starting points some hundreds of kilometers away. They took a taxi to find their mother, who was in the hospital.

Words fail to describe her pain, desperation, and horror.

Throughout those first days, Ran vacillated between two states depending on which personas were in control. When alone, he cried deeply: "where was justice, where was logic, where was truth?" In addition to these WHY's which haunted his mind, he was also plagued by the feeling that he had lost his opportunity to heal his relationship with this father.

At all other moments, he was the strong *Emotional Stoic* and the

Intelligent Problem Solver that the situation demanded, as he was the eldest son. Also his *Universal Philosopher* and *Child of the Universe* personas were absolutely sure that everything was happening according to a divine plan. Everything was as it should be.

At the wake, Ran felt a conflict between that part of himself which was very happy to see persons he had not seen for a long time, and another part which told him that he should not express happiness on such an occasion. He opted for expressing his happiness, even though he was criticized for it.

MESSAGES FROM BEYOND

His father had mentioned a number of times, that when he died, he would like to be buried in the cemetery in his father's (Ran's grandfather's) mountain village. Ironically, Ran's grandfather left Moor to die in Aland, while his father moved from Aland to die in Moor.

They traveled up to the mountain village on the winter roads decorated with bright yellow flowers. After the ceremony in the village church, they placed the body in a vault built on the cemetery grounds, because the earth was too frozen to dig. They would place the body in the earth in the spring.

Two events then took place which strengthened Ran's faith in the afterlife. A few hours after they arrived home, Ran's sister asked him to come and see her husband who was in some type of trance. His brother-in-law Mostar had his eyes open, but had no communication with the environment. After failing to bring him to, by touching him and talking to him, Ran brought a strong alcoholic beverage and put it under his nose. Mostar slowly came to. When he felt Mostar was able to talk, Ran asked him, "Where were you brother?"

"I was with Dad," was his answer.

It was a good thing it was Ran who woke him, as the other members of the family would have dismissed this as illusion.

Ran continued, "How is he?"

"Fine, he was in a long white gown. But he is concerned about Ma and about the University."

"Did he say anything to you?"

"Yea, he asked for something strange. He wants someone to go up to the mountains and oil the door of the vault because it squeaks."

Mostar was baffled. Ran looked at his sister in amazement. This was definitely a clear message from their father that he continues to exist.

Mostar was not aware of Ran's father's fetish with doors that squeak. Hardly a Saturday would pass when he would not walk around the house oiling the door hinges, so that they would not squeak. Ran shared this message with the rest of the family, and they were forced to admit that this was a very strong sign. If it had been anyone of them, they could have called it projection, but Mostar was ignorant of this fact.

Also, some days later, Ran's mother remembered that three days before the incident, she heard his father shouting in his sleep, "Ranor, Ranor, watch out he has a gun."

Ranor was the name of the other professor who was shot a few minutes earlier by the same student. It seems that Ran's father was subconsciously aware of his impending death, although his conscious mind had no awareness of this.

These facts strengthened Ran's views on the existence of the soul.

RECONCILIATION WITH HIS FATHER

That evening he had a dream in which he talked with his father. His father showed him the reality in which he was now existing. For

Ran's dream-self, it was a substantial reality much like our material reality. He asked forgiveness from his father for any pain that he might have caused him and he felt his father's forgiveness and love. He too, forgave his father and embraced him.

Ran repeated this communication a few times more during his meditations those days and felt at peace concerning his relationship with his father.

THE INSANITIES OF WAR

The civil war in Moor was escalating. There was no logic to this senseless killing of neighbors. The warring parties were supposedly divided according to religion, but the war had nothing to do with religion – it had to do with ignorance, fear, greed, and lust for power.

There was no system of law. The student who killed his father was walking around free as there were no prisons, police or courts. Some of the family's Moorish cousins offered to arrange for him to be killed. Ran put a quick end to such talk.

"There is divine justice," he told them. "If he is to be punished, life will take care of it. If you want to do something when there will be a system of justice, bring him to court." His family's pain would not be eased by killing someone else. Let the insanity stop here.

Bombs were falling regularly. One didn't know from one moment to the next where one would land. One blew a hole in the kitchen of Ran's apartment. Another slammed into the University's men's dormitory. One evening, while daring to sit outside on the verandah, a bullet whizzed by Ran's head and engaged itself in the wall.

Ran wondered how he might be useful. He went to the university hospital and offered his services. They put him in a room with a man who was connected up to nine tubes that were adding and removing various liquids in order to keep him "alive until he died." Ran's mission was to pinch the man occasionally to see if there was any reaction, so that they would know if he was alive or not. If not, then the bed and instruments would be used for the next shrapnel-packed victim of this insane war that no one would win and all would lose.

Ran pinched the man a dozen times in a two-hour period and then decided that it would be more useful to meditate and send light and love to the soul in that body. He closed his eyes and directed his awareness towards the soul occupying that body. His experience had taught him that the soul would probably be hovering in the room. He spoke to it mentally. He encouraged it to accept God's light and love, and let go of any fear and be at peace. Ran spent the next half an hour in this manner. When he opened his eyes, the man was noticeably more relaxed. He passed away during the night.

Ran, however, was beginning to realize that there was little he could offer at this time in Moor. The building in the mountains, which he had prepared, was occupied by an invading army from a neighboring country that had come to ensure "peace." Curfews were in effect for most of the day, leaving only a few hours for one to get out and get food.

BULLETS WITH NAMES ON THEM

One afternoon he heard a tremendous explosion. The bakery about a hundred meters from his house had been hit by a bomb. There had been a line of about twenty Moorians waiting for bread. A few were killed instantly, others were taken to the hospital in critical condition, others were attended to for minor wounds, and still others walked home dazed and shocked.

The insanity around him began to shake his belief in a divine plan. "Was it already agreed upon before that bomb hit, who would die, who would loose a leg or an eye for life, who would be in pain for months and who would walk away untouched? Or was it chance, chaos, events with no reason? Did each receive exactly what he needed for his evolutionary process, or was the universe out of control? Was there a God who controlled what happened, or was man's insanity the decider of events?"

Ran was shaken and confused. He sat at his father's desk, took one of his old note pads and started writing a poem, in which he described the horror and suffering, the injustice of the war going on around him, including his father's senseless death at the hands of a student gone mad. After about a half an hour of writing, that non-persona voice came into gear (it could also have been the *Child of the Universe*) and began to answer.

"No one died by chance. There is a *Universal Intelligence*, a divine being who controls every event. Each event is chosen by the soul in cooperation with the Universal Being even before it incarnates. My father knew he was going to die. He had chosen to die in this way at this time. The student was only the means, not the cause. Every bullet has its target's name written on it."

The poem ended with a sense of clarity about this point. It also triggered off another discovery for Ran. Life is fragile and temporary. He didn't know if he would die tomorrow or in 70 years. Life was to be lived as if he would die tomorrow. No more preparing, no more getting ready to do what he was going to do. He decided to get on with his life and not waste one moment of this incarnation.

At that moment, he also became aware that he had been somehow restricted by his father's rejection of his change from a scientist to a "who-knows-what." He would kid Ran when he saw him eating sprouts, "eating those worms again." Well now the chances of getting the approval he sought were zero. He had been reconciled with his father in his meditations and dreams, and now he was ready to live his life fully, according to his deepest convictions.

This experience helped Ran later when he began counseling persons. He knew that for a person to manifest his full potential, he would have to free himself from the need for his parents' approval. He would have to develop enough faith in his inner guidance so that he could love, respect and serve his parents without needing their affirmation, recognition or approval.

Ran was ready to get on with his life.

CHAPTER TWELVE

CO-CREATING A SPIRITUAL CENTER

Ran decided that he first needed to get in touch with his inner strength. He spent the first days at some monasteries resting, praying and trying to put himself together. In the monasteries, he felt much unity with the monks, even though he could not speak their language. For him they were brothers on the path.

This is what he thought until a few Alander speaking teenagers helped to translate for him. The monks did not see him in the same light. They believed that he was not a Christian, since he did not belong to the specific sect of Christianity established in Moor. This seemed strange to Ran as his thoughts were, "what difference does it make what sect we belong to, since we all worship Christ." They did not share his perception.

A CENTER MANIFESTS

As the war was scaling down but as the center in the mountains had been destroyed, Ran decided to see if there was any group interested in yoga or massage, where he could be useful. He made a few contacts and started out with an exercise class with only four persons in his small two-room apartment. After a month they started searching for a larger space. They found a basement which could accommodate a class of twenty persons. Gradually he began to offer lectures on subjects of health, psychology and philosophy. Then they started to sponsor vegetarian dinners. He now had plenty of help from those interested.

Without his noticing, he was gradually falling into the role of the teacher, counselor and lecturer. The whole process happened slowly, organically as a plant grows. Four became fifty which then became two hundred which eventually became, over the years, *two thousand.*

It all seemed so natural, as if some other power were guiding the process, as if Ran were simply the custodian of this creation, and not the source or the creator.

And, in fact, he was not the creator. The center was a creation of higher powers through the many people who came together to manifest it. Many thousands of people poured through the process, some for days, others for many years, and a few for all their lives. Ran was simply there to establish the banks of the river which gave some consistency to that ever-flowing and changing group of Alitheans who helped and also benefited from this creation.

Ran then decided that he would become a spiritual commune of one, and left his apartment and lived in the center, which moved location every few years for various reasons. He decided to receive no pay, and took only room and food.

Through the years his experience became his teacher, and he developed a series of seminars which gradually manifested as a curriculum, and which took six years for the participants to complete. The participants learned to care for their bodies, emotions, minds, relationships, souls and eventually for the society around them. The emphasis was on self-knowledge, love and service.

Gradually many other activities were included, inspired by the various participants. Teachers and group facilitators were trained, who eventually took over for Ran so that more persons could be reached and on a more personal basis.

Groups were created for emotional sharing, for meditation, for chanting, for serving the poor, visiting the orphans, donating blood, supporting those with cancer and those who had lost their loved ones to death.

Vegetarian dinners and cultural evenings were held regularly. The center began to incorporate the arts. A theatrical group was formed. Seminars were developed combining creative arts and self-discovery. Members with musical ability entertained the others.

All work was done voluntarily. No one was paid. Around 80 persons offered their services some hours each week, in the office, teaching, counseling, massaging, cooking, in the garden, and organizing etc.

Eventually a community was formed. Some forty persons passed through the experience of community life at one time or another. At one point, they had become about twenty persons – a few living in the urban premises, running the center there, and the rest in the rural retreat center, which was created for seminars and retreats.

They started a Health Food store, packaged their own food stuffs, grew organic vegetables, baked sweets with natural ingredients, and developed a small cottage industry producing various health-oriented products.

They shared hours of spiritual exercise and many hours of sharing emotions and ideas about how to improve themselves and their work. They created together.

Ran became more and more well known. He was invited on a regular basis to speak in other cities. He was invited to speak regularly on radio and was on television a number of times. His books grew in number and circulation. Over 80,000 copies of his books had been read by Moorians in Moor and all over Alithea.

Everything was perfect for Ran. He was living a life that he loved with unlimited opportunities for serving and creating. He was surrounded by wonderful people whom he loved and who loved him (except for the Church hierarchy who thought he was working for the Antichrist). Although he was working eighty hours a week, he

Co-Creating a Spiritual Center

totally enjoyed himself. One month a year he would go off to meditate, write and commune with nature. He felt useful and this was important for him.

He was very happy...

...Until his child personas staged their revolt.

CHAPTER THIRTEEN

PREMABABA

RAN'S HEART OPENS

Ran had met a number of spiritual teachers in his life. He was grateful for their presence, example, effort, selflessness and their teachings. Actually, he seldom heard something that he had not already discovered from within. But knowing something intellectually and *living* it was a totally different matter. These men and women whom he met in Aland, Moor, and Bharat were all examples which encouraged him to follow in their footsteps.

He could not, however, bring himself to surrender to these persons. He respected them and loved them, but sensed that, although they were certainly many steps ahead of him on the path, they too were still living in the subjective world and were enclosed in a system. They were not functioning from that space of total awareness and experience of the truth.

That was until he met Premababa. You will remember, that while in the Big City, driving a taxi and living in a community led by Shaktma, he had come across sacred ash being created in an apartment by Premababa from afar. He still had this man's picture and would look at it often, but he had never met him.

Two months after getting started with the new center in Moor, and few days after he moved into his new apartment, a friend came by with a gift for the occasion of his new residence. It was a small ornamental bird made in Bharat. He asked her where she got it, and she described the location: a shop which imported various items from Bharat.

The next day Ran visited the shop and, to his amazement, beheld an enormous two-meter high picture of Premababa on the wall. He could not believe the "coincidence." Of course, he knew it was no coincidence, and that this was just another hint as to in which direction to flow. The owners of the shop were devotees of Premababa, and they rekindled his already inherent desire to go and meet this man.

The following summer he did visit Premababa in his monastery in Bharat. Upon arriving in Bharat, Ran found everything so totally different than anything he had ever seen in his life on Alithea, but at the same time so familiar. Things that ordinarily would have seemed strange or objectionable seemed very natural, as if he had lived there all his life. He fell in love with Bharat and its people.

His relationship with Premababa was an internal one. At first he put him in the role of the father wanting his attention. He wanted to be affirmed as a "good boy." The teacher in him wanted also to be recognized as a teacher. The days passed, and Premababa paid no attention to him.

Ran had a room for himself and meditated most of the day except for the hours where they would wait for Premababa to come out and walk among them, collect letters, perhaps talk to them, perhaps invite them to go into his room for an interview later.

He would occasionally materialize that sacred ash, and place in outstretched waiting hands seeking this prized spiritual food. He also might materialize a ring, or rosary beads, or a medallion, sometimes crosses, or some other small object which he would then give to someone to give them a first-hand experience of spiritual power so that their faith in the spiritual and divine might become stronger.

During this first visit, Ran was somewhat put-off with the habit which the Bharatis had of bowing and touching or even kissing Premababa's feet. Ran's ego completely rejected such a possibility. Yet one day after a few weeks, as Premababa passed in front of him, he found himself falling before him and touching his feet with his two hands.

When Ran sat back up, he was overwhelmed by a flow of energy-like electrical current that passed through his hands, and up into his head, making him dizzy. Perhaps Premababa had sent him a little electrical shock to wake him up. Perhaps it was his own projection. This energy then moved into his heart, and he felt an opening of love for Premababa and all those around him.

Ran spent that first trip meditating, fasting and keeping silence. He never got the interview he wanted, but on the last day he stood up as Premababa passed and told him that he was leaving that day. Premababa smiled at him and waved his hand materializing sacred ash, placed it into Ran's hand, telling him, "eat it."

Ran ate most of it, shared some with those around him, and placed the small amount which remained in an envelope to take back to Moor with him. Every week he placed a little on his tongue until gradually it finished. Every time he took this ash, he felt a spiritual vibration pass through him.

JEALOUSY

Two years later he was again in Bharat visiting Premababa, this time with his Bharati friend Haron who had taught him yoga and who was also living in Moor. They shared a room and again it was a time for meditating, keeping silence and rejuvenating the body and mind.

One day, when Premababa was walking through the crowd, he took Haron for an interview. Ran was hurt that he was not taken, and experienced jealousy as if he were a child and his father was paying more attention to his brother. He noticed throughout the days that he was feeling jealous of those who were chosen. His interpretation was that Premababa loved them more than him. This offended him, as he believed that he was making a much more sincere spiritual effort than those chosen.

Again his trip passed without his getting the desired interview. On the last day he stood up again and informed Premababa that he was leaving, Premababa continued walking a few steps, and then turned around and said, "leaving, very happy," and again materialized sacred ash and put it in his palm. After sharing a little with those around him, this time he ate it all, there and then.

Ran was happy again. He was beginning to realize that Premababa was teaching him much more by not giving him this interview. He had seen his own jealousy and dealt with it. He discovered that he wanted the interview as a form of affirmation of Premababa's love and thus of his own self-worth. He realized how selfish and immature all this was.

He even wrote an article about his jealousy, which became one of a number of his articles published in Premababa's organization's monthly magazine. Premababa's accepting these articles in his magazine was Premababa's way of telling him that his understanding and writings were true and useful, but that he was still learning from not getting the personal attention he desired.

Ran gradually began to understand that most devotees were making a huge mistake in believing that these interviews had something to do with one's self-worth or with Premababa's love or acceptance of the individual. He realized that there were two basic principles involved.

The first was how much the person needed, or would be *helped* by this contact. Thus need, and not worthiness, was the first basic factor. The second was *usefulness* concerning Premababa's organization. Obviously Alitheans, who had incarnated to function through Premababa's specific organization, would need more specific instructions as what to do. Both reasons were totally practical and had nothing to do with special love, self-worth or one's spiritual achievements.

REJECTION

Upon returning to Moor, as he was collecting his bags from the conveyor belt, a man in a uniform came up to him and asked him if he was Ran. When he answered, "Yes," the man guided him back to the checkpoint which he had just passed. There he was told that he could not enter Moor as he was considered dangerous for the national security. This amazed him and his *Rebel* persona was outraged at this obvious injustice. The church authorities had arranged, during his absence, for him not to be able to renter the country.

After many telephone calls, he was allowed in for ten days. During those ten days those who wanted him to be in Moor managed to correct the situation. He stayed.

His *Rebel* and *Unjustly Persecuted* personas felt very hurt by this injustice. Although he was trying to help people, he was being treated like a criminal. He was reminded of his life as General Rupert.

HIS FIRST INTERVIEW

On the third trip, one month passed, and the day finally came. Premababa motioned for Ran to go in. When Ran got up, he motioned to two women who were also from Moor to come as well. Men sat separately from the women. It was only the three of them and an elderly Bharati couple. Premababa looked at Ran first and said, "You have been waiting a long time, huh?"

"Yes Baba," Ran replied, "But I know that your sense of time is different from mine."

Premababa smiled and said, "You see first I give disappointment and then I give appointment."

Ran laughed and answered, "I'm glad it was that way and not the other way around."

Premababa told him that his mind "was like a monkey moving here and there." But of course he said this to almost everyone. He asked Ran what work he did, and Ran told him that he was teaching. Premababa seemed pleased and told him that his life would be blessed. With this he placed his hand on the top of Ran's head, and Ran grabbed his hands and held them there, as if greedy for his blessings. Ran asked him about his meditation technique and Premababa confirmed that he was on the right track.

At the end of the interview Ran stooped to touch Premababa's feet uttering over and over, "thank you Baba, thank you Baba."

Premababa laughed at him and mimicked him "thank you Baba, thank you Baba." This was one of the times in which his grateful *Chooser of Goodness* persona was overdoing it with gratitude. But he was genuinely grateful.

Ran sat for hours afterwards savoring every word and motion that occurred.

On the way back to Moor, Ran was very happy, but he also realized that he had received the same energy and spiritual boost the first two times in which he did not have an interview.

He now understood that the spiritual help which one receives has nothing to do with the external happenings

A MARRIAGE CONTRACT

On the fourth trip, Ran was accompanied by Issabella whom he was interested in marrying. He was now thirty-six years of age and had not yet committed himself to marriage. This was the first woman who interested him enough. She was interested in spiritual life, was an efficient worker and liked to help others. He also found her very attractive and they enjoyed each other's company, both in work and play.

Some months previous to meeting her, while sleeping in a pyramid that they had built on the roof of the center, he had a dream in which he was told that he would be meeting the woman of his life. The woman appeared before him. Issabella was obviously this woman he saw in the dream.

Many of his personas were interested in making such a commitment. Other personas such as the *Holy-Pure-Monk* and the *Seeker of Enlightenment* had their fears that they would lose their spirituality or be distracted from their goals.

He was in conflict, and wanted his "daddy" Premababa to tell him what to do. He tried in various ways to get a clear answer from Premababa as to what he should do. All methods failed. Finally they got an interview, and again Premababa would not answer him.

After some days, Ran was sitting in the fields outside the monastery. He imagined two futures, one in which he would live the life of a monk dedicated to prayer and meditation, or another in which he would stay in the world and serve people through teaching, counseling, writing, organizing and in any other way that he could be useful.

He searched inside himself to see emotionally, physically, mentally and spiritually which he preferred. He felt more attracted to being in the world. This seemed more important to him. It was also in line with Premababa's teachings. He also felt that if he wanted to live as monk, he could do so the last twenty years of his life. He planned to live to 81 years of age, so at 60 he could retreat and have time to work on his inner development more intensely.

As the years went on he realized that many of his urges to live as a monk stemmed from the habit of his previous lives as a monk, rather than his inner voice as to what he should be doing with this life. Perhaps it was programming from past lives and not guidance. He also realized that one learns many lessons while trying to deal consciously with the events of one's external life.

Having felt now that he knew what he wanted, he told Issabella. She agreed, and they decided to make up their own marriage contract and hand it to Premababa. If he took it (he knew the contents of every letter offered to him, and he would not take a letter holding contents which he would not agree to), this would be a sign. They each wrote what they expected from the other and how they wanted to live. They then constructed the contract together so that it suited them both. They placed it between them, held hands and meditated on unity between them.

At the same time, Ran was also trying to decide whether to study yoga therapy with a well-known Bharati teacher and therapist who had offered him the possibility of living and studying with him. He had these matters in his mind when Premababa passed by him. Ran stood up and offered him the envelope with the marriage contract. Premababa looked at him with a big smile and took it saying, "very happy." Encouraged, Ran asked him, "Should I study yoga therapy with Sri Janar?" Premababa looked into his eyes and said, "Yes ."

Ran and Isabella lived in Sri Janar's house for the next 40 days, studying yoga therapy throughout the day and observing and helping out with patients who came mainly in the afternoon and evening. He did not learn many facts which he did not already know, but he did learn to put all of what he knew into an organized program and also gained much more confidence in this system, as he saw it working very effectively.

This third trip was a very important lesson in believing in himself. Premababa would not tell him what to do, because he wanted Ran to grow up and take responsibility for making his own decisions in life and have faith in his inner voice. He was told to study with Sri Janar, in order to realize that what he had already discovered on his own, was true. Conclusion: *he could trust in his inner guidance.*

Towards the end of this trip, Ran was watching Premababa from afar, holding some objects which he had bought for others. He wanted to offer these to Premababa to bless. There were too many persons between him and Premababa, for him to approach. Suddenly Ran felt a rush of energy flowing through his hands into the objects. It lasted about five minutes. Ran then realized that he was externalizing the power of the divine and limiting it to Premababa's body which was walking in the distance. Premababa insisted that the power which flowed through himself flowed through all of us. Few, however, were able to comprehend this. Ran began, in his own humble way, to understand.

When Ran and Issabella arrived back in Moor, they were considering whether to start publishing a magazine presenting subjects concerning health, psychology and spiritual life. One night Premababa came to him in a dream and Ran asked him. Premababa told him to go ahead. They did.

Ran had a number of dreams in which he asked various practical questions of Premababa and received the answers he needed. Of course, someone might say that his answers came from Ran's subconscious or his higher self. Ran was not concerned about where they came from, as long as he felt he was being guided.

He also had dreams in which Premababa would hold him, like a little child, in his embrace or in which Ran would place his forehead on Premababa's feet. He always woke up with a special energy and joyful attitude after such dreams. This positive state would last for days.

DISCOVERING PATHS INWARD

A few years later, he found himself again with Premababa, soaking up his love, and feeling his own love for Premababa. Again Premababa called them in for an interview. Baba was his usual bubbling-with-love-and-wisdom self, teaching them and giving them strength to move on in their spiritual practices.

Each visit to Premababa was an opportunity for Ran to rejuvenate himself through spiritual practices. He would sit in his room, or under a special meditation tree, and allowed himself to be guided from within concerning the form and contents of his spiritual practice.

Over the years he was guided through a wide variety of breathing control techniques in combination with special prayers and concentration on the centers of consciousness. He was also guided internally through various meditation techniques. After many years he found himself preparing the body and mind with a complicated breathing-prayer technique in which he would guide the energy through the various centers of consciousness along his spine, as he invoked a different concept at each center. This also evolved throughout the years, culminating in the following invocations while ascending the centers.

"Loving Lord Jesus Christ have mercy on us."

"Loving Lord Jesus Christ thank you for enlightening our faith."

"Loving Lord Jesus Christ thank you for enlightening our desires."

"Loving Lord Jesus Christ thank you for enlightening our ego."

"Loving Lord Jesus Christ thank you for enlightening our love."

"Loving Lord Jesus Christ thank you for enlightening our psyche."

"Loving Lord Jesus Christ thank you for enlightening our mind."

"Loving Lord Jesus Christ thank you for enlightening our unity."

"Loving Lord Jesus Christ thank you for enlightening our divinity."

"Loving Lord Jesus Christ we love you and we thank you."

He would then follow this with a meditation on the Self, rejecting every mental or physical phenomena as illusion, and coming back to pure awareness. When the mind was unusually unruly, which was not seldom, he would bring in the thought of death and would think, "Who will I be after I die? Who was I before I was born? This body and mind are going to die. All is God."

The mind would then see the senselessness in continuing its mundane line of thoughts, and he would return to witnessing and extracting himself from the illusory phenomena of the mind. When he started the meditation, he would say a prayer for those who needed help, and then in general for humanity and nature. Then he would say to God: "I am going to try to empty myself of who I think I am, to empty my mind and heart and I invite you to fill it, to come into me and allow me to experience my true self. Make me into the being You want me to be."

Then he would begin the process of letting go.

By this time, Ran was also beginning to feel that it was better not to focus so much on the particular form of Premababa. He wanted to transcend forms. He wanted to feel God's presence everywhere and in everyone. This was actually the essence of Premababa's teachings, but few were ready to make this transition in perception as most chose to remain in the role of the child, externalizing and limiting the divine.

Ran was also feeling the need to reconnect on a deeper level with Christ. He felt no conflict between these forms. When he prayed, he prayed to Christ. This did not create any conflict for him as Premababa had clearly said, "I have not come to change your religion. I have come to make you a better follower of the religion you already belong to."

Thus Ran did not feel the need to return soon to Bharat. He focused on feeling God in every one and every situation.

PREMABABA ACCEPTS RAN'S BOOK

Issabella and Ran returned again to visit the ashram and bathe in Premababa's love and spiritual inspiration. This had become a second home for them.

At one point Ran decided to offer Premababa the Center program and a cassette of their chants in Moorian. Premababa accepted both with a large smile, indicating that he was pleased both with he Center's work and with the fact that they were chanting to the Christ in their own language.

At another point, Ran handed him the book that he had written about Premababa's teachings. Premababa took it in hand, looked it over and then signed, "With Love, Premababa." Some weeks later Ran received permission from Premababa to have the book translated into other languages. That gradually happened.

They passed a peaceful month, bathing in the love they felt for this being who had given so much to all of mankind. There was no more anxiety about having an interview. Ran was satisfied simply to feel his love for Premababa. He would sit there and feel his heart opening with such joy and gratitude towards this gentle, and yet, all-powerful being.

At one point he felt his heart open so much that he could not contain the energy which was flowing. This became for Ran a point-of-reference for what it means to love. He had not felt this way for anyone in his life until now. He felt so happy that this being simply existed without wanting anything specific from him.

They were called in and again Premababa performed various miracles materializing sacred ash and rings and various other objects. He gave them his love in this way and spoke to them about spiritual life. Ran simply sat and loved, he had nothing to ask for. He was blissful. He was learning how to love *without wanting something* from the one he loved.

AN ALL-EXPENSES PAID TRIP

After a few years, Ran was invited to be the main speaker at a five-day International Convention of Yoga Teachers in a country on the other side of Alithea. They paid for his way to come and all his accommodations. Bharat was on the plane route, and thus he managed to have a free trip to see Premababa again.

On this trip the testing began again. Bantof, a young Moorian man who had a history of psychological problems, started to act strangely in the monastery. As the administration office was aware that Ran spoke Moorish, they asked him to speak with the man. Ran tried to calm him down. He believed that he was the Christ and that Premababa was the Antichrist. He started wearing long gowns and speaking aggressively.

Eventually the administration asked Ran to help the young man leave. Ran, with much difficulty, managed to get him on a bus to return to the airport in Moor.

This was one of the reasons that Ran had come to prefer spending the summers in Moor, focusing on the divine through the formless. Every time he was in Bharat, he, by the nature of his position in Moor, was asked to take care of various practical problems for Moorians. These responsibilities distracted him from the spiritual focus he wanted to create during this short period of time which he had, when he wasn't working 80 hours a week.

After two days, he received a message that the young man was now in a mental hospital two hundred kilometers away. Ran and Issabella took a taxi with another Alander whom they met there, who was also a psychotherapist. They found Bantof in an asylum.

Ran was amazed at the innocent faces he saw in this asylum. They were the most angelic faces he had ever seen. He spent some time with Bantof who was quiet now that he was drugged. But what to do now? How was he going to get home? Ran and Issabella had to go on to the convention. Bantof had to return in the opposite direction.

The psychotherapist suggested that they put him on a plane by himself and have him picked up in Moor. Ran could not agree with this. Then the psychotherapist offered to take Bantof to another destination in a country near Moor where he would be passing on his way back to Aland.

All of this depended on incredible timing and the ability to get one of Bantof's relatives go and meet him at this other airport. This sent them running first to the police (Bantof had pulled out a knife and threatened someone in the hotel he had been staying), then to the court judge to get an affidavit allowing Bantof's release from the asylum under their custody. Then they had to call his parents in Moor, something like calling the other side of the universe from Bharat in those days. Then back to the asylum twice a day to bring him food and keep him company.

The Alander psychotherapist left without their being able to make the connection. Ran and Issabella were left holding the bag and had to leave the next day. Now back to the court judge to cancel the order, back to the police to return his belongings. Back to the asylum and also to call his parents before they left to tell them what they must do.

All of this occurred at a time during which Ran wanted to be meditating and preparing. In a few days, he would be speaking for five days to 150 Yoga teachers from all over the world.

ADMIRED AND ACCUSED

The rest of the trip was heavenly. They visited a number of cities while giving lectures and seminars. They then went on to the convention, which was a great success, and they were much loved. It was at this point, the *Teacher* persona began separating itself dangerously from the other personas, as it received ever-increasing amounts of attention.

He also learned from this trip to let go of his need to prepare himself energy-wise for lectures and seminars. He saw that it was his insecurity that caused him to believe that he needed to prepare himself. It was sufficient to pray for guidance just before starting to speak. It became a natural habit to ask for guidance whenever he spoke or counseled. He prayed that he express only what the others needed to hear to be benefited spiritually, nothing more or less.

When they arrived at the airport in Moor, Ran was once again not allowed to enter. His name was on the computer black list noted as a person dangerous to the national welfare. The church authorities had once again played their hand in their attempt to get rid of him.

The contrast was amazing. Being treated in one country as a celebrity and a person who has much to offer others, and then in the other as a criminal for the same reasons that the others considered him to be something special.

Ran realized how silly it was to identify with the one role or the other. Both were mistaken. He was nothing special and also he was not a criminal. Nor was he the victim as the *Rebel* and the *Unjustly Persecuted* wanted him to believe. All was happening for a reason. He preferred none of these roles. Neither to be someone special, nor to be hated and feared. But it seems he needed to learn through these experiences.

He had to remain in the airport a considerable time until his wife was able to manage again to get him in.

His residence was arranged and everything was wonderful again. He had everything he needed. A fine wife, who shared with him this common effort and creation; multiple avenues for creative expression: the Center, a magazine, a publishing company for his books, a community of like-minded Alitheans, a health food store, service to the orphans, the poor, the refugees and the blind and so many people being helped through the center.

He enjoyed working and creating. He also enjoyed the month in the summer when he could prepare lectures and seminars, write books, meditate more, and commune with nature.

Almost all his personas were satisfied.

Everything was under control.

Until the revolution.

CHAPTER FOURTEEN

PERSECUTION FROM THE CHURCH

Two years after starting the new center, he had received an official notice to appear at the aliens' bureau. When he had gotten there, they had informed him that he was considered to be dangerous to the national security and therefore, he was an "undesirable," and would have to leave in three days.

He was shocked. He could not comprehend what this meant. To whom was he dangerous? His only desire was to help people. He felt hurt, injustice, fear and anger as the *Rebel*, the *Sacrificing Hero* and the *Unjustly Persecuted* monopolized his mind space.

Many of those involved with the Center moved into action. They found out that the church was responsible, and particularly Father Malloor – a zealous priest and theologian who was responsible for protecting the church members from these "dangerous heresies." Ran requested an investigation into these false accusations, which were subsequently found baseless.

Again after some years, the same scene occurred. He was told to get out of the country in ten days. The order that was again instigated by the church was rescinded when upon investigation, the accusations were again found to be false.

Twice, as already mentioned, he was refused entrance into the country. Each of these four incidents was a trying time for Ran. His *Rebel* and *Unjustly Persecuted* personas were troubled and magnified by these events, which to himself, and the thousands that knew him, seemed clearly unjust.

Each test, however, was an opportunity to develop many of the spiritual qualities that he valued. As the threat of being evicted from the country was a continual reality, he learned to let go of attachment towards external stability in terms of a home and source of living. He learned to leave the outcome in God's hands.

He learned to fight injustice without harboring negative feelings towards the perpetuators. He learned to forgive and to love those who hated and misunderstood him. He learned to attempt to communicate with them without attachment to the result. He definitely gained much from these events.

He sent to Father Malloor and to the Holy Synod, the guiding Hierarchy of the Church, detailed explanations of their activities along with letters, books and lectures on cassette and video.

He sent them a detailed survey, with questionnaires filled out by the members of the center, in which they indicated that they had come much closer to their religion through their contact with the Center. Ran invited Father Malloor and any other members of the church hierarchy, to come to the Center to discuss their fears and objections.

He never received any answer. Over the years, 18 official letters were sent to the Church Hierarchy by the Center's board of trustees as well as a number of personal letters and cassettes to Father Malloor. The answer was always the same – none.

The situation worsened as the Church started an all-out campaign to "protect" people from centers such as the one created by Ran and his friends. There were frequent articles in newspapers and magazines, radio and TV broadcasts as well as pamphlets handed out in the churches stating that these centers, listing Ran's center along with many others (and often even referring to his name personally), are centers which use people, misguide them, have sexual orgies and worship Satan.

Ran didn't even believe that there was a Satan. His love was for Christ, God, man and nature. He gradually got used to this type of false accusation. It helped him learn all of the lessons mentioned above.

Father Malloor wrote a book about these "dangerous heresies," referring to Ran and his center on sixty pages of the book. Ran wrote a book in answer to this book, but his friends felt that it was too dangerous to publish it. Ran's position in Moor was already fragile. He did not have the rights that other citizens had. Because he was an Alander and not a Moorian, he could be thrown out of the country by the Secret Service without a court trial (as they already attempted four times).

He learned that children were being taught in their religion class at school about these "Satanistic" heresies, often referring specifically to Ran's center. People were being programmed with fear and hate towards a group of people they didn't know; a group of people who simply wanted to help others.

An orphanage that had been receiving help from them for ten years informed them that now that they have learned that they are worshipers of Satan, they did not want their help anymore. Citizens called and cursed them on the phone.

Whenever Ran appeared on TV, the Church Hierarchy would call and complain and make sure that it would not happen again. There were a number of bomb scares in which they had to stop classes and evacuate the building. Finally Ran's car and even the center were set on fire and his life threatened by an anonymous caller. He was told to get out of the country or else he would meet with an accident.

This was all very tiring for Ran, as he was particularly vulnerable to injustices from his lives as Rupert and Shala. His *Unjustly Persecuted* persona grew in size. He sometimes felt like returning to his own country where he had the same rights as all others. There, at least, he could have dealt with the matter legally, forcing those who made these accusations to prove them or be silent.

On the other hand, he felt very useful in Moor and loved the country and people. It was a very strange experience for Ran, who very much wanted to have good relationships with everyone, to have tens of thousands of people hate him because they were misinformed about what he was doing. Moreover, he was learning and gaining so much by being persecuted in this way. He learned to let go and surrender to the Divine Will. If he was to leave, he would leave, if he was to stay, he would stay – this he left to God.

He sent love and light to Father Malloor. In one meditation he even had a message that they had been brothers in a past life, and that Father Malloor was doing him this favor by testing him in this incarnation. He actually felt a tenderness towards this elderly gentleman, who apparently believed what he said.

Ran gradually learned to ignore all of this and continued to feel very happy with his life, enjoying the center, the community, his wife and his month in the summer, where he would go to the mountains and write. His greatest happiness came from seeing how many people were being helped so effectively by the center, the books and the cassettes. His dream was coming true. He wanted in some way to be useful in humanity's transformation, to work for a better world with greater love and unity.

He felt his life blessed and balanced.

Everything was perfect.

Until the revolution of the suppressed personas.

And then it happened.

CHAPTER FIFTEEN

THE REVOLUTION

THE FIRST BATTLE

Ran loved his wife Issabella. However, because of Ran's character their relationship consisted of 95% work that they shared and 5% of personal contact. Their exchange of affection was more on the level of brother and sister, or parent and child than husband and wife. This was due mostly to Ran's decision not to "lose energy" on sexual activity. Issabella accepted this, made this sacrifice for which Ran was grateful.

They put all their energy into their work. They created a magazine together and then a publishing company. Ran was in love with Issabella; whenever he saw her he felt his heart open. He was happy that they were living and serving together in this way.

For the first nine years of their marriage everything was perfect. He enjoyed the variety of their lives. The Center, the publications, the seminars, the way of living and sharing in the spiritual community, the service to the surrounding society. Life was perfect.

And then it happened.

Ran began to notice other women. He was very pleased with Issabella. She was as physically attractive as any other woman; she worked hard, she loved him, he loved her, and they had managed to create a harmonious and fruitful life. Why was his mind focusing on other women?

He noticed that his mind tended to focus on women who were more emotional and rebellious, more "alive" to their emotions than he. For about a year, he just watched this. Then one day while counseling, he found himself more attracted to a young woman, but avoided making any advancement. After a few sessions, she confessed being in love with him. He then admitted that he too felt an attraction. They held each other for about five minutes and it was over. Ran had learned to enjoy allowing energies flow between himself and others. He considered this an innocent alternative to erotic contact.

But in subsequent "innocent" embraces, he began feeling his erotic nature awakening. He had suppressed this part of himself for about 18 years. His wife understood and helped him in this, but it seems that some of his personas were not satisfied by this solution. The *Rebel,* the *Poor Unloved Child,* the *Prankster,* the *Erotic Woman Dancer* were creating an overthrow of the governing personas.

This contact with this younger woman lasted about two months and never reached the level of sexual intercourse, but his rebelling personas were definitely reawakened. Issabella sensed all this and was extremely hurt and unhappy.

She confronted him with this a number of times, but he could never admit it. He did not want to hurt her, nor was he dissatisfied with her so as to want to separate. He also could not admit to himself that there was a part of himself which sought this feeling of freedom through erotic play or just through being free to do what he wanted. He was feeling suppressed without anyone else being at fault.

He was in conflict. He loved Issabella and wanted to be with her, and never wanted to hurt her, but on the other hand these personas were reacting strongly. They perceived her as the obstacle to their free expression.

Ran could not admit this to himself and thus could not admit it to others. He thought many times of doing so, but feared that they would reject him and never understand him as they obviously expected much more from him, as he did of himself. He wanted to be an example of ethical behavior. He wanted to show that Alitheans could grow spiritually in a marriage relationship. He was ashamed of himself but could not share it with anyone, except with God in his prayers and meditations.

This upsurge of the revolting personas passed and Ran was not bothered by them for two years. During this time Issabella was still very much hurt by what she knew had happened but could not deal with, because Ran could not admit it. She began to naturally distance herself from him and the Center. Ran felt badly about this, because he did not want to lose her, and he also needed to feel that they were working together on this project.

THE SECOND BATTLE

Two years later the same thing happened with Brenna. While counseling her, he began to feel that same affection. He was touched by her sensitivity and wealth of emotional expression, as well as her rebellious nature. The *Rebel* awoke again seeking to express his "freedom" to do whatever he wanted. His erotic self had now been suppressed another two years, because of his own inability to accept that his erotic nature was also God-given. The *Holy-Pure-Monk* and *Seeker of Enlightenment* had prevented him from expressing this nature even to his own wife. The *Teacher*, the *Writer* and the *Organizer* left him no time or energy to feel it. But it was there imprisoned in the vault of his subconscious. It awoke again.

He explained, and Brenna agreed, that they would share this intimacy for only ten days and that he could share affectionate embrace but not sex. Ten days became a month, and a month two, and two finally became three. Their contact became ever more erotic and emotional, without ever being consummated in the act of sex.

Ran was in turmoil. Although he was able to perform all of his functions as a teacher, organizer and counselor with clarity and efficiency, he was in deep inner turmoil. He loved two women, and wanted to hurt neither. He needed both. He knew that he must let go, but he couldn't. On the other hand it was as if the conspiracy of rebelling personas wanted to destroy the roles of *Teacher, Husband,* and *Monk,* because they had been suppressed for so many years under their rule.

He even mentioned to Brenna that he was destroying his role as teacher and husband in order to be who he really was. His various personas made various excuses such as:

"As we are not engaging in the act of sex, then it is ok."

"How could loving another aspect of the divine hurt others?"

"Just a few more days and we will stop."

"By loving, I am adding love to the universe."

"Brenna needs me."

The other personas scolded him:

"You are doing to your wife what you would not like her to do to you."

"You are not doing what you teach."

"You are not being honest."

"You are not a spiritual person."

These two camps of personas were at war.

Ran prayed many times a day for help to stop. He asked God to guide him. The more he prayed, the more intense became his feelings for Brenna. He loved Issabella also very much and did not want to hurt her, but his rebelling personas now saw her as the enemy, the oppressor, the obstacle to their freedom of expression.

And then the moment of truth came.

His wife found out.

DESTRUCTION

What ensued was the most painful experience of Ran's incarnation on Alithean.

CHAPTER SIXTEEN

THE CRISIS

CONFESSION

Ran sat before the thirty people he loved most in his life. He had in a few short hours been transformed in their minds from their beloved friend, guide and teacher to their disgraceful, betraying, two-faced enemy. He was deeply ashamed, not of his feelings for Brenna, but of his inability to share his situation with the others. He had been afraid to.

He felt horrible that he was now causing so much pain for people he loved so much and who were so important to him, most importantly his wife. He confessed as well as he could, still trying to cover his weakness and fears. His phrases were short, confused and often lacking continuity.

"My head is spinning.

"So many feelings flood my mind simultaneously.

"I feel hurt that they do not understand me.

"I feel love for all those who come to my mind.

"I feel sad for all those whom I have caused to become disillusioned with the spiritual path.

"It is okay to be disillusioned with me but not with what I have taught you.

"I feel weak and helpless against the forces of my subconscious mind.

"I feel horrible for the pain I have created for my wife Issabella, and for so many others.

"I feel love as my broken heart opens.

"At last, I am humbled. Finally, comes my release from the role of the teacher, and my need to be perfect, not for myself but for others.

"But which are those weaknesses and mistakes?

"That I loved another? No, love can never be a mistake.

"My mistake was that I was not able to accept or admit my feelings, and that I did not have the power to raise that love to a purely spiritual level.

"The more I prayed to be released from my attraction and attachment, the stronger they became, as if all this was destined to be. In order to destroy me.

"I prayed to God numerous times each day to remove this desire.

"After each prayer, the thought came that perhaps all this had to happen in this way, and I ended the prayer with the phrase, 'Let your will be done.'

"How many times I looked at my wife Issabella with love in my heart, wishing that she be well and happy, only to be unable to express those feelings to her.

"Now although she hates me, and rightly so, I love her and I want her to be happy.

"It was as if a part of me had gone crazy, and proceeded towards total destruction of all that I had created.

"So many times in the past I had the power to prevent this erotic impulse from expressing itself. But not this time.

"I am tired. I feel very tired. I have become entrapped in the roles of the *Teacher* and the *Savior*. I have become their victim.

"I feel responsible for everyone and everything.

"I feel responsible for the young men and women in the commune, for the students, for all the groups and activities which have been created.

"On the other hand, I gave all my time and energy life. I held back nothing.

"I am leaving you all and the Center with empty hands, but with a full heart.

"Despite my weakness, I did what I could.

"It is as if I had decided to destroy it all, as if God has planned this moment.

"I feel very concerned, however, that you not reject the teachings which we have all seen help thousands of people.

"I do not feel guilty for loving another fellow being. My guilt lies in wanting to protect myself by hiding my feelings and weaknesses, and therefore my inability to express what was going on within me.

"I am guilty of fearing rejection from others.

"Of course, I am learning a great deal from all this.

"Some of the lessons are easy, such as forgiving those who hate me and want to hurt me or have revenge on me.

"Another lesson is to face leaving so many friends whom I truly love.

"Hundreds of persons, whom I love, come to my mind.

"Although it is extremely painful, I accept having fallen in their eyes.

"There is paradoxically a certain freedom for me in that. I am freed from the need to be perfect in their eyes. That myth is now shattered, and we are all set free to grow together in the truth that we are all spiritually equal and that the Divine exists with in each of us. We can now grow in the truth that there are no teachers and no students, but that *we are all manifestations of the one Divine Creative Consciousness and that we are all learning and all teaching.*

"A part of me feels hurt that after trying for so long to serve people, caring for them and wanting them to be happy and well, that with one mistake, they suddenly forget all the love that transpired between us, and remember only the disappointment, and hate me for that.

"I accept the consequences of my actions and understand your feelings.

"I have faith that what is happening is exactly what I need for my growth as a person.

"I was attached to my work.

"I never took time for myself as a person. I wanted to be beyond that.

"Only it seems a shame that so many others had to suffer and perhaps become disillusioned with the path.

"Our Center is a light; an example in society. We have achieved much. You can be proud.

"It must continue, now without me.

"For a long time now I have felt the need to work on myself as a person.

"I want to be able to help others, not through techniques or what I do, but rather through what I am. I want to become a humble source of love.

"I feel a fire in me which is burning whatever is useless.

"This is a very powerful lesson for me; to try to feel well even though there are so many persons who do not believe me and even hate me.

"I have felt very lonely these last months.

"I have grown tired of being misunderstood and accused by a whole society.

"On the other hand, I am grateful for the opportunity to learn to love and accept myself regardless of others' rejection.

"I feel especially sorry for the young members of the commune. I am so grateful for their cooperation in creating what we have manifested together. I love you all very deeply, and I hope that you will continue. If you chose not to, then I wish you lives full of love and growth. If you ever need me in the future, I will be there for you.

"I feel an aversion at the moment towards the idea of teaching again.

"I feel the need to be the simple person I have always been on the inside.

"Perhaps to cultivate the soil; to pray, to communicate with nature, to serve others with love.

"I would like to write and express my personal self through feelings.

"I feel the need for a humble type of life.

"I feel released from so many responsibilities which weighed heavily upon me.

"I thank God for this humbling moment.

"I thank God for this rejection which I am receiving.

"I thank God for the hate which I am receiving.

"I also thank God for the love and forgiveness which I feel from some of you.

"I thank you, and I ask you to pray for me."

REACTIONS

Some understood, others were very angry. He received much hate for a number of months. The next day he issued a confession to be read in all the classes. He announced his retreat from the Center for an unknown period of time. He emphasized that they should not lose faith in the teachings, the system, or the techniques, that this was his personal failure, which had to do with one of his personal weak points and not with the system or philosophy that was being taught. He encouraged them to continue without him.

After ensuring that the Center could continue for those who did want to continue, he moved into semi-seclusion until he left again for Bharat.

SECLUSION

In those two months, he lived by the sea, meditated many hours and tried to figure out what was going on within himself and what he should do. He felt a strong aversion towards returning to teach. He wanted to be anonymous. He didn't want to live any more with the pressure of knowing that other people wanted him to be perfect. He wanted to be himself.

He connected with Brenna a few times in those two months. He loved her and cared for her. But he was not happy. She was not at fault. He was in great inner turmoil. He had to find out what was going on in himself. He had to be alone.

The spiritual community dissolved, only five of the twenty members remained and in the following year and a half they became three. As a result of Ran's persona revolt, they lost the main building of their retreat center.

The urban center, however, survived. Only about fifteen percent of the members left, mostly the newer ones. Most of those who had been there over a year and knew Ran, remained. The Center was able to continue without him.

While in retreat, he received about 150 letters from students expressing their love and asking him to please return soon. Ran was grateful for these letters, but they did not help him much. If he didn't love himself, how could he feel their love?

One letter by a young woman stuck in his mind. She mentioned a place in Bharat where she had recently participated in some seminars that helped her. This place was run by a group of persons whom Ran, until now, had considered to be following an illusory spiritual path. Ran still held his opinion, but the letter remained in his mind.

DIVISION

The members of the center were divided. Most understood, but a handful were very unhappy and angry and wanted to burn all Ran's teachings, books, cassettes and videos. They wanted to ensure that he would never be among them again. One woman even told him, "I would like to kill you." Ran understood all of these reactions. A number of his own personas agreed with them.

The church was overjoyed that finally there was "proof" that he was the evil person they had been saying he was. Even the Premababa centers found this opportunity to verify that he was not following the right path. While the Church accused him of being an agent for Premababa, who they believed was the antichrist, the Premababa centers accused him of not following Premababa's teachings by adding various psychological processes such as childhood regression, psychodrama and work with the subconscious. Both groups were against him and found him to be evil for the opposite reasons. But the basic reason was that he did not conform to their beliefs and path.

REJECTION

Ran was overcome by many powerful feelings. This was a new experience for him. He felt shame that he was not able to live up to his teachings. He felt that he had failed as a teacher, as a husband, as a spiritual aspirant. He felt guilt for all the pain and confusion that he had created for others. He felt rejected, unworthy, unloved. He also felt injustice, somewhat like a tree that had offered a thousand sweet fruits, and now was being condemned for producing one sour one.

He felt that no one understood him. He had in mind hundreds of examples of men and women who had fallen into such an illusion for long periods of time and with full sexual relationships, who had not received such treatment. Most were still married.

He, like his environment, was divided. One group of personas saw him as the abuser, while an other saw him as the abused. He wished he could have turned the clock back a few months and change all that. He could not.

He was most pained by the fact that members of the community, whom he dearly loved, were very hurt and very much against him. They felt betrayed, and rightly so, and now they were trying to break away by perceiving him as an evil person. This allowed them to create the distance they needed. Ran understood this, but he still felt pain.

Ran also felt betrayed by God. After so many years of prayer, meditation and analysis, he had expected to receive more help when he prayed to be released from his desire to be with another woman. He felt that he had made an intense and disciplined spiritual effort for 25 years, living simply, praying and serving as much as he could. He had prayed so intensely those days to be given the strength to stop, and felt more and more driven rather than released.

Still another part of his multifaceted group persona saw all that was happening as exactly what he, and everyone else needed for their evolutionary process. He felt that he was actually *pushed by some higher power to fall into this trap, for everyone's good.* Many lessons would be learned by all.

He needed to learn not to identify with the role of the teacher and be himself. He had often said, "I am not perfect, I am not enlightened, I am on the path with you, I have many faults and weaknesses which I am working on." But he never had the guts to share those specific weaknesses with others. He wasn't even aware of their magnitude until the revolution.

The others would learn to focus on the spiritual process, the teachings and the techniques, and not on the person. They would learn to internalize their power. *This became an opportunity for Ran to become even more humble, and for others to own their power by developing their innate abilities.* This is what happened.

ILLUSION

This was obviously his so called "mid-life crisis" which men and women are known to pass through. Ran felt that his position was even more difficult. Yes, on one hand it was a mid-life crisis but, according to most of his personas, and all those around him, he and all others who people put in the role of the spiritual person are not supposed to be subject to this illusion. They are supposed to have overcome their physical nature.

In the following months as Ran had time to occasionally read newspapers and magazines, he began to become aware of how many priests, bishops and spiritual teachers fall into this trap not for a few months, but for many years and with multiple relationships. He wondered about this as he conceived these persons as much more spiritually in control than he was. Many of them had been lost in this confusion of a double life for ten and twenty years.

Thinking about this, he realized how vulnerable people in such a position are. When someone opens his heart to you and trusts you, you see their beauty. As the love factor is often well developed in these teachers and counselors, they care for the person who comes to them for help. They begin to respect, admire and love that person, to see their inner beauty and they fall into the trap of wanting to be with that beauty, to share it and to offer their affection to it.

In addition, they are subject to all the ancient biological and psychological needs and instincts, which make men and women feel attraction. Also the move towards something more intimate is often initiated by the person "being helped," who frequently puts the teacher into a father or mother role and falls in love with him or her, often expressing these tender feelings to the teacher or counselor. This is a stimulus that can easily trigger the teacher's need to receive and give affection and love. A teacher might also fall into the trap of not wanting the other to feel rejection after such a confession.

Thus, souls who are evolving through this role of the teacher or counselor are much more susceptible to falling into this trap. The trap is not of loving or caring, but crossing over the border to the physical expression of that love. Yet society is much harsher in judging them for this. Thus they are in a very difficult position.

RETREAT

At this moment all his personas were in an uproar, and he was very confused.

He had to get away.

He returned to the Center for one week, entered each class in order to ask for their patience and understanding, explained that he was not ready to return and that he would be leaving Moor for some time. He asked for their forgiveness again and departed.

CHAPTER SEVENTEEN

HEALING

SEEKING HELP

Ran started his trip with a visit to a monastery in Northern Moor, seeking help from a Christian Monk elder there who was known to have spiritual clairvoyant powers. He wanted to ask the elder to help him discover what had actually happened. How was it that, although he was so disciplined and had made so many years of spiritual effort, he was still vulnerable to these personas and was able to lose his clarity? After a two-day journey, he arrived only to find that the elder had left the monastery and was seriously ill in the hospital. No help from here.

He then left for Bharat. Premababa's monastery was very much changed. There were many more people, more cement, and hundreds of police and soldiers as the president of Bharat was visiting Premababa, seeking his blessings and advice.

Ran had three basic needs. One was to get an answer from Premababa as to whether he should return to Moor and whether the Center should continue as it was presently structured? Or should he make major changes in his life and/ or in the Center? After what had happened, he was plagued by self-doubt.

His second need was to meditate, to transcend, to reestablish that inner contact which he had experienced often in his life, but which he had presently lost.

His third need was most probably a prerequisite for the second. He needed to cry. He felt that he had many emotions in him that he had not yet become familiar with, let alone express. He had no idea how he was going to do this. He needed catharsis. He had realized that meditation and prayer can often bypass these emotions and create a spilt personality; in his case, a split in his group persona. Some personas had proceeded intellectually and spiritually, while others were still afraid, still in doubt about their self-worth and were experiencing pain, which the other "spiritual" personas would not allow them to bring to the surface and express.

His first need, however, was to get confirmation from Premababa as to how to proceed. During the first days, his contact with Premababa was very loving and assuring. Ran was afraid that he would be rejected or scolded. He had reverted to the role of the child and was again putting Premababa in the role of the father who was going to tell him whether he was a good boy or not and whether he loved him or not.

Fortunately for Ran, as he could not stand any more rejection, Premababa was kind to him, taking his letters, blessing objects for him, smiling at him. After about a week, Ran decided to get a clearer answer about the Center. He put the Center's program in an envelop with a letter which said "If you do not want me to continue with this Center, or if you want us to make changes in the way it functions, please do not take this letter. If you do agree to the way it is functioning and want it to continue as it is, then please take this letter as a sign."

Ran was anxious as Premababa came towards where he was sitting. He could accept closing the Center if the letter was refused. He could accept starting a new life on a totally different basis. But he preferred to continue where he was, as so much work had been done and he felt useful, and enjoyed what he was doing. He preferred this to starting all over from the beginning with something totally different. But he was resigned to follow whatever message he got from Premababa on this account.

Premababa approached, smiled long and deeply at him, and took the letter. Ran was relieved; he was getting a second chance to do things right this time. Afterwards those who were sitting near came over and asked Ran, why Premababa had smiled to him in that way. This too was Premababa's way of answering him, by making these people emphasize the fact that the answer was, "yes."

Need number one was satisfied and Ran felt better now. Although he still had all the emotions he had brought with him, he was happy that he was being given another chance. Now it was time to meditate and, if possible, go through a catharsis.

However, his knee was bothering him terribly, making meditation difficult, as did the fact that there was very little peace in the monastery with so many devotees, police and soldiers.

Ran thought about traveling to the north and staying at a monastery that focused more on meditation, to go more deeply into himself. But he had never gone anywhere else in Bharat. He felt that it would be strange to leave Premababa's monastery and go to another. Yet a voice in him said that this is what he needed. Another voice told him that all monasteries are dedicated to the one God and lead to Him. But there was resistance in his personas, many of them wanted to stay or, more accurately, felt that they should stay. But this was exactly the cause of Ran's revolution. He had made many decisions based on what he should do and ignored a deeper voice that was closer to the truth.

He called his Bharati friend Haron who lived in northern Bharat now, and asked him if he would be interested in making a pilgrimage to a monastery for meditation. Haron had visited many of these monasteries and knew them well. Haron was interested.

But Ran was still unsure what to do. He enjoyed the atmosphere of devotion and love in Premababa's monastery. In the evening, sitting out in the open space, devotees gathered, singing songs of love to God in many different languages. Some had guitars and drums. It was a deeply touching sight. He would cry, thinking, "Why couldn't all the world be this way."

A COINCIDENCE

While visiting with a homeopathic doctor who worked at the monastery, he asked him if he had ever heard of Dr. Voran, a famous Moorian homeopathic doctor. The doctor smiled at the coincidence and said, "yes and he is coming today, this evening." Ran had met Dr. Voran a number of years earlier and recently had been encouraged by one of his group facilitators to go to him for help during this time of crisis. Ran respected him but did not go, as he preferred to work this out within himself, without the help of external energies, even if they were natural.

He was happy to see Dr. Voran again. He and his wife had been invited by Premababa to spend a few days at the monastery. Ran passed two wonderful days with them, and then came time for them to leave. They would be leaving by plane, avoiding an exhausting three-hour taxi ride and then a flight to their destination.

Ran thought of leaving with them, but knew that there were no vacant seats. He decided to leave it up to fate. He put his name on the waiting list. Number twelve. If he was to leave, there would be space. If not, he was to stay.

Although the odds were against it, he found a seat and left.

MORE COINCIDENCES

He took a taxi to Haron's house and was met by his beloved friend and his lovely wife, Promil. They received him, tired, confused, still feeling guilt and failure. They took him in and gave him their love. He ate the delicious Bharati food that Promil prepared with love. He meditated and began to recover.

One afternoon, Ran asked, "Haron, I see that you have some books by Rashor; what do you think about him?"

Haron replied, "They are great, excellent." Promil agreed.

Ran was shocked. Both were yoga teachers trained in the strict Bharati tradition. Rashor was a very controversial figure, who rejected most religions and traditions, advocating freedom from all systems (although creating his own) and also freedom for all types of expression including sexual. He had been thrown out of some twenty countries as no government wanted him there. He had accumulated a large amount of personal wealth donated to him by his followers.

Ran had a negative opinion of all this. But yet many had a negative opinion of Ran without knowing him. Ran was, however, very surprised that Haron and Promil thought positively about this Rashor.

Then Ran remembered a letter written by one woman that stuck in his mind. He realized now that she was referring to a seminar center created by Rashor's followers some one hundred and fifty kilometers from Haron's home. Rashor had passed away, but his followers had created a university of "techniques for body, mind and spirit" there.

Ran was set to thinking by this strange twist of events. He looked through a brochure, belonging to Haron, which indicated that Rashor's followers were involved in catharsis techniques. This interested him. He called and found that they had no accommodations in the monastery and that Ran would have to live at a hotel while there.

This was enough to make Ran decide not to go, as he was not at all sure about this place, and did not have money for hotels and did not like living in hotels, while doing inner work. So as he walked back to Haron's house after the call, he had decided not to go.

Then Promil remembered that she had a good friend in that city whom they could stay with. His excuse was destroyed. Okay then, they would go for a few days just to see what was going on.

The train ride was like a three-ring circus. Vendors passing through the aisles selling everything imaginable from soft drinks, popcorn, sandwiches, cakes, coffee, and tea to fruits and even vegetables. You could do your week's shopping on the train.

Ran was troubled by the poverty in the slums that lined the train route for the first five miles of the journey. He could not imagine how people could live their whole lives under a piece of cloth strung up on four sticks. Each rain and wind just dissolved it. His own problems seemed so small, and he, so ego-centered to be worried about them. Each, however, has his own evolutionary path through which he struggles and grows.

The countryside, once they got out of the city slums, was magnificent. The air cleared as they traveled three hours up into the mountains. It was chilly when they arrived in Ranu, the site of the Seminar Center. They stayed the first two nights with Haron's friend.

CATHARSIS

As they approached the Seminar Center, they noticed people, mostly young foreigners, both men and women, wearing maroon robes. The frequency of these robes increased as they approached the entrance. Ran thought to himself, "they will never get me to wear one of these robes." He always had an aversion towards "uniforms," towards being like every one else. His ego reacted towards this elimination of his uniqueness.

At the reception area, they browsed through the numerous pamphlets explaining the various activities and seminars. Both Ran and Haron were impressed. These people were quite organized and seemed to have a certain expertise on the subjects and techniques that they offered.

Ran was divided as usual. A few personas, especially the *Monk* and *Teacher* had reservations about their teacher Rashor, even thought he had passed away a few years ago. On the other hand, the activities that were being offered centered on catharsis, which was exactly what many of his personas needed.

He decided to try the place out for few days. The first hurdle he had to overcome was the fact that he was required to wear a maroon robe on campus. He soon found himself in a robe, which he actually enjoyed because it reminded him of his days in Moor where he would often wear such a robe when at home.

The next obstacle was to find a place to stay. Hotels were too expensive and also dirty. They decided to look for a short-term apartment. They were standing in the doorway of a shop where the owner had gone to see if one of his apartments would be free soon.

Suddenly a three-wheel taxi stopped outside the store and a young man got out and came up to Ran and called him by his name. Ran, startled at first, then recognized Ganor, who had lived in their community in Moor for six months. He was God-sent. Ganor's roommate was leaving that day and Ran could move in the next day, paying a very small rent. Ganor was shocked to see Ran there, as he knew Ran's opinion about Rashor.

This was another of the many so-called "coincidences" which helped Ran to overcome the fears that he had made a mistake in leaving Premababa's monastery. It was clear that he was being guided to be here at this time.

Ran was impressed and helped by the various activities. There were many opportunities to release cathartically through dance, movement, shouting, singing, laughing and crying. Very little teaching was done. The seminars were 95% experiential as opposed to intellectual.

He found it difficult at first to get out of his intellectually-oriented focus. Others made fun of his intellectual tendencies. One of the group leaders asked him if he was a priest.

Ran answered, "Not in this lifetime." They all laughed.

At another point, the leader encouraged him to let his inner child free to play. Ran explained, "that is what I did a few months ago and he fell in love with another woman, and now my wife wants a divorce." They laughed again.

Although he felt like a stranger, that he didn't fit in there, he also felt that there was an emotional part of himself which had to come out now or never. If he couldn't get in touch with his emotions now, when he was feeling so hurt, guilty and sad, he would never be able to.

They helped and pushed him to express his emotions in various ways, usually by focusing on the body and the energies flowing through the body and allowing them to flow outwards expressively, first through words and then through crying, shouting, laughing or any other form of expression. Without knowing it he was being introduced to a system called "Body-Centered Psychology" which he would use extensively after that for helping others. He worked on releasing the traumas and shame stored within him.

In one session, all participants were asked to remove all their clothing and walk around the room. This was a very releasing experience for Ran, for he had always felt shame about his body, which he believed was not attractive. As he walked around, he gradually overcame his shame, experiencing a oneness with those around him. When the group leaders asked them to express their thoughts and emotions, Ran expressed that he felt comfortable with all of those who were also naked, but not with the group leaders who had their clothing on. He became more clearly aware of a mechanism that also works at an emotional level in psychology groups. When the group leader does not also expose himself or herself emotionally, the participants cannot feel totally comfortable with him or her. This was a lesson for him later on, while working with groups.

Afterwards he realized that this was the type of activity that had made Roshar such a controversial figure, and thrown out of so many countries. He understood, on the other hand, how releasing it was for him, how many barriers had been destroyed allowing others to see him, physically and emotionally. There were absolutely no sexual overtones. They were forty children playing in the nude. Overcoming their shame in this way, they regained their innocence.

LEARNING TO CRY

Ran was a hard nut to crack, but eventually he let go and cried. He cried deeply and extensively for a week. He cried for the pain he created for his wife Issabella, and also for Brenna, and for all the people he loved. He cried for his failure to be who he wanted to be. He cried because he felt abandoned by God, who he felt hadn't kept his promise to him, that if he tried hard, he would be helped to proceed.

He cried because he wasn't enlightened. He cried because all the rest of humanity was not enlightened. He cried for all the pain on the earth, all the unhappy people, the poor, those who live in war, in fear, those who were ill, the orphans, the elderly, the handicapped, the lonely, those in prison, the emotionally disturbed. He cried for all those who had lost their loved ones, especially their children. He cried because he was not able to create a better relationship with his father. He cried because he was not given all the attention and love he wanted when his younger brothers were born. He became an infant crying for his mother. He cried for the seeming injustice of this creation. Then he cried upon perceiving the beauty of all creation.

One day, walking to his crying session, he collected from the ground some of the most beautiful orange and red flowers he had ever seen. He looked at them for a long time. Later, as he was crying out to God for the seeming injustice which He allowed to transpire on Alithea, expressing both his pain and anger at God for not enlightening everyone and allowing so much pain to exist, he remembered the flowers and then cried at the beauty of this creation. It was at moments like this that he thought he was going mad. He was not especially afraid of going mad, as he saw it a state of freedom from his intellectual prison.

He also laughed. He laughed for a whole week, three hours a day.

He laughed at the beauty of those who laughed with him. He laughed at the "Divine Joke" which had been played on him in which he took everything to be serious and real. He laughed because all of his pain was an illusion. He laughed out of love for life. He laughed about the goodness in people. He laughed looking deeply into the eyes of those laughing with him. Then he came into contact with the source of causeless joy, joy without a reason. He laughed because he was happy, for no reason at all, because happiness was his nature.

In the process of laughing and crying, Ran discovered much about his resistance, fear and stereotyped thought processes. He was able to break through his fear of showing emotion or enthusiasm. Then came the week of meditation, in which Ran had the opportunity to meditate about five hours a day, going deep into himself to bathe in his inner peace. He felt himself being healed. He was grateful.

In the evenings, all the participants viewed together video lectures by Rashor. Ran was not able to totally dissipate his resistance towards Rashor's tendency towards criticizing other teachers, systems, and religions, or his tendency to exaggerate or his various inconsistencies. Thus, although he could not accept the master, he marveled at the devotees' methodic system of catharsis and physical - emotional healing. He was not able to accept Rashor's "negativities," but he was grateful to him for what he created.

Ran learned again the lesson of not judging something that he had not experienced first-hand. Ran who had said he would stay only a few days, left only after six weeks, completely rejuvenated.

THE FINISHING TOUCHES

His three needs had been fulfilled. He had received the message from Premababa to continue his work at the Center, he had cried, and he had meditated. He still, however, had some anxiety about what would happen in Moor. He had called his wife a few times, encouraging her to consider the possibility for them to work it out and be together again. She was still very hurt and was not open to such a possibility. But he felt he could persuade her upon returning.

He wanted everything to be as it was.

During the last days in Ranu, Ran visited Narik, a teacher who helped him go even deeper into the experience of his universal self. Ran had known for many years now that spiritual techniques alone would never liberate him. They would simply raise his vibrational level so that he would eventually be able to detach himself altogether from the ego, which is trying to get free with these spiritual exercises. This teacher was a living example of having achieved this detachment.

Each evening about twenty seekers would gather at his home, in the suburbs of Ranu, where they would meditate for about forty minutes and then listen to him answering questions posed by the group. The atmosphere was blissful and Narik was exquisite in his ability to bring them to the realization that there is no personal self, and that all personal spiritual ambition, even the desire for enlightenment itself, is an ego trap that will keep the ego in its separateness.

Spiritual techniques can be performed, but not with the goal of getting free. For as long as we are identified with the one who is seeking to get free, we can never realize that we are actually the one who is already free. Ran and Haron felt much love and gratitude towards Narik for his teachings, love and hospitality, for after each session, Narik's lovely wife would serve them excellent Bharati cuisine.

This was the topping of the cake. After getting the okay from Premababa, six weeks of catharsis through crying and laughing, and then another week of meditation, the healing process was sealed with the highest of teachings.

The train ride back was exquisite, as Ran gazed at the countryside rolling past him, while listening to inspired Bharati music on his headphones.

Ran left Bharat once again, now for the seventh time, overflowing with gratitude towards the land that always healed and renewed him. In was the land of opposites, of endless variety in which one is free to be himself and not be noticed or condemned.

He took leave of his dear friends Haron and Promil and returned to Moor.

CHAPTER EIGHTEEN

A SECOND CHANCE

NEW LESSONS

His wife Issabella met him at the airport to ensure that he got into the country, as he had been denied entrance twice previously. He was very happy to see her. On the way back from the airport he received his first shock. She had moved out of their apartment and that there was no possibility of their continuing. It took him a few days to adjust to this new reality.

After unpacking he went to see what was going on in the Center. Those who had remained still loved him and cared for him. Yet he still felt strange. Feelings of failure came to him often in those days. As he visited each class for the first time again, he repeated his request that they forgive him for his mistakes and any pain or disillusionment he had caused them.

Gradually as he continued his classes, he once again began to feel useful and creative. Having been humbled, his teachings were simpler, more accessible. They were now beginning to understand that he was a person like themselves, simply trying to improve himself.

There were still seven persons living and working in the community. Then one by one they announced that they would not be continuing... each for his own different reason. Each time someone left, Ran was filled with doubts about himself. He felt that he was unable anymore to inspire people towards living this communal life of selfless service. They sold the health food store.

The little energy that remained now went towards running the classes and seminars. Ran was still plagued frequently by self-doubt. The slightest criticism or sign of failure made him fear that he was not the proper person for the work that he was doing. Two thoughts kept him going. One was that Premababa had taken the letter indicating that he should continue. The second was that people who came to the Center were very satisfied and were being helped effectively. He felt useful.

Ran was caught between these two opposites; the obvious benefit which the members of the center were receiving and, on the other hand, the dissolution of the community which ran the Center. He was caught between self-doubt and a desire to be of use to others.

He began to share with his group facilitators the basics of "Body-Centered Psychology." They were retrained along the lines of effectively helping people to release their suppressed emotions. It had become very obvious to Ran that he had become a split personality. That his personas were at war, that he had ignored certain personas these last eighteen years, and that they still lived in him and had caused this revolution which had turned his life upside down.

With the help of the group facilitators, they revamped the whole six-year seminar, making basic changes, introducing more movement, dance, expression and catharsis so as to help others avoid the trap he himself had fallen into. The facilitators themselves went through the same process. The seminar and the center, and all those who passed through it, were very much benefited by Ran's crisis. This was unequivocally obvious.

REBUILDING

But Ran still had doubts about himself as a person. Although he perceived that he was an effective teacher, writer, creator and organizer, he doubted his own purity. He wasn't sure if he was a good person.

These doubts were not based on any observations which he had made concerning his character, but rather on events such as criticism from others, or members of the community leaving. His self-doubt was based on external stimuli and not on inner data about himself. He realized this, and could not understand why he was doubting himself so much. His *Bad Unworthy Child* had come clearly and intensely up to the surface.

He was now forced to perform many physical tasks that the other members of the community had covered previously. At times he found his *Teacher* persona complaining and feeling humbled for having to deal with so many "unimportant" details. But he knew deep in himself that this was exactly what he needed.

He frequently enjoyed his humble role of cleaning, building, working with cement, the plumbing, the electrical problems. He became the maintenance man for the Center. His mind was at ease while performing these functions, and the *Cooperating Server* persona enjoyed serving in this way. Some did not want to see their "teacher" humbled in this way, but this is exactly what they all needed. He would ask his *Teacher* persona, "what do you want to be – a teacher, or a simple soul in the evolutionary process?" The answer was the second.

The retreat center had to be rebuilt. The changes which had to be made were very demanding economically and physically. Ran mobilized his energies and with the few members who had remained to help, they recreated their seminar center. Once again he witnessed the miracle of Divine support.

Although they were few, the right persons appeared with the right talents at exactly the moment that they were needed. They were able to once again create a fine retreat and seminar center. In only three months, Alitheans were benefiting from the summer seminars once again in progress.

DILEMMAS

Ran still received much criticism from those around him. From the Church, from the Premababa centers, and from the old members of the community. He even had to admit committing adultery to thousands of viewers in a TV interview.

He tried to understand the reason why he was creating this situation. Was it that he must change the way he was thinking and acting? If so, the problem with this possibility was that each group that criticized him, wanted him to be something different from what the other group wanted. They were criticizing him for totally different reasons.

Another possibility was that he simply needed to learn to accept and love himself even when there were so many people who thought negatively about him. This was a difficult test, but he was beginning to be able to do so, to believe in himself and in his truth, regardless of what those around him thought of him.

Another dilemma that bounced back and forth in his mind was whether to have a conscious love relationship with a woman or not; to have a partner or not. His personas were split on this subject. Some personas definitely felt the need to share their love with a partner. Other personas believed that this would be an obstacle to their spiritual growth and perhaps to the dynamics of the community as it began to grow again.

He needed to receive and give affection and love. But he also needed to be alone to meditate, pray and transcend his personas.

Thus, although the center had recovered and was functioning very well and everything had returned to normal in his life, there were still basic inner conflicts which needed to be worked out. The questions which needed answering were:

1. Am I pure enough to be in this position?

2. Is the criticism I am receiving there to make me change, leave or

learn to accept myself as I am and believe in myself?

3. Am I to learn to become more austere and selective in placing people in positions to help others?

4. Should I be in a conscious love relationship or not?

5. How should I divide my energy between teaching, writing, counseling, helping the poor, and my own spiritual practices?

6. Should my emphasis be on accepting who I am or on changing who I am?

7. Should I make efforts to change or leave my transformation up to God?

His main questions behind all these questions were: "Does God want something more from me, or am I on my road to Him?" and "Is the path to God through denial, or through seeing and loving him in everything that I encounter?"

He could not distinguish whether the voices advocating denial of food or a relationship or other external sources of fulfillment were his inner self guiding him in the present, or the voices of past programming, causing him to limit the Divine to specific places, persons and situations.

He needed to answer these questions, but was getting conflicting answers from his various personas.

He decided to call a conference of all his personas and allow each to express itself as they sought as a group to find a solution...

CHAPTER NINETEEN

RAN CALLS A CONFERENCE
OF ALL PERSONAS

SELF DOUBT

Ran had so much to be grateful for. He was living a blessed life. He had food, shelter, and so many people who loved and respected him. He had ample opportunities for creativity. He had his health. Although he had no personal wealth, no house, nor land, he had so many persons who were willing to allow him to use their summer homes when he needed a place to meditate or write. He had accomplished much with his life personally and socially.

He had every reason to be happy and grateful. And he was.

But... always the eternal "*But*."

Those questions were still nagging him in the back of his mind, including doubts as to whether he was living his life as God wanted or not. Whether God wanted more from him and if so, what? Should he be more un-worldly, denying the pleasures of the world or should he learn to see the Divine in each experience and activity?

Was the path of denial a programming from past lives, or his inner guidance for his present path towards freedom? Were his personas, who advocated retreat from the world, actually guiding him towards enlightenment, or preventing him from seeing the Divine in all things, including himself?

He was also at a crossroads on a practical level. Were the difficulties he was having in securing stable residence in Moor a message to leave, or simply a test for him to learn to live and feel safe and secure in uncertainty while not knowing whether he would be asked to leave the next day? It was definitely a wonderful spiritual test; to serve and give all one's energy without any payment; to create something so large, to keep nothing for one's self and know that any day he might not be allowed to partake in that creation, or that it might disappear altogether.

Was he to continue in his evolutionary path toward God alone? Or was his path to God through a deep love relationship? Was his reluctance to be alone rooted in his previous life spent in prison, or was it guiding him to be in a love relationship and face an aspect of life that he had ignored for many incarnations.

Although his life was fine and he had many reasons to believe that he was being guided from within, he had a dose of "spiritual anxiety," or self-doubt.

Ran decided to do a retreat in a friend's mountain home near a river. For the first weeks, he meditated, walked in nature and proof-read some of his books. After that he spent his time meditating more intensively and communing with nature.

He then decided to hold a conference of personas – a psychology group in which each persona would be able to express itself freely, with the hope that they might come together and agree on some of these points that were unresolved in Ran's mind.

THE GUIDELINES

It was decided that the *Seeker of Truth* would be the group facilitator, as he was the most objective of all. The *Seeker of Enlightenment* and *Savior-Teacher* personas were ruled out because they were too identified with their roles and images of how they must be.

They sat in a circle and meditated a few minutes, breathing deeply in a synchronized way since they shared the same lungs.

As they were connected in this way, the *Seeker of Truth* reminded them of the guidelines for incarnation on Alithea which they had been read by the Angel of Light before incarnation. These truths were passed on by the ancient sages of Alithea.

"1. All personas will all share one mobile compartment.
It will have two legs, two hands, one head, one brain and various other organs and systems necessary for you to perceive and function on the material plane.
a. No persona will be able to leave it individually.
b. No persona will ever be able to go anywhere alone, you always travel together.

"2. You will all share one energy system
a. Thus each uses the energy that belongs to all of you.
b. What each does with this energy affects all of you.

"3. You will share one consciousness
a. Although you will each have your own beliefs and thoughts, you have only one screen of consciousness on which to project them.
b. These thoughts, however, can be projected in succeeding order with such rapidity, that it may seem to you that they exist simultaneously.
c. The thoughts projected by each, will, in many ways, limit the others' mental freedom.

"4. The lines which separate you and give you the feeling of individuality are imaginary, mutable and often disappearing.

"5. You must find happiness together, or not at all.
You will never be able to find happiness
a. by fighting each other .
b. by suppressing one another

c. or by ignoring one another.

"6. Your source is one and your separate identities are illusion.

"7. You will all evolve together.
The balance of powers and strengths between you will be dynamic and ever changing.

"8. Each of you and the nature of your relationships with each other will be continuously reflected in the world and events around you, especially by others' reactions to you.

"9. You have three powers with which to become free and happy.
a. love - acceptance
b. truth
c. awareness

"10. You will forget all this upon birth.
You will believe that you are one,
until one day you fall apart
and realize that you are many
and then really become one."

The *Seeker of Truth*, then concluded, "well it seems that we have arrived at this point of falling apart so that we can become one again. Let us address ourselves to this process."

THE MONK

He then asked the *Holy-Pure-Monk* to initiate the conference with a prayer.

The *Holy-Pure-Monk* closed his eyes and prayed, "Dear God, please guide us and all other beings in our efforts to understand your will for us. We don't want anything else but that; to be as You want us to be."

With this he broke out crying, sobbing. "Maybe we are not how You want us to be? O, how much we love You. How much we miss You. We have been seeking so many years. You have abandoned us. Why? We have tried so hard. When will You come? When will You grant us the vision of Your being, the experience of Your presence? What else do we need to do.?"

The *Bad Unworthy Child* and *Poor Unloved Child* cried with him.

The others all waited for their crying to subside. Then the *Seeker of Truth* approached the *Holy-Pure-Monk* and asked, "what are you feeling?"

He answered, "I am tired. I feel abandoned, weak, unable to succeed in my task. I feel rejected by God, and also guilty that I am not able to reach Him."

"Where do you feel these feelings?"

"In my solar plexus and a little in my chest"

"Monk, please breathe into the area which is most tense – breath in and out and allow the energies to move into those feelings."

The Monk breathed deeply, opening the diaphragm area as his breath increased and emotions expanded.

"I feel dizzy. I am going to faint – all this energy is rushing to my head."

The *Seeker of Truth* encouraged him to continue, as this was a sign that the energy pattern was breaking up, and that he would be free if he continued.

The monk cried out in desperation, "God where are You, why have You abandoned me? I have done everything You have asked, why have You not come? You have not kept Your promise! You said You would be there for me."

The *Seeker of Truth* whispered "What promise?"

The *Monk* spoke, "I am Franz from our past life. I live in a monastery, and I have sacrificed all my life. I have denied the pleasures of the flesh. I have suffered deeply. I have spent sleepless nights fighting with my desires. And I died with nothing, with nothing, I never had the Vision..."

The Seeker of Truth whispered into his ear, "What vision?"

"The vision of God."

"And how is that vision?"

"My Lord Jesus Christ, of course."

"Why do you need this vision?"

"Then I will know that He loves me."

The *Bad-Unworthy-Child* and *Poor Unloved Child* were sobbing again as they identified with the *Monk's* feelings.

The *Seeker* continued to verify what he was hearing, "You need a vision to be sure that God loves you? You are not sure that He loves you? You are not sure if you are worthy of His love?"

When the *Monk* heard these words, he realized that his desires and complaints were ego-centered, that he was not loving God, but wanted verification of his worthiness through some sign from God. He had sacrificed material desires, but he was full of spiritual desires. He was actually seeking affirmation of his self worth and of God's love for him.

He realized that, just as others sought verification of their self-worth through a woman's love, or money, or professional success, or through their intelligence, he was looking to be affirmed by a vision.

The *Seeker of Truth* asked: "*Monk*, can you love God and serve Him and have faith that God is love, and feel His love without a vision? Have you ever thought that you are not crying because some child in Moor, or Bharat, or any Alithean country has not seen God? You are not crying because some child does not have food. You are crying because you have not had the vision, the *verification*. You are not crying because your brother in the other cell, who is praying like you, is not having it. In fact, you want to have it before him, because you think that then you will be more worthy."

"*Monk* can you see that you are like those who seek to have the attention from their spiritual teacher, not simply because they love him, but because then they will be verified. They will be 'good boys and girls.' They will have had found their self worth."

"*Monk*, what do you want to do?"

The *Monk* responded, "I can see what you are saying. I understand. I see that my desire is selfish. But, I still feel that need. I suppose the truth will slowly seep into me. What I can do is to leave Ran to live his life. I had my chance hundreds of years ago in that previous incarnation. I am projecting onto him my old perceptions. I will try to let him find his own way."

THE BAD UNWORTHY CHILD

The Seeker of Truth looked around the circle and asked if there was any one who has something to express.

"I do", responded the *Bad Unworthy Child*. "I can identify totally with the "Monk" and I can see now that he is my creation, my projection. I have not learned to love myself, nor to believe in myself. My childhood and previous life experiences have programmed me in this way. Independent of Ran's and even Saram's accomplishments and efforts, I have chosen to perceive and register only those experiences which verify that I am not worthy and not loved.

Thus I am also the creator of the *Poor Unloved Child*. I am at the core of every persona's effort to verify its self-worth. Each of you tries, in your own way, to confirm that you are good and worthy. Only then do you feel successful. Except for a few exceptions, you are all my children, my creations."

The *Seeker* answered, "This may be true, *Bad Unworthy Child*, but each of us has other needs besides the need for affirmation. We desire to grow, to learn, to serve, to help, to love and even to unite with God. We experience a number of desires and motives simultaneously. Perhaps it would be useful then, before we go much deeper, for each of us to express our needs and desires and beliefs, especially as they correspond to basic questions upon which we want to agree at this time. Let me remind you. They are:

"1. Whether it is better for us to proceed alone or through a conscious love relationship?

"2. Whether it is best for us to stay in Moor or leave?

"3. Whether we can proceed more efficiently by living a more secluded life or by serving in the world?

"4. Whether our emphasis should be on trying to change ourselves, or on accepting ourselves as we are?

You can add any other themes that are important to you.

"Let us move in the circle from left to right. Would you like to start *Poor Unloved Child*?"

THE POOR UNLOVED CHILD

The *Poor-Unloved-Child* shared his feelings, "I need love. My main focus is to get it from women, as they substitute my mother, but also from older men who replace my father. My need for a relationship is not for sex or other pleasures but rather for attention, affection, and to be loved unconditionally, with all my weakness and faults. Thus, for these reasons, I would prefer to have a relationship. The rest of the questions do not interest me.

"I suppose I would chose that we learn to accept ourselves as we are. If I were able to do that, I would not need to find someone to fill my emptiness, by making me feel that they love me. Also, I would like to add that I need exclusive love. Otherwise, I get jealous. It seems that I feel that I am verified in a relationship only if she loves me exclusively. If she loves everyone or also loves some other man, then I loose my feeling of self-worth.

"If I could accept myself as I am, then I could love others unconditionally, and not need to seek or control the love that I receive. Their love for me would be a natural reflection on my love for them. I also would never be jealous.

"I think that my evolution is through a conscious relationship in which I can work on loving and being selfless. Until now I have been very selfish.

"Also I have a complaint for the other personas. I often feel rejected by them. They accuse me of obstructing their disciplines, and their attempts to be self-sufficient. They accuse me of slowing down their evolutionary process, that my needs for attention and love make *us* more egocentric than they would like us to be.

"What can I do? Can I be other than what I am? By rejecting me, they are simply worsening my condition and making me even more insecure, and then I feel even more unworthy and more unloved.

"I need love, not rejection. If these other personas would have patience with me, especially the *Monk,* the *Savior-Teacher* and the *Seeker of Enlightenment*, I would feel better about myself and would not need to seek so much attention and acceptance from others, and then we would all evolve much more smoothly.

"When I do not get what I need from you all, I necessarily must seek it from outside."

The other personas were obviously impressed by the *Poor-Unloved Child's* reasoning. They reflected on what he said.

The *Seeker of Truth* kept up his role as facilitator, "Thank you *Poor-Unloved-Child*. We will skip you temporally *Bad Unworthy Child*, as you have already spoken. We will get back to you."

THE GOOD OBEDIENT BOY

The *Good Obedient Boy* started to speak. "Well, the *Poor Unloved Child* pretty much covered my needs. We are very similar. I would agree that we are creations of the *Bad Unworthy Child*. I agree with his statement that he has created a number of us. I share, with both of them, the doubt about who I am and whether I am worthy to be loved and respected, both by my fellow Alitheans, and also by God.

"Thus my basic need is to always appear 'good' in other peoples' eyes. I usually manage to do this by suspecting what they want from me and giving it to them. I find it impossible to say no. Also, I frequently obstruct our other personas from expressing themselves when I fear that their behavior might make people see me as *not* good, and thus not love me. This holds especially true for the *Playful Prankster,* the *Righteous Rebel* and the *Erotic Female Dancer.* I would like you to take this moment to ask your forgiveness, for I have frequently stifled your expression."

These personas nodded acknowledging his request for forgiveness.

"I feel guilty as I have not allowed us to be our natural selves. On the other hand, because of my self doubt, it is not easy for me to overcome this reflex action of trying to be the good boy."

The *Seeker of Truth* intervened in order to clarify, "What do you mean by good? You have seen, throughout our lives, that you have been criticized and rejected by whole groups of people for actions and behaviors that were considered exceptionally good by others. How then can you actually gain your self-worth through other peoples' opinion? You will have to choose which group you want to be good with, and then you will not be good to the other."

The *Good Boy* answered, "You are right. I have noticed this over the years, and especially the last two years after the crisis. Many people forgot immediately all of our positive interactions and remembered only our faults. I also recognized what you just mentioned, that we were being accused by various groups and people for completely different things. Trying to satisfy the one group, would have made us even more wrong to the other.

Being rejected in this way, after trying to be good to everyone, has helped me considerably to decide to allow us to be ourselves. I am much freer today than three years before. And you all will be too, because I will strive to suppress you much less, and eventually not at all.

"Have patience with me, I am in the process of growing up."

The *Seeker of Truth* acknowledged the *Good Boy* and thanked him for his honesty. They proceeded.

THE PLAYFUL PRANKSTER

The *Playful Prankster* took the stage. "I love to play. To play with words; to laugh, to joke about life and about the rest of you more serious personas. Many of you are much too serious for me and I feel stifled. Especially after the *Savior-Teacher* developed and started monopolizing all our time. Between the *Teacher's* monopoly on the mind-body complex and the *Good Obedient Boy's* prohibitions, I was feeling very much suppressed. Because of this I was probably one of the main personas responsible for that crisis two years back. I was suffocated by the role of the *Teacher* and of the *Spouse*. These two roles made me feel that I had no right to exist, let alone express myself.

"Together with the *Rebel*, the *Erotic Dancer* and the "Child personas" we started the revolution which turned everything upside down. We managed to confuse most of you, even the *Savior-Teacher*.

"I am personally very sorry for any pain which others may have felt, especially Issabella and Brenna, and the members of the community. I am sorry that so many were disillusioned. But I am not sorry for all of you. You needed it. We were not able to move as one, as long as there was no equality or balance. You were all trying to be something that we were not yet. We might be soon. But we were not then. We had become split into two camps.

"Thus I do not ask for your forgiveness. Although I may have messed things up for us on the outside, I have done us all a big favor on the inside. You are lucky I have not been more active. Many times I have felt the temptation to do something totally out of context, often when the teacher was teaching, in order to shake everyone out of their complacency. I would just love to see their faces if I said something totally inappropriate, or if the *Erotic Dancer* danced for them... I can see their faces now."

All had a hearty laugh, as they imagined the expressions on all of those faces trying to place what they were seeing in the context in which they had put Ran, the *Teacher*.

Prankster continued, "As far as the question about whether or not to have a conscious love relationship, I am *for* it. This is the space in which I can play the most. In personal love relationships, the *Teacher* relaxes and needs not control all the time, while the *Good Boy* is not afraid of being rejected.

"I like to tease and also to play erotically. Sex is not important to me; we can do without that if other personas have objections, but playing erotically makes me feel free and able to do what I am not supposed to do. I live in such a seriously-oriented persona group, that I need this play, and *all* forms of play for my balance.

"I also like to play with the energies which flow between us and a conscious love partner. I think we have still much to learn and gain through such a situation. Concerning staying in Moor or not, I would suggest that we allow the Divine to decide that. If we are to be elsewhere, let us be moved by the *powers of life* themselves as we have been so many times in the past."

"One more point I would like you to consider. We have been placed together in order to work in balance. When the *Monk* and *Good Boy* suppress us, and the *Teacher* and the *Efficient Worker* leave us no time for expression, then it is natural that we will move to the other extreme in order to balance things out. This is not a threat for further revolutions, but a suggestion for more harmonious coexistence.

The *Seeker of Truth* closed jokingly, "Thank you *Prankster*. I hope that you will keep us amused in less destructive ways from now on."

He nodded to the *Fascinated Wonderer*.

THE FASCINATED WONDERER

"I need to have contact with God's creation. I love to get lost in fascination and wonder at the beauty and inconceivable intelligence and intricacy which holds this universe together. I see this everywhere – in man, chemistry, physics, and biology, but most clearly in nature. Because of our previous life as *Phantom Healer*, I am healed and fulfilled most by sitting next to rivers.

"It is here that I feel God most. No church or monastery has helped me feel God more than nature itself; especially the elements of water, air, earth and fire. I enjoy most falling into a reverie – a combination of imagination, meditation, prayer, contemplation and talking with God and the beings of nature.

"I understand us and others better when I see us within the mechanism of nature. It is then that I get answers as to how we must live and proceed... it is then that I am recharged and revitalized.

"We have not given ourselves enough time for consultation these last years. I too would like to lodge a complaint to the *Savior-Teacher,* the *Efficient Worker,* and the *Monk* personas. You have really left no time for the rest of us. I have been given no time at all throughout the year.

Only in the month of September am I given about an hour a day. All of you are so result-oriented. You have been given time because the hope is that you produce either on the material or spiritual realm. You are all effort-oriented. Even the *Monk* is making effort when praying and meditating.

"I may not produce results, but I am essential for our balance. Without balance we cannot proceed as a group. The split between us was a natural result of giving time only to result-oriented personas.

"I can certainly understand the revolution which took place, although I wish it could have happened with less pain for the others. Perhaps, however, that pain was exactly what they needed for their growth.

"Concerning whether to have a conscious love relationship, I would like to explain that I find it difficult to fall into my state of wonder and fascination when there is someone else around. The *Loving Friend* is afraid that the other might feel ignored or left out and I cannot get lost in my fascination. Thus, in such a case, it would have to be with a woman who would understand my need to be alone at these times without feeling rejected. Otherwise I would prefer that we be alone. I like Moor, but wish it had more rivers. And cleaner ones.

"But I can recognize that some of the other personas are very useful here and that it would be better for us to stay, until as the *Prankster* put it "The Divine throws us out."

The Seeker of Truth then gave the word to the *Efficient Worker*.

THE EFFICIENT WORKER

He quipped jokingly towards the Wonderer, "I heard you – you want to take my time away. Well I must agree that I sometimes wonder whether you might be right. I actually feel that I must be in continuous action. I ease up only when the personas have been especially productive and it is past eleven at night.

"I often wonder why. One answer is that I believe that I am on this earth to help, to create, to work, to manifest. That is the purpose of my existence. I often say, 'I will rest when I die.' As long as we are here in this body, we are here to work towards creating a better world.

"I see no sense in wasting time in social contact, idle gossiping, watching TV or any other such pastimes which I feel do not serve our evolution or improve the quality of life for those around us.

"I am sure of what I believe. I can quote you a number of passages from Christ's teachings that affirm what I am saying. As we are healthy and able to work at this pace, I see no reason not to do so.

"Also I would like to point out that I am not the one who occasionally seeks recognition through our work. It is the *Bad-Unworthy-Child* and *Good Boy* who seek recognition through me and also through many of you. I would like to ask them to allow us to perform our functions as workers, servers, teachers, writers etc. for the motives that we ourselves have, and not stick in their little noses after we have finished in order to verify their self-worth.

"I would suggest that we help them to feel their self-worth as they are, and not through our actions. Let us help them learn to love and accept themselves unconditionally, so that we can perform our functions with the purity of our own motives and not with theirs.

"I hear a lot of talk about balance. I must admit that I can understand what you are saying. Until our recent revolution, I thought that we had balance. I was not aware of any symptoms of imbalance. But as the revolution was definitely a reaction to the suppression created by some personas, I must agree to discussing how we might live in greater balance. However, I would like to have specific suggestions, which would not reduce our hours of work."

"About a relationship: I am not interested, unless she can work with us and produce. I do not want to allocate time for all that relationship stuff. If she can work at our rate, okay.

The *Seeker of Truth* smiled as did the others, humoring his obvious attachment.

He nodded to the *Righteous Rebel.*

THE RIGHTEOUS REBEL

"I hear a lot of hot air here. A lot of words. There is a war going on out there. People are unhappy, poor, homeless, people killing each other, suffering with real problems, and you are complaining about unequal time use of the mind-body complex.

"I have a need to rebel against the hypocrisy and the stagnancy which I perceive in society. When I see the same thing happening in here, I do the same. That is why I united with the *Prankster,* and started that revolution. We did what we were not supposed to do. For me that is freedom. Are you all free? You are blinded by your motives and needs.

"Well I need freedom. I couldn't stand hearing from the various personas, 'O you cannot do that because you are living in a teacher's body, or because you are living in a husband's body. I was suffocating with all those 'not this, 'and 'not that.'

"Our life had become a museum for me. I thrive on change, on being able to do crazy things. I, like the *Prankster,* am ever-ready to shock people, to do something out of context, as we did when we were Babu in that previous life in India.

"I want to shock them out of the idea that we are some teacher, that we are something different. I want to shock them out of their complacency and fixed ideas. For me fixed ideas are the cause of all our Alithean problems.

"We need core changes, not simple analysis and affirmations. I cannot suffer any more living a belief system that is not totally mine. All that the *Teacher* teaches and the *Universal Philosopher* thinks and writes are truth for me, but I think that we have made many concessions to a society which lives in ignorance. We could teach others in a more radical way.

"It was that quality of rebelliousness and the desire to shock others which I saw in Brenna and which attracted me to her. I say that in many ways she was freer than we are. She was able, in many situations, to be herself even where we were not.

"When I made my revolt, I was attracted towards the ideal of our being ourselves. I even told this to Brenna. I said I am now destroying our roles as *Teacher* and *Husband*, because they are suffocating me. It was as if I was consciously destroying everything we had created, because it was the only way I knew to free us.

"I, too, am sorry for the many who suffered or were hurt. But we have asked forgiveness enough times. If they cannot forgive and go on with their lives, that is their own creation from here on. I suggest that we examine everything we do and determine whether it is free from roles, and exactly who we are at this point of our evolutionary process.

"Frankly for me, it is a bit difficult living in Moor. But if the rest of you believe that we are useful here, then I agree to stay until we are shown otherwise. As far as a woman is concerned, I have my reservations. In general, I feel suppressed by women. I feel that they want to limit me. I do not want to do anything immoral, or cheat on them. I just want to know that I am free to express myself in any way that I feel.

"We have all come to realize that we will not find our happiness in some other person. I want to be free to show my love to other persons, without our partner feeling hurt. I do not need erotic contact with them, but I feel totally suppressed when I see another woman, which I respect and love and want to show her love or attention, with or without erotic undertones, and I am afraid to do so because our partner may feel hurt or jealous. I do not want to play any more 'you looked at that other woman games.'

"So I would prefer not to have a partner, unless she is very self-confidant and secure in herself and can stand seeing me also show love to others.

"I also feel suppressed when we fast. I cannot stand to feel that I cannot eat if I want to. Not that I am so hungry. It is the idea of being limited. You must all remember that I was born in a prison cell in our many lives ago as Rupert. I felt deprived of everything, and have related all deprivation and external control with being done injustice to, and with being weak and helpless. It is not easy for me to get free from these feelings so easily."

The facilitator responded, "Thank you *Rebel* for your input. May I ask you a question?"

"Go ahead"

"What is freedom?"

"It is being able to express what you are without changing it for the sake of the environment."

"Fine, let me ask you then, are you free to change or limit your expression for the sake of the environment, if that would offer something to others or your own inner growth?"

The *Rebel* was caught off guard. "Probably not. I have been so obsessed with the freedom to express and not to change; I never thought that there was also the freedom to change or to not express if that serves some purpose. Thank you. I will think about it."

But the facilitator was not finished. "Also, can you feel free to be who you are even when the people you love or give importance to, do not agree with you or even reject you?"

"I can, but the *Good Boy* intervenes, and does not let me."

"Thank you and good luck in your quest for real freedom."

"Okay, it is your turn *Unemotional Stoic*."

THE UNEMOTIONAL STOIC

"I need to conceal emotion, both negative and positive. For me both are signs of weakness and vulnerability. This I have learned throughout the ages in various incarnations but also in this present one from our father, who was also like this. I need to be always in control, distant. I protect myself in this way from being hurt. Of course, this does not work internally. It is silly a mask I wear. But I am stuck in it.

During the last years I have gradually begun to express my feelings, both positive and negative. It was impossible for me to say 'I love you.' Also it was impossible for me to express pain, hurt, fear, anger. Fortunately, we did not have these emotions very frequently. Our life has been very blessed.

"After our crisis, I have learned to express my pain *and* my love. We seldom have anger and fear, and thus I have not had to confront this problem. My belief was that people would not respect me anymore if I showed my emotions. This also included enthusiasm. Although I feel enthusiasm frequently, I do not show it, but rather keep an even tone of voice and expression. I fear I might be considered silly or fickle if I showed my enthusiasm.

"Also, I often feel deep love for various persons, or gratitude for their presence or respect for their being. I express about two percent of these feelings.

"I have, until now, severely suppressed our emotional expression. This, in part, has been one of the causes for the revolt two years ago. You see we were attracted to women in general who were very free in their emotional expression. This balanced us.

"I suspect that I will have to free myself from this fear of showing emotion (when we have them of course), so that we may be more balanced inwardly and not need to seek someone to balance us externally... because then we will force that person to express double emotions – theirs and ours – through the connected 'barrel effect.'

Conference of all Personas

"I feel that we still have much to learn by being in the world, and working and expressing ourselves in the material world. I think that it would not be practical to think about withdrawing yet. Perhaps in about ten years.

"As far as a conscious love partner is concerned, I think I would have a lot to learn by having a partner to whom I could learn to freely express my emotions. She would at first, however, be able to see my love in my actions, and not need to hear it from me many times a day. When I feel pressured, I bottle up. My actions speak more clearly than my words."

The *Seeker of Truth* then gave the word to the *Anxious Worrier*.

THE ANXIOUS WORRIER

"If the *Unemotional Stoic* was born of our father, I was born of our mother in this incarnation. Of course, I have been learning to be as I am for many incarnations now. All of humanity has mastered my art. I worry. My nature is to think about the worst things that can happen – to fear that things will not work out as we want them to – and to pass various scenarios through our mind as to what we must do in order to avoid catastrophe.

"I do not worry only about material matters, but also about spiritual. I even worry because we are not enlightened.

"Over and over again, I have seen that all my worry was for nothing. Now of course, I am much better that I used to be. But I still exist and occasionally waste some minutes of a day with my anxiety. I ask your help. I want to come into full contact with the Divine and see for myself that there is only God everywhere, as our *Philosopher* and *Child of the Universe* keep telling us. When I see that, I will be free. But I need to see it with my eyes. Their teachings do not help me.

"We have been through a lot together. I thank you for your patience with me, and ask for your continued understanding. I am very old; much older than all of you. I existed when we were only in the animal stage, and in the primitive man stage of our evolution down on the Earth. Most of you were dormant seedlings then. My roots go deep and thus, I will be the last to disappear. But eventually the light of the Divine will burn me and transform me."

The *Seeker of Truth* felt that a transformation of thought form was necessary here. He guided the Worrier into a state of deep relaxation and asked her to visualize the emotion of worry or anxiety.

"What do you see?" he asked.

"A hunched up woman sitting out in the cold darkness."

"Ask her what you can do to help her."

"She says to embrace her, but she is ugly."

"Begin to send her light and love, accept her and wish her to be well."

"Now she is straightening up. She is getting warm inside. Her face is relaxing. She is still old and it is still cold and dark, but she is radiant and beautiful. She has faith. She is at peace."

"Good, embrace her now."

"We are already embraced."

"Now let her peace and faith flow into you, and remain in that state as long as you like."

After about five minutes, The *Anxious Worrier* came out of his relaxation with a radiant face. "That was wonderful."

The *Seeker of Truth* explained, "you see, you fear because your thought forms cause you to. Whenever you feel anxious or worrisome, bring this image of that radiant woman with her faith and peace to your mind and draw from that image those qualities."

"Thanks, I will. Let us move on now. I have taken up much time."

Now it was the *Understanding Listener*.

THE UNDERSTANDING LISTENER

The *Understanding Listener* presented himself.

"I was born during our adolescence when our friends would naturally open up to me with their problems and deepest thoughts. I had the ability to see and accept everything as natural. I was seldom critical. I just listened and tried to understand what they were feeling.

"I like to help people, to befriend them, to allow them the opportunity to express their emotions, needs and thoughts. I like doing this. It gives me a sense of meaning, and it is what I was born to do.

"In these later years, we have been doing less of this as we have been spending more time on teaching, organizing and writing. This is a decision we will have to make – whether we will listen to people or train people to listen to people. In the last years, we have moved in the direction of the second option. I can see that this is wise and fruitful as more persons are helped. But I sometimes think we have overdone it.

"Perhaps we should move back in that direction of listening to others more.

"I too was involved in the revolt incident. I was probably the one who made it possible. I was our contact with Brenna before there was any physical or emotional attraction. Even after we began having those feelings, I continued on in this role of listening for a considerable percentage of our time together.

"Then the various other personas began to feel more personally interested. This, however, did not diminish my role as a listener.

"I, too, agree that we have much to learn in the material world, but perhaps I could agree to retreating in about ten years so as to give all our energy to the lessons learned by being alone. As for a conscious love relationship, I am for it.

It was now the *Efficient Organizer's* turn.

THE EFFICIENT ORGANIZER

"I love to make order, to plan, to create a structure where there is none. I like to make things more efficient and improve them. I like to manifest ideas on the practical level.

"I need the freedom to move and make decisions. Many have criticized that I do not consult the others enough, but just make decisions on my own. They are right. But, I do not mean to exclude them. I just get carried away, and when they complain, I see that I have done it again.

I also get many complaints from the *Disciplined Meditator*. I might as well say it before he does. I use his time quite frequently, because it is in meditation that there is peace, and I can get inspired solutions from our inner self. I agree that I should find my own time, but no time has been allotted. For this reason, I steal moments in meditation or deep relaxation or just after sleep when the mind is still quiet.

"I, too, would like to express my grudge to our children personas. I have noticed that they sometimes use my efficiency to affirm their self-worth. As has already been expressed, this diminishes my joy. I organize because I experience it as a creative service to the world around me, as putting order to chaos.

"I, too, would suggest to them that they realize their divine nature and not seek to find their self-worth in our accomplishments. It creates double motives. Fortunately they usually do not show up in the process of working, but only after-the-fact.

"I enjoy being in the world and organizing. I do get frustrated when others are not consistent with their promises or not reliable concerning the responsibilities they have accepted. But here I am learning detachment, acceptance and perseverance. I learn to grow through disappointment.

If we connect with a partner, it would have to be one who would share our work. It would be difficult for me to live with anyone else. Such a relationship for me would also be a work partnership. Otherwise I am not interested. I would prefer to be alone. It would not be enough that we worked together. She would have to take responsibilities.

Saram

CHAPTER TWENTY

THE CONFERENCE CONTINUES

The *Seeker of Truth* then gave the word to the *Cooperating Server*.

THE COOPERATING SERVER

"The purpose of my life and that which gives me happiness is to serve others, to be useful in any way to others, including animals, plants and insects. I also enjoy cooperating with others in this process. I feel extremely happy when I see a group of people working together for a purpose of any type. It could be feeding the poor, building a house, or cultivating the earth, painting, etc.

"For me, serving together is the highest form of communion and communication. I experience much more unity with others through working with them for a common cause than through talking about 'who we are and what we do.'

"It is not important for me whether or not we are working in the same place or at the same task, as long as some ultimate goal unites us. One could be typing a text, another in the kitchen cooking, and another in the garden, while still another is giving a massage. As long as we are aware of each other and dedicated to helping others through what we do, we are united.

"My problem is that few people feel this way. Most are enclosed in their family units and are not interested in the larger community. I occasionally feel disappointed, as did our previous incarnations as Rupert the general and Hans the Doctor. This is my basic problem – disappointment.

"I am the persona who very much pushed for creating the community. I believe in community life, perhaps because our experiences as Karan with the Essenes and Shala with the first Christian communities. I want to live that simple communal life, working for the whole, without payment. I believe that this offers us many opportunities for growth.

Family life is difficult, but community life is even more difficult, as you have a much larger family, with a much wider set of beliefs and needs. The ego appears very clearly in such situations, and then with the communication techniques available, we have the opportunity to grow by facing where our ego conflicts with the others. Thus, I obviously believe that we still have more lessons to learn through interaction than through retreat.

"I have conferred a number of times with the *Organizer,* and we agree that we would like to manifest a place for the poor and shelterless; a place, however, in which they can learn to work and use their own energies to support it, thus regaining their sense of self-worth and dignity.

"Lastly, if we are going to have a partner, she should be willing to live a simple life, without material possessions, and be willing to work side-by-side with others for the common goal.

The *Seeker of Truth* then gave the word to the *Disciplined Meditator.*

THE DISCIPLINED MEDITATOR

"I believe that our freedom lies in stopping the mind completely, so that no persona at all is functioning. Only then can we experience our true self, which is beyond the sum total of our united personas. I felt frustration, when all I ask for is an hour or two a day for this most important process, and then you all usurp into my time space to fantasize or plan according to your own needs. This is especially true of the *Efficient Organizer*, the *Teacher* and the *Writer*. I realize and accept what the *Efficient Organizer* already said, that this is a time in which we are all closer to our source of inspiration, and that these three personas need this source in order to perform their work with quality.

"But the fact remains, that subsequently the moments of transcendence are few and short. If you would all be quiet during this time, we would be able to make such a deep contact that you would have continual inspiration and support from the higher levels of our being. I interpret that it is your insecurity in the roles that you play that does not allow you to let go during this time and have faith... faith that your instructions from above will come when you need them.

"The fact is that not even the child personas give me so much trouble in meditation. It is you, workers, who obstruct the emptying of the mind! I ask you to think about this and act accordingly."

"Now you all know my beliefs about contact with the world and having a partner. I am against both. I believe that we can proceed much more quickly by retreating and by not having a partner who will simply distract us. I know that many of you feel that you are not ready for this, or actually believe there will be greater evolution through contact with the world and a partner, but this is my opinion."

Some personas, especially the *Rebel*, were fidgeting with the idea of total seclusion.

The *Seeker of Truth* then gave the word to the *Erotic Female Dancer*.

THE EROTIC FEMALE DANCER

"It is fitting that I should speak after the meditator. First of all, I resent that name. I am not simply a dancer. I am the tip of the iceberg of your enormous *Anima*, which consists of the memories of all your female incarnations, which you have blocked out in this obviously," as she looks around the room, "male incarnation."

"You would not have had to suffer that revolution two years ago if you had more contact with me, and allowed your feminine side to express it self. You seek other women, because you ignore me, your inner woman. You need an external partner to balance you because you have suffocated your inner partner.

"I represent not only your ability to let go and dance erotically, which you haven't let me do since we were three years old, but also our whole feminine nature, our ability to express our emotions." She stared at the *Unemotional Stoic* – "or our ability to flow with life and not try so hard at every thing we do."

"You have made everything into a work timetable – even our hours of prayer and meditation! Nature does have its rhythms, but it also has its storms, its earthquakes, its fires and its floods. These purge and create new beginnings. These create opportunities for growth, just as the revolution did.

"Learn to express your love. Learn to be human before you try to be divine. Be a simple person. Remember our life as Shala the dancer. She was totally immoral by society's standards, but she loved Christ more than *they* did. Her prayer was to dance with him. How many of you dance with Him?

"You call for Him. You cry for Him," she nodded to the *Monk*, "You empty yourselves and ask Him to fill you with His presence, you serve Him by serving His children, you offer Him the results of your efforts, but do you ever dance with Him?

"I am for giving more time and mind space to our female qualities of love, simplicity, humility, power, affection and, most of all, freedom of expression," she smiled at the *Rebel*.

"Now concerning your having a relationship with another woman," she took an austere look and they all laughed, "You probably need to because I have observed that when we are alone, you all go into the *Monk* and *Meditator* mode and you will probably never develop those qualities in this way. You could if you gave more time to me, your inner woman. That for me would be the best solution, if you have the ability to do it.

"Living totally secluded, doesn't excite me at the moment, even though I would have you all to myself, because, except for a few exceptions, you are all a bunch of bores."

There was a certain amount of commotion as they laughed and exchanged comments on her remarks.

The *Intelligent Problem Solver* now had his turn.

THE INTELLIGENT PROBLEM SOLVER

"I am the part of us which imagines being stranded on a desert island, and then trying to see how comfortable he could make life, by inventing various solutions for shelter, water, climate control etc.

"I get a kick out of solving problems. I like the challenge. It is like playing sports, but the adversary is the problem to be solved. I also share many interests with the *Joyful Creator*. We have worked on many projects together when the goal was not so much to solve a problem, but to create something that did not yet exist.

"I am probably an obstacle to your search for enlightenment. I enjoy the world and its challenges. I would accept having a conscious love partner if she too would participate with me in manifesting solutions and creations."

The *Erotic Dancer* laughed, "Each of you wants something different from this woman. Where do you expect to find this dream woman? And have you ever thought that you could grow much more quickly having a relationship with a woman who is the opposite of what you wanted? Then you would really learn conscious love, to love some one as they are, not as you want them to be.

"Also understand this – you can only attract what you are. Thus each of you must be or become what you are asking to have. The law of sympathetic vibrations and the mirror of life will bring you what you are, not what you want."

The *Seeker of Truth* attempted to restore order. "Thank you Dancer. Now it is your turn *Unjustly Persecuted*. I think it would be fair to everyone if we kept our comments until the second round."

The *Dancer* winked at the *Prankster* and *Rebel*, "Yes Mr. Chairman, always order, always routine."

THE UNJUSTLY PERSECUTED

The *Unjustly Persecuted* spoke.

"I have the belief that I am misunderstood or being unjustly criticized, condemned or persecuted. The roots of my being start with our life as Shala, the dancing woman, who was not understood at all by those around her, but even more intensely in our being thrown into prison as Rupert the General.

"In this life, that woman accusing us at the age of four of looking at the girl being dressed, and our father's giving us his right hand when we asked for our rights – are just a few of the experiences which have created this belief and myself as a persona.

"These last years we have received much criticism by persons who have not even met us or tried to understand what we are doing. I feel unjustly accused by these people. I also feel unjustly treated by the Church, which has persecuted us for the last eighteen years. This is in spite of the fact that we have made innumerable attempts to create a dialogue with them, which they have refused.

I sometimes wonder whether these events are created from my expectations or whether they are there for us to grow through. At any rate, with the help of the *Universal Philosopher* and the *Child of the Universe*, I have gradually changed my perception. I now realize that everything happens according to a divine plan and that

I create whatever happens to me.

"I am at peace with myself and these people. I find it very easy to forgive and love them. I believe that I have learned my lesson in this life."

"I hope so", shouted the *Rebel*, "because I am not into being persecuted any more so that you can learn lessons."

Despite the facilitator's efforts, laughter filled the room again. It seems that they were getting tired and they needed a break. The facilitator suggested that they take a break now.

"Wait a minute," protested the *Unjustly Persecuted*, "you see how I attract injustice. I am not finished yet."

"Oh yes, excuse me, continue and we will break immediately afterwards," amended the facilitator, amused at how the *Persecuted* really did create his own reality.

"Well now my concentration has been broken," he complained, enjoying being the victim again. He had conquered all the major injustices but was still susceptible to the small ones. We are all this way with some small things.

"I guess I have nothing much else to say. I would prefer to stay in the world some years more and have a conscious love partner who would really want to communicate deeply so that we could understand each other. Thank you, for listening."

CHAPTER TWENTY ONE

AFTER THE BREAK

After the break it was the *Socializer's* turn to speak.

THE SOCIALIZER

"I, like the *Macho man* and the *Hero,* have atrophied. I went into seclusion at about the age of 24, when we started to take this spiritual path more seriously. At times people have pressured us to reactivate my place in the group of personas. They even claim that we are not balanced without it.

"Somehow I accept that I have no further role in this incarnation, although at times, I wonder if I am hiding for some reason. On the other hand, the *Worker, Teacher, Organizer* and *Writer* personas, do not leave any time free anyway.

"If people had more meaningful ways of socializing, I would perhaps be interested.

"Leave me out of the discussion unless at some point, you feel that my role might become important again.

The floor was given to the *Loving Friend.*

THE LOVING FRIEND

"I need deep friendship. To love as much as to be loved. I need to know that there are persons with whom I have connected, who love me as I am, and whom I love as they are. I need to connect with persons with whom I can communicate without misunderstanding each other. That does not mean that we must agree, but that we understand what the other is saying, and feel unity with him even when we do not agree.

"A loving friendship for me means that we are free from social games. That we can talk or not talk, depending on our moods. That we can be together or ask for space according to our needs. This type of friendship has nothing to do with being together frequently, although this too is wonderful.

"It happens that, in this life time, our best friends live in other countries, and we seldom see them. This has probably been designed so that we could have more time for our work. I suspect that the *Teacher,* the *Organizer* and the *Monk* had something to do with this.

"I have, however, no complaints. I feel satisfied on this level.

"I would like to mention that the role of the *Teacher* does not help me much. Other people put him in a special place in their minds, and that prevents real friendship based on equality. They cannot see us as simply another friend in the process of evolution.

"Time is, however, our main obstacle. What would happen if we had a friendship relationship with the 2000 people we know? Obviously nothing would get done.

"So I can understand the *Socializer's* giving up his position. I am, however, satisfied on this level.

"I was deeply saddened by the revolt in that I was not able to be a good friend to our wife. The *Rebel* had gone so crazy and had gained so much control over us that I could not express my love to her. She had become, for him, a symbolic obstacle to his imaginary freedom. He did allow me, however, to be a friend to Brenna for at least a short time.

"I would like to stay in the world of work and interaction. I am still learning. A partner for me would be an opportunity to have a friend close by at all times.

It was indicated that the *Joyful Creator* should now speak.

THE JOYFUL CREATOR

"I feel blessed in this lifetime. We have had many opportunities and avenues to express our creativity. Composing songs and chants, creating seminars, lectures, writing articles and books, developing a spiritual center, a health food store, and a community, just to mention a few.

"Mostly I have worked in conjunction with various members of this group of personas. I would like to thank you all for your help and cooperation. I am satisfied, except for the limitation of time. Not that I do not get enough time sharing on our body-mind system, for we are always in the process of some type of creation. I am grateful for that.

"But the external time frame for work is simply not large enough for me. You have all heard me say that if only we had five simultaneous incarnations – five mind-body systems – I still would not be able to complete what I have in mind.

"Thus my test in this incarnation is learning to make choices, as to which avenue to give our energy in each moment. It is difficult to decide sometimes whether to teach or write or compose songs or work on improving our retreat site. All must be done, and I enjoy all of it.

"But to complain of such a problem is ridiculous when others have serious problems which make them unhappy. I will simply have to learn to get free from my creativity greed.

"I must also clarify that I do not consider that I am the source of any creation whatsoever, but simply the channel, the connecting link between the divine source and the material world. I simply have been put here to manifest materially what already exists on a spiritual level.

"You can imagine then that I am for staying in the world of action where I can enjoy the purpose of my life: creativity. I could accept a partner who would participate in that process with me and not inhibit me with ideas about what can or cannot be done."

"Thank you *Creator*, we are grateful for your joyful presence among us."

The floor was given to the *Chooser of Goodness*.

THE CHOOSER OF GOODNESS

"I am a sucker for goodness. I cry when I see people loving or helping each other. I cry at movies. Of course the *Unemotional Stoic* doesn't let me be noticed by others. I want to see a world in which all love each other, in which all support each other. It was perhaps I, more than any of you, who created our first revolt at the age of 22 when we fell into that depression and ended up resigning from our job, to search for a meaning in life. Although I am not a philosopher, I knew that I could not live in that world I was seeing on TV.

"I wish and pray for world peace, and want us to do something about it. It is I who managed to persuade you all to forget your grievances with others and forgive and love them. It is I who eventually forced you to choose cooperation and love, even when various personas were hurt or insulted.

"I believe, as does the *Child of the Universe*, that goodness will protect those who protect it. I am willing to take that risk and live as much as the rest of you allow, according to that one law of love. You, and others on the outside, laugh at me often, that I am naive and gullible. You may be right, but also I may be right.

"I hope that in the future you will listen to me more and more. Goodness is God. He who lives with goodness will be protected by goodness.

"Excuse me for preaching.

"I also cry often in gratitude for what we have. I consider it a blessing that we have water, shelter, food and so many other blessings. I feel grateful for the wonderful people we know, for nature, the sun, the light, water, and the flowers.

"A partner would be for me an excellent opportunity to grow, as personal relationships are often the place where it is most difficult to choose goodness.

"I feel that I have failed in my test of choosing goodness when I was not able to be faithful to our wife. I resent the *Rebel* for causing me to become so blind. I believe that I have learned my lesson and will not fall into that illusion again.

"Thank you and may you all be forever immersed in the light and love of the Divine."

"Thank you holy one," quipped the *Prankster*, as he mocked a reverent bow "for your blessings."

The *Holy-Pure Monk* was next in the circle, but as he had already pretty much expressed his needs and his problem, when he broke down crying after his prayer, it was decided to continue on with the *Seeker of Enlightenment*.

THE SEEKER OF ENLIGHTENMENT

"I seek enlightenment, freedom from ignorance, from the illusion that we are this body and mind. I seek to experience our Real Self, which is beyond time, space and matter. I am very much with the *Meditator* and the *Monk* on this issue in that I believe that we need to meditate and live in seclusion from people and activity, so that we can focus exclusively on the process. I must admit that I have a degree of anxiety about this. I had hoped to achieve that state by this age. I often feel disappointed in myself and in the rest of you. I feel frustrated that we cannot direct ourselves more intensely towards that goal.

"For a five year period about 20 years ago, we gave more time to personal retreats and inner work like this conference. Once the *Teacher* and *Organizer* and *Writer* came on the scene, they did not leave much time for this process of getting free from the mind and its various games and attachments.

"Now, during some discussions with the *Child of the Universe*, he has pointed out to me that a desire for enlightenment is also a form of attachment and, to some extent, an ego-centered desire. I can see this now. I can also see that my attachment to becoming enlightened had created much of the pressure that ended up in the revolt.

"It was I, along with the *Body Maintenance Man*, who demanded our version of celibacy for those seventeen years, allowing very little outlet for our erotic energies, creating a climate of oppression for the personas who eventually revolted. But I am convinced that the loss of semen is a major energy drain that delays our freedom from the mind. We cannot generate enough energy in the system so as to transcend the mind.

"Thus I thank you all, especially those personas who sacrificed their needs for that restriction. I hope that you will agree to continue with that policy regardless of what you decide about a conscious love partner."

"Oh great!!!" exclaimed the *Dancer*, "now you want her to be a nun. You guys are crazy, where are you going to find such a woman???"

"May I continue? My ideas might not be liked by all of you, but I believe what I say. My only doubt is as to whether I am being controlled by programmings from previous lives as to how to approach the matter of enlightenment.

"The *Child of the Universe* has helped me to accept that we might never get enlightened in this lifetime, no matter how much we try. He is now helping me to consider whether my ideas about enlightenment itself might not be a restricting mechanism. I have a specific idea of what it must be and how we must approach it. That may or may not be the process for our times, or for our specific group of personas. I am considering this, but have not come to a final conclusion."

"According to my perceptions until now, I would prefer that we live in seclusion and meditate many hours a day, perhaps write a few hours a day, so that other personas would feel satisfied that we are offering something to the world. My vote is that we do not engage in a conscious love relationship. If however, the others decide to, consider my restriction."

The floor was given to the *Savior-Teacher.*

THE SAVIOR - TEACHER

"I have heard my name mentioned repeatedly and often accompanied by complaints and accusations. The same is also true in the outside world. I am often tempted to give up. As the *Loving Friend* has already mentioned, people put me in another category and either place me beyond themselves or reject and criticize me. It is a very lonely position. Very few see us as a simple Alithean who is evolving along with everyone else.

"How I got created in this life is still a mystery to me. It started so naturally by explaining meditation to one person and exercises to another, and then listening to another person's problems. Then it became more efficient to make groups for exercises and for psychological and philosophical subjects, and then to write about them and lecture about them.

"It was all a very natural process. But I, within myself, was the same simple being. Others put me in this position, and I somehow fell into it, and then became trapped in it. Much good was being done. I was good at explaining things in a simple way that helped people understand. Models and examples came to my mind while teaching or answering, and often I would have no idea where these wonderfully clear answers were coming from. I was learning as I talked.

"I often reminded others that I am not enlightened, that I have many weaknesses and faults, and that I am working along with them. I never, however, mentioned which specific weaknesses or faults. I suppose I feared that they would leave. Also it is one thing to mention my weaknesses to a psychology group and another to large audiences, who would spread everything I said over the grapevine to thousands of people. Then the next day I would hear a version completely different of what I said. The same was true if I talked even with one person. It is very lonely being a figure that all look up to and talk about. It has tired me.

"I feel inadequate. On the other hand, I know that I am being used by some higher power. I am not anything extraordinary; I have no special powers, except inner peace, a desire to help others, and the ability to use my energies effectively. Being a teacher has been our largest test in this life.

"We have been criticized, persecuted, condemned, and, on the other hand, made into a God by others. Both are problems through which we are learning. For a long time now I have passed on all compliments to the Divine, where they belong, and then ignore them. On the other hand I have learned to love those who condemn us. This has been useful.

"I partially agree with the *Seeker of Enlightenment*, the *Meditator* and the *Monk*, that we need more time to be alone and make contact with higher aspects of our being, in order to offer more to those around us.

"For this reason, I have already begun the process of replacing myself as much as possible, without endangering the quality and effectiveness of our Center. I continue to believe that it offers so much invaluable help to those around us. I have literally seen thousands of lives, throughout the years, changed for the better.

People begin understanding themselves, they begin forgiving themselves and others, they learn to believe in themselves. They return to God, and often even to the Church.

"I am willing to sacrifice our enlightenment for that which we are offering. You all complain about the hours that I monopolize, but you are all selfish; consider how many persons have been helped through these classes, techniques and writings.

"I agree to search for a greater balance, so that no more revolutions are necessary. This, however, would have to take place at a pace that would not put the Center in danger. I too want to work much more deeply on myself.

"The revolution was a very traumatic experience for me. I did resent that we were forced to do something which I did not believe in, and which was totally against what I taught and still believe. I had prided myself in living in accordance with my teachings. I was very humbled by this event. I will take every measure that it not be repeated. I felt very guilty for some time, and occasionally still do, even though we have asked forgiveness so many times.

"One thing which has helped me to overcome it to some degree, was reading very frequently in magazines about other teachers much more advanced than I, and even priests of many years' standing, coming out and admitting that they had numerous affairs and for long periods of time. I know that this does not excuse what we did, but it does make me realize that it is a common trap on this path. For actually it is the trap of love. You love someone else, and this love causes you to want to spend intimate time with them. And you justify to yourself saying, 'well, who am I harming by loving another person?' Well the fact is that it is not the love that is the problem, but that we are doing to someone something we would not like them to do to us. This must never happen again.

"I would also say that I enjoy very much being in the opposite role, to become the student at some other seminar, or sit at the feet of Premababa when in Bharat. I feel more relaxed when I am one of the crowd and do not need to be someone special for the others, and feel responsibility for what is happening.

"I too would like to ask our *Children* not to use me and my abilities and people's admiration for their sense of self-worth. We will have to give them more love and acceptance, so that we can be free to do our work; free from any such second motives.

Concerning your questions, I can accept more time in seclusion but not at the risk of the Center's work. I can accept a conscious work relationship only if she does not need much energy from me but is willing to put energy into the work."

The *Dancer* shook her head in disgust.

The floor was then given to the *Disappointed One*.

THE DISAPPOINTED ONE

"I have learned to feel disappointed in myself and others. I have expectations of myself and of others. I must admit that the concept of evolution has helped me to accept mine and others' limitations at our present stage of evolution.

"Occasionally, however, I do still feel disappointment in myself although less in others. I believe that I should have been able to do better with my life. Of course, many would say 'but you have done so much with your life; you have written so many books, you have helped so many people, you have created so much.'

"All this means nothing to me. I still feel that I have not manifested my potential that there is much more in me to be manifested. I guess I have a type of spiritual greed.

"I try to remember what Premababa told us in our first interview. 'No appointments, no disappointments.'

"I have managed throughout the years not to let this disappointment stop me from giving all my energy to what I am doing, both spiritually and externally, in the world. I am happy for this. I have not let disappointment stop my effort; I have learned perseverance.

"I am indifferent as to whether we live in seclusion or not, or whether we have a partner or not."

The next in the circle was the *Seeker of Truth,* but as he was facilitating, he asked to be allowed to speak at the end. And thus the floor was given to the *Responsible for Everyone.*

THE RESPONSIBLE FOR EVERYONE

"I feel responsible for everyone's happiness, health and harmony. This is one of the reasons we do not spend free time with others. I cannot relax as long as there is someone else around who might need something. I cannot free my mind from someone who might need some help at a certain moment.

"I have made a struggle through the years, mainly because there are so many people who need help, to learn to leave them to God's custody. I help as much as I can without taking responsibility. I have made a distinction between helping and being responsible for. I cannot make anyone else happy, but I can wish him to be happy and offer him whatever I can so that he might be. The greatest thing I can offer him is to help him understand the lesson he must learn in order to be happy.

"I have become virtually free over the years and do not consider that I have a problem at the present. I enjoy living alone, but living with others is also a challenge not to feel responsible for them. This is also true for a partner. I think it would be a wonderful challenge to be in a committed love relationship without feeling responsible for the other's happiness. It is not easy."

The floor was then given to the *Loving Husband.*

THE LOVING HUSBAND

"I have lived amongst you for the first nine years of our marriage to

Issabella. I loved her and enjoyed being with her very much. We lived and worked together with considerable harmony considering that we were very different persons. We complemented each other. I enjoyed being the husband she could depend on. I enjoyed expressing my affection, waking her with a song in the morning. For the first nine years of our marriage I felt that all was wonderful, and never would have ever imagined that we would not be together today.

"Even after the revolt, my desire was that we stay together and work out what had happened. But she was too hurt, and I can understand that. I do not know if I will ever become active again in this incarnation. If so, I will not allow the *Rebel* to confuse me in that way. I am also beginning to understand the mechanisms of a conscious relationship more clearly.

"I am still in a state of shock. I am not afraid of being hurt, but rather of hurting others again. I would have to see that all our personas are completely stable before taking such a step."

The personas called the *Loving Son* and *Loving Brother*, passed as they had been living away from their family for 20 years and had little to do with this specific conflict.
The next in turn was the *Scientist*.

THE SCIENTIST

"I will be brief. I was more active in the beginning of this incarnation, and still enjoy learning about how the universe functions from a scientific viewpoint. I find that physics is converging with the spiritual point of view and this excites me. Just give me a little time, if only just before we sleep at night to read a page, not more, of such information.

"I have no opinions on the other subjects. Thank you."

"Just like a scientist, one, two, three, thank you. Now we can move on to the *Body Maintainer*." The *Seeker of Truth* expedited the conversation.

THE BODY MAINTAINER

"I have a number of complaints and requests. As you know, I have been given the job of keeping this body functioning properly, so that we can continue our evolution and our service to the society around us.

"Basically we have a healthy body and a clear and peaceful mind, considering how cluttered it is with personas. If we didn't exercise and meditate daily, we would probably be living in an insane asylum.

"This, however, is just the point. Due to our heavy workload, we have not left as much time for exercise and breathing as we used to. The *Teacher* and *Organizer* are responsible for this. They and the *Writer* do all their work sitting, and the body does not move enough.

"All of these minor problems can be solved by an hour's walk every day. I don't know where you are going to find the time, but this is my recommendation.

"Also we have gained weight and this does not help. I admit that we are not consuming large quantities of food, but we are eating before sleeping. I would like to have all of you consider some program changes that would allow movement after the meals, and not sleep.

"Lastly, I agree with the *Seeker of Enlightenment*, we cannot afford the loss of semen. It is a vital energy that takes at least three days to totally replenish. It is just not worth it. So, if you are still interested in a conscious love relationship, the poor woman should be warned of this fact.

"I find that, when we live alone, we have more time to care for ourselves physically. But I do not want to be selfish, this body is going to die anyway, irrespective of what we do.

The floor was then given to the *Enjoyer of the Senses*.

THE ENJOYER OF THE SENSES

"I enjoy the various sense inputs. Through them I relax, forget our inner tensions, or get a feeling of joy or stimulation. I like to eat, to watch TV (comedies to be exact), to enjoy erotic sensual contact, to listen to music, watch a sunset.

"Except for a few meals a day, I have been given very little time during the last 20 years. That is why I conspired with the *Rebel* and the *Prankster* in the rebellion. I felt completely ignored and empty. My needs were not taken into consideration. The *Efficient Worker*, the *Teacher* and the *Writer* would leave me only a few minutes to have a meal, and even then they would read or organize at the same time. Or I would be allowed to watch the news before going to bed. I was allowed to exist only when the body and mind had no more energy that they could squeeze out of it.

"I know that many of you do not consider me to be useful or important. But as long as I exist, and until I go into retirement as some of the other personas have, you will have to recognize my needs. Otherwise, very naturally, pressure will build up and there will be other revolutions. I will disturb your meditations, or your life, as before.

"I, like all personas, will gradually evolve and desire more ethereal sensuality of the inner senses, but that is something which will happen naturally, just as a fruit grows ripe and falls off the tree. It will not happen because the *Seeker of Enlightenment* considers me to be an obstacle or because the *Efficient Worker* does not consider me to be productive.

"Consider these thoughts and act accordingly.

"I personally would like to have a personal relationship in which we can share affection. Someone to hold me and to hold and to enjoy the peace we both feel in an embrace. I obviously do not want to live in seclusion at this time."

The floor was then given to the *Writer*.

Saram

THE WRITER

"I enjoy combining words as others like to combine colors or musical notes in order to convey concepts and feelings which are floating intangibly in our collective subconscious. I need to make the imperceptible perceptible, the hazy concrete. I like to use words to break through the clouds of confusion, allowing the light of clarity to show through.

"Words are my playthings and communication my purpose. We are born in the sign of Hermes the messenger. Thus our purpose is to connect with the just-beyond-reach spiritual truths and make then reachable. I am a transformer and a transmitter – not a source. I am a vehicle of expression for something greater, and not the creator himself.

"When I sit, I have no idea what is going to come out. I learn and read as it flows out – I do not know from where. It is like watching a mystery movie. I really do not know how it is going to develop and end.

"I too would like more time. I have been allowed only one month a year. I still have books written five years ago which I have not had time to proofread. I have many impulses in me that have no time to come out. I feel like a woman pregnant with triplets who is told 'wait two or three years until she gives birth to them.'

"Books are like children. They have their own inner reality they are already whole. They are simply waiting for time and space to manifest and develop. They have already been written on a spiritual level and are simply waiting for a birth channel. A child is already grown on a spiritual level and is simply waiting for a birth channel to come through.

"Just as our children are not ours, neither are our books, our music, or any other creation which comes through us. It is for this reason that I have never placed in any of our books a phrase prohibiting its reproduction. How can I restrict the reproduction of something that does not belong to me but to the universe?

"I have often spoken with the *Efficient Worker* about taking time from the *Teacher* and giving it to me. With one book we can help thousands of people. With the seminars only tens or hundreds. My belief is that we should move in the direction of writing and not in teaching or organizing.

"I agree with the other more productive personas. I do not feel good when I notice that one of the children is using our ability to write to feel good about himself. The *Unworthy Child* must definitely learn to love himself.

"I would prefer to live in seclusion, where I can write without disturbances and responsibilities. I would prefer to live alone without a partner, unless she was very self-sufficient and allowed me ample time to write, without feeling rejected or ignored. She would also have to be able to live in seclusion, at least some months each year, as only there can I be totally connected."

The *Dancer* was obviously disgusted by each persona's egocentric demands to be placed on this unfortunate woman, if she existed anywhere.

THE UNIVERSAL PHILOSOPHER

"I am the *Universal Philosopher*. I believe in the spiritual truths that we teach. I search ever deeper for the connections between those things that superficially appear unconnected. I believe that there is one universal consciousness behind all of the phenomena of this universe. I believe that we are expressions of that consciousness.

I do not believe in evil. I see that it is ignorance that appears as evil. There is no power but God's. I do not see God as a person, as does the *Monk,* neither do I separate men into spiritual or not spiritual. I do not share the *Seeker of Enlightenment's* anxiety about enlightenment.

"I realize that all is happening as it must and that we need only to attend to our growth without worrying about the results. You are all so result-oriented. You are all so ego-centered. You all want time for your needs, and at the same time you all feel so guilty.

"Why?"

There was sudden commotion in the area where the *Unworthy Child* was sitting. He was doubled over, apparently with pain.

CHAPTER TWENTY TWO

THE UNIVERSAL CHILD

THE UNWORTHY CHILD

The *Seeker of Truth* went over to the *Unworthy Child* as did the *Child of the Universe.*

The *Seeker* spoke, "*Unworthy Child,* are you in pain?"

The *Child* did not answer but moaned.

The *Seeker* continued, "Breathe into the area where you have pain. That's it, take deeper breaths and allow the pain to spread out, to expand."

His instructions to the *Unworthy Child* were spoken about twenty seconds apart, allowing the child to experience what he was saying. The *Child of the Universe* had placed one hand on the *Unworthy Child's* back.

"Keep breathing more fully as you let the breath move into and out of the area which pains you.

"Now allow the pain to expand to get larger, to magnify.

"The pain is spreading out and moving within you."

The Unworthy Child moaned, "It's moving up into my head. My head is aching. I feel dizzy. I am going to faint, I want to stop."

The *Seeker of Truth* encouraged him, "You are in no danger, just keep breathing, more lightly if you want, but stay with the breath and the pain. Immerse your self in it. Swim in it. Be dissolved in it. Accept it."

The *Unworthy Child* started crying, shaking and convulsing. This went on for about five minutes. Then he began crying and shouting, " I don't want to live! No one loves me! I am evil. I hate myself. I do not deserve anything good. I do not deserve to be a teacher, nor enlightenment, nor a happy relationship. I am not who they think I am! I am not the good person they think I am. No one would love me if they knew the truth about me. They love me for the rest of you. Because you are teachers and writers and organizers. They do not love me, no one loves me. I am nothing. I am not lovable as I am. If they knew me, they would reject me!"

The *Seeker* allowed him to go on in this way for about ten minutes until he had nothing more to say. He then spoke gently to him.

"Child please allow your attention to focus on your feeling of unworthiness. You will notice that this feeling can be felt somewhere in your body. Let your attention go to that part of your body.

"Breathe fully into that part of the body.

"Now just allow your the mind to be free to accept images or feelings or thoughts."

"Thousands of images are passing through my mind. I see Shala the dancer being rejected by those around her. I see Franz the Monk feeling guilty for his sexual fantasies. I see Rupert the General feeling self-rejection for his failure. I see Hans the doctor rejecting himself for not being able to heal more effectively. There is Babu, the wandering monk, feeling guilty about his pranks.

"I see that woman who is pointing at me, indicating that I am evil. Now, I see our father giving me his right hand, when I was asking for my rights. There is that child telling me that the devil wants to get in my mind. I see myself as an adolescent, feeling guilt about my sexual activities. I see myself feeling guilty even when I am not. When others criticize me, I feel guilty. I see how easily I lose my sense of self esteem."

The *Child* continued for some time in this way externalizing dozens of incidents which had undermined his sense of self worth.

When he had stopped, the *Seeker* asked him to select one of those incidents and to bring it clearly into his mind.

The *Child* began to speak, "She is pointing her finger at me and telling me that I am evil."

The *Speaker* encouraged him on "Who is this...?"

"That woman who was dressing her daughter when I and her daughter were four years old. She is throwing me out of the house. I feel horrible. I feel dirty and evil. I also feel misunderstood and confused as to what I have done."

"Would you like to tell this woman something?"

The *Child* moaned, "Why did you throw me out? I wasn't doing anything evil. What could I, a four-year-old child, know of these things? You have destroyed my self-image. I hate you!"

The *Seeker* then asked, "do you have anything else you want to tell her?"

The *Child* shook his head indicating, no.

"Now *Child*, try to take responsibility for what had happened and speak to her again. Imagine that the child you were at the age of four had the knowledge which we have today and speak to her."

The Universal Child

The *Child* spoke slowly and hesitantly at first, searching for words. "I have chosen, for some reason, to create you in my life. I have allowed you to shadow my self-worth for too many years. I release you from your role. I declare to you, that I am not an evil person, but a person who has sincerely tried to be good in his life. I declare to you that the human body is not an evil thing and neither are sexual impulses. They are an integral part of creation. I also inform you that I free you from every responsibility for this incident, and I free myself from the thought forms that resulted.

"I free myself from the idea that I am not worthy.

"I free myself from the idea that people will not understand me.

"I free myself from the idea that I will be expelled and that I am not wanted wherever I am.

"I free myself from the idea that the female body is something forbidden and thus something to be given importance to.

"I free myself from the idea that sex is evil."

The *Seeker* and the *Child of the Universe* were smiling at each other.

The *Seeker* asked, "is there anything else you would like to tell her?"

"Yes, thank you for the opportunity to grow and realize my self-worth from inside."

The *Seeker* went on, "Child, I would like you now to allow the emotion of unworthiness to take a form in your mind. Imagine it as something separate from you which is positioned across from you."

"I see a small beaten child. He is dirty and refuses to look at me."

"Ask him when and how he got born in you?"

"He won't look at me, but he indicates that he already showed me in the series of events which I saw earlier."

"Ask him now, how you can help him. What does he need from you?"

"He still won't look at me. He seems both hurt and angry at me."

"Why is he angry?"

"Because all these years we have paid no attention to him. We have left him feeling unworthy."

"And what does he want from you now?"

"To love him, to play with him and to accept him and love him as he is."

"Can you do that?"

"He is very dirty and repulsive, and he does not help because he will not look at me."

"Accept him as he is and send him love and light from where you are. Let your love and light flow out to him and surround him and permeate him."

"He is changing. He is standing up. He is becoming cleaner. He is now turning towards me. He is becoming larger."

"Keep showering him with your love, your acceptance and your light."

"He now has a radiance, a light which is shining from his chest and around his head, like a hallow. He is now beckoning me to approach him."

"Go ahead, go to him."

The *Child* stopped talking. His face showed that he was in bliss, at peace with himself.

They all sat in silence and allowed him undisturbed to enjoy the embrace with his transformed feeling of unworthiness.

After about ten minutes of silence the *Seeker* spoke to him gently, "*Child* are you ready to come to now?"

He nodded, "yes."

"Then gradually let your awareness come back to our circle.

When he opened his eyes, the *Child* tried unsuccessfully to describe the bliss that he felt while embracing transformed feelings of unworthiness and accepting himself as he is. He thanked all of them for their attention and patience.

The *Seeker* added a few words, "*Child*, if you ever find yourself feeling unworthy again, bring this image to yourself, this feeling of embracing that child with unconditional love. In this way, this illusion of your unworthiness will dissolve in time.

"Thank you, I will," he responded as he cuddled in the *Child of the Universe's* embrace.

THE SEEKER OF TRUTH

The *Seeker of Truth* looked back at the *Universal Philosopher* and asked, "You were interrupted, do you want to continue?"

"No go ahead, you have all heard my beliefs hundreds of times. Let us continue."

"Fine then, that leaves myself and the *Child of the Universe* who have not spoken. As he is occupied at the moment, I will say my piece.

"I seek truth, wherever I can find it. I use many of you in the process. I use the *Wonderer* in nature, the *Scientist* in his readings and deductions. I use the *Understanding Listener* to learn from people, and of course the *Universal Philosopher*.

"I am different from them in that I am never satisfied. I never draw conclusions but just accumulate the facts. My mind is open to hear and see more. I am the eternal student who seeks to understand. I can learn as much from a child as from a professor, as much from a prostitute as from a priest. There are no boundaries for me. All of creation is my laboratory in which I seek to realize the truth.

"Most of all I use the *Meditator* as during those moments of silence I grasp things totally differently. I see union where opposites appear. I see one where there are many.

"I have no complaints as I use all your time. I am forever watching, forever learning through each of you. Whichever persona is using the mind field, I am there too, witnessing and learning through his experience. Thus I have no absolutes no limits, no requests.

"I thank you all for your company all these years, and I want to say that it has been a pleasure to travel in the same body with such a wide variety of personas.

"Now I hope that our *Children* have enjoyed their embrace as it is now time for the *Child of the Universe* to address us.

THE CHILD OF THE UNIVERSE

The *Child of the Universe* let go of the other *Child* and sat comfortably there where he was. He sat erect, but with no effort and no sense of self-importance, naturally.

"I and all of you – we, are children of the Universe. The Universe is our creator. We are divine. We can never be anything else. Nothing that the Divine creates can be other than divine. I am divine. I live in a divine universe. A universe in which there is only the divine, only goodness and no opposite to that. You, in my universe, are divine. All beings in my universe are divine.

"In that divinity I feel complete safety, as I am surrounded by God in all his forms. In my universe, all things come from God, the pleasant and what you call unpleasant. In my universe there is no question of worthiness. Can the Divine be unworthy? Can anything that the divine has created be unworthy?

"In my universe there is no enlightenment as there is nothing to oppose the light. There is nothing to be enlightened. We light up something that is not lit enough. There is no liberation, because there is nothing bound to be liberated. The seeking for enlightenment is based on the veil of ignorance that causes you to be blind to your divine nature.

"Would the Divine cry out for enlightenment? And who will be enlightened if the *Seeker of Enlightenment* gets enlightenment? Just him and the *Meditator*? What about the rest of us? As long as the rest live in fear, ignorance and feelings of unworthiness, no one in here can be enlightened.

"I will show you. Will the real Ran please stand up."

They all started to stand, but looking around at all the others in the process of standing they all sat down.

"You see. The real Ran and Saram is something much greater than the sum of all of us. The real Ran is none of us. The real Ran is *Universal Divine Consciousness*, which has temporarily projected itself into the material world into order to express its divine nature.

"You are all parts of that process. I am the latest in that evolution of personas, and there will be others after me. Ran is the banks of the river and we are the water running through. Ran is ever changing as we change and evolve.

"Many of you have asked, 'Am I the way I am supposed to be? Am I the way God wants me to be? Must I do something more? Must I be something else than what I am?'

"Does the water in a river ever ask the banks, 'Am I in the form I should be? Am I as you want me to be? No, it just allows itself to be formed as it is by the riverbanks, by external and internal forces, and flows towards the sea, until it eventually disappears losing all form, being immersed in the formless sea.

"You are as you should be at this moment. Guilt, fear and self-rejection will not change who you are. Love, acceptance and selflessness, however, will. You are all overcome with the desire to be better, to produce more, to serve more, to have more results, to be better meditators, better teachers, better writers. All of this is ego-centered. Just be a piece of water in the river. He will shape you into the *Meditator* or the *Teacher* or *Writer* you must be.

As long as you perform spiritual practices in order to get free, you are functioning from the ego. Perform them because you enjoy them, as you enjoy eating and sleeping. As long as you seek enlightenment through having or not having a partner, or living or not living in seclusion, you are desiring from the ego. Yes, even the desire for salvation is desire. It is for your salvation. You are conceiving yourself as something separate from creation and asking for salvation for your personal ego, not for the egos of all the other beings on the planet.

"Pray for all beings to be enlightened. Pray for the planet to evolve. Perform your spiritual practices but with no goal in mind. The results will come when you are ready. There is no enlightenment or salvation of the personas. There is simply the realization that our real identity is *not* these personas but the Divine. No persona will wake up enlightened.

"The divine consciousness in this group of personas will simply have experienced its separate existence from its various personas. Thus, it matters not whether you have a partner or not, or whether you live in seclusion or not.

"What matters is that you love, that you are humble and selfless and care about everyone, and not only about yourselves. For spiritual ego and spiritual greed are the worst obstacles because they are the most invisible. They seem holy.

The Universal Child   253

"The key is self-acceptance. Accept that you are created in the image of the Divine. That you have been created as the Divine wants you to be at this stage of your evolutionary process. But just as the river; two meters downstream, you will be changed if you allow it. If you are, however, identified with your roles, saying I am a *Teacher*, I am a *Writer*, I am an *Organizer*, a *Perceiver of Goodness* or an *Unemotional Stoic*, you will never flow. You will never change.

"You will also never change until you accept your present nature as God-given.

"There is an unworthy child in each of us. Each of us has learned to doubt his worthiness and to doubt God's love, and thus God's protection and the goodness of the universe.

"This universe has only one creator – God. Nothing He creates can be evil.

"So, unless you come from some other universe and are created by some other god, you cannot be evil. You are a flower bud in God's garden. He comes by and prunes the plant, cutting away what is not useful, so that energy can flow up into that bud and make it bloom. Rejecting ourselves because we have not yet bloomed is like rejecting a rose bud, accusing it of not being worthy of God's love because it has not yet bloomed. Realizing that it has not yet bloomed and that its purpose is to bloom is natural and useful. We then have a frame of reference and know that we have not yet become what we will become. But rejecting ourselves, because we have not become what we will become, is silly and counter-productive. In this way we cut off the juices and energies flowing to that bud and it will never bloom.

"By accepting it, loving it, giving it our attention, we help it to come into contact with its center of power and it automatically transforms itself. You saw that in the transformation of emotions which the *Child* (We will remove the epithet 'Unworthy' from now on) and the *Emotional Stoic* experienced visually when they sent love and light to their emotions."

UNIFICATION

The *Child of the Universe* stopped as if inspired with an idea of something he would like to do. The rest were quite flabbergasted that this child was talking to them in this way. He was obviously right. They all saw that.

"I would like to guide you all through a deep relaxation process. Do you agree?"

They were all tired anyway, and they jumped at the idea of lying down.

"Only I would like you to hold hands with the personas next to you. This is for two reasons. One is that it unites our energies and the other is that one can squeeze the hand of the other in the case that he falls asleep."

They laughed as they complied, joking that the *Unemotional Stoic* was the greatest snorer in bunch. One quipped that this was the only way in which he expressed his emotions. Gradually they settled down.

The *Child of the Universe* instructed them to breathe more slowly and deeply for some minutes. Then he took them through all the parts of their mutual body and had each of them let go of that part of the body, until all the body was completely relaxed. His voice was very gentle but also very commanding, sure of itself.

"Now breathe slowly and deeply. Focus on your breath. Feel it coming in and moving out. Feel energy come in with the inhalation and allow tension to flow out with the exhalation.

"Now, as you breath in, imagine that you are receiving energy and love from the persona to your left; and add your love and, while exhaling, send this energy with your love to the persona on the right.

"Inhale receiving love and energy from the left and exhale allowing your energy and love to flow to the right.

"Continue in this way feeling the flow between you."

After about five minutes, he continued.

"Now feel yourself as energy, or as consciousness. Let go of the body feeling and feel your energy. Feel yourself as energy, without a body.

"Feel yourself as a consciousness without a body, like air, like space.

"Sense that the Persona to your left has also lost its form, and is now an energy-consciousness without form.

"Now imagine that, as energy-consciousness, you are shifting towards the left and merging with the energy-consciousness to your left. Two energies become one, two consciousness unite and become one consciousness.

"Now sense that the Persona to your right has also lost its form, and is energy-consciousness without form.

"Now imagine that as energy-consciousness, you are shifting towards the right and merging with the energy-consciousness to your right. Two energies become one, two consciousnesses unite and become one consciousness.

"You have lost all sense of limitation. You have expanded beyond the boundaries of your 'selves.' Feel yourself as energy-consciousness in a sea of energy-consciousness.

"Experience that unity and freedom.

"Now remain in that state of expansion and unity as you allow these affirmations to pass deeply into the center of your being.

"I am God's child.

"God loves me exactly as I am.

"I am easily lovable as I am.

"The universe smiled when I was born.

"I deserve love and respect from all beings.

"I accept and love myself and others exactly as we are.

"I express my true feelings and beliefs.

"Others love and respect me when I show them my real feelings.

"I enjoy the play of creativity and love.

"I am loved for my playful attitude.

"I experience work as a creative love-offering to the world around me.

"I am internally free in all situations.

"I feel safe and secure when sharing my emotional world with others.

"I enjoy the unity of deep interpersonal contact.

"Meditation is for me a spontaneous reunion with God.

"I feel my self-worth regardless of what others think of me.

"I create my reality in such a way as to flower into the divine being that I am.

"I am totally responsible for my reality.

"Everything which is happening in my life at this moment is exactly what I need to experience as a stimulus for my growth process.

"There are unjust actions, but there are no victims.

"I feel comfortable with all people.

"I feel comfortable in all environments.

"I feel comfortable in all situations.

"I trust in continual divine guidance and inspiration.

"I do what I can and let go, and let God take care of results.

"I feel God's continuous love in all situations.

"God is love, and His love for me can never diminish what I do.

"God is the consciousness within me.

"I am not this body and mind. I am eternal, divine consciousness.

"I love and serve those around me, starting with my family.

"I place the truth above all other needs.

"I create a healthy, harmonious and vital body.

"I create a peaceful, clear and perceptive mind.

"All parts of my body and my being are divine creation.

"I am a unique expression of the Divine consciousness on Alithea.

"I am goodness.

"I am love.

"I am peace.

"I am bliss.

"I am the Divine Consciousness expressing itself through this body-mind."

The *Child of the Universe* allowed them to remain in this state for another five minutes, and then continued.

"Now as one energy-consciousness, you are moving upwards into the sky. Higher and higher...

"Feel yourself moving up out of the atmosphere of Alithea, out towards our star of light, Savitur. Move closer to Savitur, and allow its cosmic energy flow into you.

"Emerging from the center of Savitur, a being of light approaches you. He is your *Light Guide*. He knows you since the beginning of creation. He knows all your mistakes, faults and strengths, and loves you exactly as you are.

"In his presence you see your whole life before you. You see what you learned and what you failed to learn. Observe as your life passes before you.

"Now the Being of Light takes you further into the center of the universe. You approach a large illuminated hall. There you become aware of all of your previous lives and what you learned and failed to learn there.

"Witness all of your previous lives pass through your awareness.

"Now you experience all of these lives and all of time occurring simultaneously.

"You experience your 'self' as the eternal witness of all these lives. You realize that you are none of these incarnations. Just as the light of the film projector is not the images that appear on the screen. You are the light; the images just appear, because of your presence, your projection. You are the light before it passes through the film.

"In the same way you realize that you are not your personas. They are temporary projections of your consciousness, just as your dreams when you sleep.

"Your personas are dreams of longer duration. They last lifetimes. But you are not your personas, just as you are not your car. They are vehicles for your expression in the material worlds.

"Feel your real self, free from all incarnations and personas.

"Now you experience the presence of the Divine, before you, around you – in you."

He allowed them to enjoy that state for another ten minutes.

"Now you may allow your consciousness to gradually begin to focus towards Alithea again where your body is lying on the floor of a cabin next to a river in the mountains of Moor.

"Bring with you that feeling of expansion and unity. Gradually allow your body to awaken to the first day of the rest of your life."

A PROJECTION

They took about ten minutes to come to. Most of them simply stared blankly up at the ceiling.

After about another five minutes some began to whisper softly to each other what they had experienced.

It was at this point that the *Female Dancer* asked for their attention.

"Now I am going to guide you all in a positive projection technique so that you can visualize and manifest your conscious love partner."

They smiled knowing that she was putting them on. But they went along with her. Soon their speculations quieted down and they sat with their eyes closed and spine straight. She proceeded to guide them into a very short relaxation just to get their attention focused on her voice.

"Now imagine this woman in your mind as I describe her based on your prerequisites."

The *Dancer* started, hardly able to keep her voice steady, as she was inwardly laughing heartily.

"She is loving like a mother towards our child. She accepts us exactly as we are. She allows us to spend time alone in nature to wonder. She will participate in problem solving. She will leave us alone to write for long periods each year.

They were smiling and giggling but not yet outright laughing.

"She is willing to work side-by-side. She will know that we love her by our actions. She will allow us to express our love freely to others without feeling jealous. She will take on responsibilities in the work that we do.

A few had their eyes open now and were laughing silently.

"She will not need us to tell her that we love her or express our emotions easily, but on the other hand will challenge us to express our emotions. She is willing to live a simple communal life without possessions, but she is also willing to live in seclusion. She will enjoy embracing and allow energies to flow between us. She must be willing simultaneously to be celibate, be teased and play erotically."

With the last description they all had their eyes opened and were laughing freely at their demands and the impossibility of such a person existing.

After a few minutes, the *Child of the Universe* shouted out, "You know the funniest thing is that, in my universe, she exists."

The *Prankster* rebuked, "then invite us to live in your universe."

The *Child of the Universe* looked lovingly into his eyes and answered, "You already are!"

CHAPTER TWENTY THREE

AT PEACE WITH HIS SELVES

The conference took place the last three days of their month in the mountains by the river. During those days, Ran naturally, without programming it, began fasting. It appears that the *Rebel* had relaxed by simply having been heard.

As he drove down from the mountains, he felt a deep inner peace. His personas were at peace with each other. He was extremely grateful for this opportunity to attend this conference of personas. Much had been realized, communicated and resolved. The personas were on very good terms.

In the following months he noticed a clear and stable sense of balance and peace. There were many more tests than before, but whenever he noticed one of the personas reacting with negative feelings, he did not reject it, but rather searched inwardly to see which persona was not happy and asked it what exactly was the problem. He talked with it, and expressed his love to it, and promised to help it, to support it. One part was accepting the other.

He was not enlightened, but he didn't care. He had left that to God. He was able to enjoy his disciplines without obstacles from the revolutionary personas. On the one hand the disciplined personas had much more love and understanding for the personas who needed love and affirmation. On the other, the needy personas were more understanding of the need for discipline and independence. The group persona was cooperating harmoniously.

The choice to incarnate on Alithea proved fruitful. Only in this way by increasing the distance between his personas, and making them very specific and specialized, was he able to reunite them.

HOW ABOUT YOU?

If you have an unruly group of personas who want very different things, you might want to incarnate on Alithea. Or you might want to try a personas' conference on the Earth.

Good luck to all of you.

CHAPTER TWENTY FOUR

TECHNIQUES FOR RECONCILING PERSONAS OR SUBPERSONALITIES

Having witnessed in our story how Ran's personas were born, developed and ended up in conflict, we will discuss here more generally how we can understand their development and effectively reconcile them.

First of all, we need to understand that it is our various *emotional survival mechanisms* which lead to the development of the diverse personas or "subpersonalities." We are not talking here about clinically ill persons with split personalities, but the average person, including you and myself.

In response to early childhood experiences (and if you believe so, previous life experiences) we develop various inner emotional responses in an effort to maintain a feeling of security and self-worth. These then grow in their own separate ways manifesting as parts of our personality that have their own personal beliefs, logic and identity. We can call these roles, "personas," or subpersonalities. Throughout this discussion we will refer to them as personas.

Each persona has it own core belief that creates and sustains its existence in our larger identity. This core belief will have something to do with the need for security, pleasure, affirmation or freedom, or in a few special cases, other less common needs such as the need to be useful, or for salvation or enlightenment. In some cases, the basic needs may be distorted and in conflict with survival or growth, such as the need to harm ourselves or others.

In most cases, however, the needs that create these personas are our needs to verify our safety and self-worth, usually through other persons or possessions. The following chart (fig. 50) will help us understand how these mechanisms develop.

MECHANISMS OF EMOTIONAL SURVIVAL

1. EVENT

2. IGNORANCE - CHARACTER - UNDERSTANDING

3. CHILDHOOD EXPERIENCE

4. CONCLUSIONS (MY WORTH AND SECURITY ARE IN DANGER)

5. FEELINGS
GUILT - FEAR

6. CONCLUSIONS - CONVICTIONS
(1. I' M WORTHY ONLY IF... 2. I' M SECURE ONLY WHEN...)

7. FEELINGS
(REJECTION, GUILT, FEAR, INJUSTICE, BITTERNESS, DISAPPOINTMENT, JEALOUSY, ANGER, HATE)

8. REACTIONS, BEHAVIOR, ROLES

A. ADDICTION > PRESERVATION
1. To play the same role (VICTIM - OPPRESSOR)
2. To play the opposite role (OPPRESSOR - VICTIM)
3. To try to satisfy the expectations of others (SUCCESS)
4. To degrade himself (SELF-REJECTION)

B. RETREAT > CLOSING IN
1. To be blocked to situations he goes through (DEPRESSION)
2. To isolate himself emotionally (MASK & AUTISM)
3. Not to trust others (DISTRUSTFUL)
4. Not to trust himself (FEAR - DEPENDENCE)

C. AGGRESSION
1. To attack others (AGGRESSIVE)
2. To be antagonistic for worth and position (ANTAGONISTIC)

D. NEGATIVITY - REACTION
1. To abandon every effort (INDIFFERENT)
2. To reject society (REBEL)

E. SELF - DESTRUCTION
1. To destroy his health, happiness, success and relationships (SELF-DESTRUCTION)
2. Not to help himself (UNDISCIPLINED)

The mechanism starts with (1) *an event in the childhood years.* The child (2) *experiences the event through his already formed character or tendencies with which it is born.* Some may say that this is a result of the genes he has inherited. Others might say that these genes simply transfer the traits, tendencies and thoughtforms that have already developed in previous lives. These tendencies, along with the being's ignorance of its real spiritual nature, cause the being to interpret and understand this event in its own unique way. This is why siblings who experience similar childhood events and situations often react very differently to those events, developing different personality or character traits in response to those same experiences.

These (3) *understandings or interpretations of what is happening create what we call the child's inner experience* that then leads it to come to (4) *conclusions* which soon become automatic and subconscious. These conclusions cause the child to begin to doubt whether he is safe and/or worthy for love and respect.

These doubts lead to (5) *fear and guilt or shame.* These feelings then lead to (6) *more specific conclusions or convictions* which become more conscious and state that "I am worthy only if...." and/or "I will be secure or happy or free only when/if ...."

A few basic examples would be:

1. "I am worthy and/or safe only if others notice me, accept me, respect me, affirm me, care for me, love only me."

2. "I am worthy and/or safe only if I am more attractive, intelligent, capable, powerful, affluent, spiritual than the others."

3. "I am worthy and/or safe only if I have plenty of money or possessions or more than others."

These conclusions then lead to (7) *a wide variety of feelings such as rejection, guilt, fear, injustice, bitterness, disappointment, jealousy, anger and hate* as we attempt to establish our lost feelings of security, satisfaction and self worth. These feelings then lead us to (8) *develop various strategies for getting what we need from life.* These strategies gradually get ingrained and become automatic behaviors or reactions that manifest as our roles or personas.

Let us look at some of these reactions.

a. ADDICTION - PRESERVATION

1. In this type of reaction, the growing adult seeks to maintain that which is familiar, which means that he adopts the role which he experienced as a child such as the victim, the abused, the ignored, the fearful one, the one who makes mistakes, who is stupid, rejected or uninteresting, etc. Or the child may have been the "responsible one" or the "good boy," the "strong one," the "intelligent one," or the "attractive one" who received attention for his or her appearance. On the other hand, in some situations, the child might have been the "oppressor."

In such a case, the subject might find himself playing roles such as the victim, the unloved, the abused, the intelligent, responsible, or the obedient one, accordingly.

If the subject does not go through a process of conscious transformation, he will, for the rest of his life, attract these kinds of situations or imagine them to be real even when they are not. He will continue to evaluate himself in terms of those criteria he learned as a child.

2. Another possibility is to play the same game but now playing the opposite role becoming the oppressor, the unattractive, the unintelligent, or the irresponsible one. So many children who swore they would never act like their parents, find themselves behaving in the same way to their children. Victims become oppressors. The weak become the "strong." The fearful become the "fearless," etc.

3. In the case of the roles in which the subject has defined his self-worth and security in terms of what other people think of him, he will seek to play various roles which will appeal to those around him, so as to be "successful" or "good" or "acceptable" in their eyes. Thus the subject may find himself adopting such roles as the "yes" person, the successful businessperson, the socially "in," the intelligent and informed, etc.

4. In the case that the subject has become very used to being rejected or demeaned, he may continue by taking on this role towards himself by degrading himself when there is no one else to do this. This is something which he may do inwardly as he undermines his self-worth to himself continually. In other cases, he may undermine himself openly before others so that they will respond with some positive comment towards him.

B. RETREAT - CLOSING IN

1. In this type of reaction, the individual becomes blocked towards any situations that may have hurt him as a child. When confronted with such situations, he will find ways to avoid contact with anything that might cause him pain. He might ignore or deny that the situation exists or sink into depression in order not have to deal with anything.

2. He might isolate himself emotionally in various ways such as over-working, drinking, eating, drugs, incessant activity, reading, watching TV, or simply by living alone.

3. He may develop a distrustful stance in life, and simply not be open or sincere with anyone.

4. He may even lose trust in his own self and thus fear activity, change, growth, new activities, or perhaps become totally dependent on one or two persons.

C. AGGRESSION

1. He may react by becoming an aggressive or offensive personality that protects itself by keeping others at a distance through sarcasm, criticism, rejection, condemnation, and in general, behavior which demeans or hurts others.

2. Or he might get into antagonistic roles where he is competing for his self-worth and power in various ways with those around him.

D. NEGATIVITY - REJECTION

1. The subject might adopt roles that abandon every effort in life, living without goals, responsibilities or purpose. He feels safer here, because there can be no failure, as there is no endeavor which can end in failure. This may occur when a child has very dynamic parents, who make the child fear that he will never be able to rise to their heights of achievement, and thus, gives up all effort and drops out of the game.

2. Another reaction is to become the rebel who rejects society and its values not only by dropping out, but often by rejecting and actively resisting, or even undermining the status quo. Such persons may also become anarchists. Often their need to rebel is so strong that they refuse to participate in activities that they themselves would enjoy because that same activity is accepted by society or more specifically their parents.

E. SELF-DESTRUCTION

1. Some, having interpreted that they are not worthy, may decide that they must harm or destroy themselves through drinking,

drugs, overeating, broken relationships, financial disaster, etc. Others may do the same simply to get back at their parents whom they feel are responsible for their unhappiness. Destroying themselves is the only way they satisfy their need for revenge towards their parents.

2. In other cases, this reaction may not be so intense, but simply act as a mechanism that would prevent the individual from successfully maintaining positive disciplines for any significant period of time. He cannot make positive efforts for himself.

These various reactions to similar childhood experiences causes each individual to develop his own unique mechanisms for "protecting" himself and his needs. Many of us get addicted to these roles and keep on playing the same games. Some play the opposite roles, "getting back" as it were. Others retreat and isolate themselves from real contact with others. Still others rebel and reject the social values, while others become anarchists or destroy themselves in various ways. We play roles that we hope will protect our needs.

We can generalize that these reactions have the following motivations:

1. ATTEMPTING TO PROTECT SELF FROM POSSIBLE DANGERS. (We must remember that what is known and habitual, although unpleasant, feels safer than the unknown even if that unknown holds the promise of happiness).

2. TO SATISFY VARIOUS NEEDS: security, safety, pleasure, affirmation, power, esteem, expression of inner impulses, love, meaning, evolution, etc.

3. TO PREVENT PAIN: fears, hurt, rejection, or the loss of important persons, possessions or positions.

4. TO HIDE OR ISOLATE WHAT MIGHT CAUSE REJECTION: weaknesses, fears, needs, real feelings, beliefs, etc.

5. TO ENSURE AFFIRMATION by being what we believe others want us to be in order to accept us.

6. TO PROVIDE AVENUES TO CREATIVITY - PRODUCTIVITY

7. TO ENABLE US TO MOVE FORWARD THE EVOLUTIONARY PROCESS

These reactions lead to what we earlier called roles (fig. 51), personas or subpersonalities and to which we will, from here on, refer to as personas.

AN ABBREVIATED LIST OF SOME BASIC PERSONAS

(Here we are supplying you with a short list of personas and their core beliefs. Please refer to the more complete list in the next chapter which also includes their ways of behaving, the beliefs which are supported by those roles, the conflicts they often have and the childhood experiences which most often lead to their creation.)

We have grouped the personas using various names. In some cases, only one or two of the names might be applicable.

1. The Good, Righteous, Spiritual person
 a. I am worthy and safe if I am (or appear to be) good, right or spiritual.
2. The Perfect, Capable, Strong person
 a. I am worthy and safe if I am (or appear to be) perfect, strong or capable.
3. The Victim, Abused, Unjustly Persecuted
 a. Others create my reality; they are to blame for my situation.
 b. The wronged person is right and correct and worthy because the wrong-doer is wrong and evil.
 c. I am not worthy of something better than this.
4. The Weak, Incapable, Ill, Fearful, Dependent, the Child

a. I am not capable of coping with life by myself.

b. Life is difficult.

5. The Guilty, Sinner, Bad, Unworthy

a. I am Guilty, unworthy, evil, a sinner.

b. I do not deserve love, acceptance, help from others or God.

c. I am in danger (Without protection – vulnerable to punishment).

6. The Parent, Teacher, Savior, Responsible for others and everything

a. I am responsible for the others' reality – happiness, health, security, success, well-being.

b. The others cannot proceed or take care of themselves without me.

c. If the others are not well, I am to blame and have failed.

7. The Rebel, Reactionary, Challenger, Competitor

a. My freedom is in danger.

b. I must fight for my freedom, safety, or self-worth.

c. I actually need the others.

8. The Intelligent, Informed, Superior, Knower, Counselor

a. He who knows most is superior.

b. If I show them that I know more than they do, they will love me and I will be safe.

9. The Indifferent, Irresponsible, Free moving, Disruptive, Insensitive, Lazy

a. Whoever has responsibilities and/or does not fulfill them is in danger.

b. I will suffer or fail if I take on responsibilities.

10. The General, Dictator, Aggressor, Abuser

a. My safety and/or self-worth are in danger.

b. I must protect myself and others in the battle of life.

c. Power and the offense are the solutions.

11. The Spouse, Husband, Wife

a. My self-worth is dependent on how well I am accepted and recognized in the role of the spouse.

b. I must be accepted in this role in order to be accepted and safe.

12. The Woman, Man

a. My self-worth is measured by how much I am accepted in the role of the woman/man.

b. My self-worth is decided by how much I am respected and wanted by the opposite sex.

Any particular person may, however, in his self-analysis, break these major roles into a wide variety of parts, which differ in varying ways.

Here is a list of personas offered by Gay and Kathlyn Hendricks in their book <u>Conscious Loving</u>:

1. CONSCIENTIOUS: DO THE RIGHT THING
2. SUPER COMPETENT : HERE LET ME DO IT
3. DEVOTED : I'LL ALWAYS BE THERE FOR YOU
4. DRAMA QUEEN / KING : YOU WOULD NOT BELIEVE THE DAY I'VE HAD
5. RAMBLING' GUY / GAL : DON'T FENCE ME IN
6. VICTIM : POOR ME
7. PERFORMER : THE SHOW MUST GO ON; LOOK AT ME
8. CRITIC : I TELL YOU WHAT IS WRONG – EVEN IF YOU DON'T ASK
9. LONER : BY MYSELF
10. SPACE OUT : HUH?
11. MR. / MRS. NICE GUY : I MUST
12. DEPENDENT : I NEED YOU
13. MR. SICK / MS. ACCIDENTS : I AM NOT WELL
14. CARETAKER : LET ME HELP YOU
15. STOIC : I CAN TAKE IT
16. PETER PAN / TINKER BELL : I'LL NEVER GROW UP
17. HOSTILE : OUT OF MY WAY
18. SELF-RIGHTEOUS : I AM HIGHER THAN THE REST
19. CHAMELEON : WHATEVER YOU SAY
20. TRUE BELIEVER : THIS IS IT; I KNOW THE TRUTH
21. SHY : PLEASE DON'T NOTICE ME
22. FLAMBOYANT : THIS IS THE LATEST THING
23. MARTYR : I'LL SACRIFICE MYSELF
24. REBEL : I DON'T AGREE

And in our story, Ran, our hero, found the following personas:

POOR UNLOVED CHILD
BAD UNWORTHY CHILD
GOOD OBEDIENT BOY

PLAYFUL PRANKSTER
FASCINATED WONDERER
EFFICIENT WORKER
RIGHTEOUS REBEL
UNEMOTIONAL STOIC
ANXIOUS WORRIER
MACHO MAN
UNDERSTANDING LISTENER
EFFICIENT ORGANIZER
COOPERATING SERVER
DISCIPLINED MEDITATOR
SACRIFICING HERO
INTELLIGENT PROBLEM SOLVER
UNJUSTLY PERSECUTED
SOCIALIZER
LOVING FRIEND
JOYFUL CREATOR
EROTIC FEMALE DANCER
CHOOSER OF GOODNESS
HOLY - PURE - MONK
SEEKER OF ENLIGHTENMENT
SAVIOR - TEACHER
DISAPPOINTED ONE
RESPONSIBLE FOR EVERYONE
LOVING SON (BROTHER)
LOVING HUSBAND
LOVING FATHER
SEEKER OF TRUTH
SCIENTIST
BODY MAINTAINER
EROTIC FEMALE DANCER
RIGHTEOUS CRITIC
ENJOYER OF SENSES
WRITER OF BOOKS
UNIVERSAL PHILOSOPHER
CHILD OF THE UNIVERSE

We can see that there are various ways of understanding and labeling these personas. *It is not so important how we name them, but that we recognize their existence in the totality of our identity and then learn to identify them, understand them, accept them and gradually help them to function harmoniously within us, with each other, and also in obedience to our Central Being.*

INNER CONFLICTS

These roles or "personas," which develop subconsciously, create a variety of beliefs and subsequent needs and emotions. Most personas manage to find a semblance of symbiosis so that we can function without serious inner turmoil. But there are times in our lives when we experience inner conflicts in which two parts of our being have conflicting needs.

Many of these conflicts have to do with the differing needs between our "spiritual" personas and our "material" personas. We place these words in quotation marks because all personas live in ignorance and thus are all material. The so-called "spiritual" personas are trying to be spiritual or, in some cases, only to *appear* spiritual.

Let us divide our ego structure, for the purposes of this discussion, into (1) the part that wants to improve our character and lifestyle and to proceed spiritually and (2) the other part that wants to remain in the familiar and conditioned types of behavior and activities where it finds security, pleasure and affirmation. Let's call the first part the "spiritual ego" and the second the "material" ego.

In the end, we want these two to meet, to open up to each other and become *one*.
We do not intend to imply that the spiritual ego is higher or more spiritual than the material ego.

In some cases, the opposite may be true, as the spiritual ego might be simply seeking security, pleasure and affirmation in other ways. The spiritual ego may occasionally be even more afraid or more attached to persons and situations than the material ego. This is not always the case, however.

SOME SAMPLE CONFLICTS

Let us look at some examples of the inner conflicts which may disturb our peace.

1. One part of ourselves may feel the need to spend more time in our **professional life** while another part may believe that we should be spending more time with our **family**.

2. On the one hand, a part of ourselves may want to open up to a **conscious love** relationship, while another part **fears** being abandoned or hurt, suppressed, manipulated, or not being able to say "no."

3. One part of ourselves may want to give those around us (children, spouse, friends) total **freedom** to pursue their happiness in their own ways, and another part may **fear losing control.**

4. The part of ourselves that wants to **please others** may come into direct conflict with our **own needs**.

5. We may, on the one hand, want **others to support us,** but on the other, feel that they **restrict us** with their support or advice.

6. One part of ourselves may **want spiritual growth**, while another may feel the need for **material security**.

7. We may, on the one hand, want to **help** a loved one or a friend, but on the other, feel that perhaps we are doing them harm by bailing them out continuously and not letting them **solve their own problems.**

8. One part of ourselves may feel a need to **protect the planet** through a simple life with very little consumption of energy and products, while another part may want to enjoy all the **comforts** of an energy-consuming, pollution-producing lifestyle.

9. We may, on the one hand, want to take a **job,** or leave a job that we have, while another part of ourselves wants the **opposite** for different reasons.

10. One part of ourselves may believe in **cooperating** with others, while another finds it **difficult**.

11. We may have a desire for various objects or situations as a source of **pleasure**. Another part of ourselves may feel, however, that this is a **sin**, or that we are **not spiritual** if we partake in such pleasures. Or it may feel that this type of pleasure seeking is a **waste of time** and **energy** considering our spiritual goals. Thus these two aspects of our own being conflict.

12. One part of ourselves may feel the need to have an **exclusive relationship**, in which our happiness and security depend on another person (usually a mate). Another part of ourselves may find this an obstacle towards its need for **independence**, self-dependence, and freedom.

13. Similarly there may be a conflict between the need for **personal love** and the need to develop **universal love**.

14. The need to **forgive** may conflict with the need to hold on to **negative feelings** towards someone.

15. The need to employ various **disciplines** may conflict with the need to feel **free** to do what we want when we want to.

16. The need to **follow** our **inner voice** in some cases conflicts with the need to be **like the others** and be **accepted** by them.

17. The need to **express our feelings** as they are can conflict with our need **not to hurt anyone**.

18. The need to **express our real feelings** and thoughts might clash with our need to have the **acceptance** of those around us.

19. The need to **follow a spiritual guide** might conflict with the need to **rebel** against all types of advice or control.

20. The **need to control persons** and situations in order to feel secure, and the need to **let things flow** and allow others to act freely.

21. Our need to **never show weakness** can come into conflict with our need to **share our weaknesses** with others.

22. One part may need **not to ask anything** from others, while another may need to have their **help** and **support**.

23. A part of us might need a **stable routine** for our balance and growth while another might need **variety** and **change**.

24. A part of us needs to **play our familiar emotional relationship games** while another part wants to **get free** from them.

25. One part of us wants to **face and overcome our fears** and blockages while another prefers to **avoid** them and **hide** from them.

There are certainly conflicts which we haven't mentioned, but most will fall into these categories.

WHAT YOU CAN DO ABOUT INNER CONFLICTS

1. Get to know these various parts of yourself by keeping a daily diary in which you refer to them by their names, needs, emotions, reactions and beliefs.

2. Keep a separate list for each persona in which you can list its particular needs, desires, fears, emotions, reactions and beliefs.

3. Discover for each persona the core belief that creates, sustains and drives it.

4. Accept each persona as a natural development in your evolution process. Regardless as to whether there is use for its continued existence, at some point it served some purpose in your search for equilibrium. Perceive each persona as one of your children, *whom you accept and love regardless of its immaturity.* Your purpose is to now educate that persona and help it to manifest its higher potential.

5. Express each persona's nature by allowing it to dance, write, or draw in its own unique way.

6. Now **let them communicate** between themselves.

a. By writing a dialogue like a one-act play in which they communicate back and forth expressing complaints, needs, feelings, beliefs, as well as questions that they have for each other. This is a regular conversation, in which questions are asked and then answered by the other party. Or perhaps arguments or accusations made on the one part can be rebutted by the other. Attempts are made by each part to get what it needs from the other.

The ultimate purpose is to create an atmosphere of *communication, understanding* and *cooperation* between these two personas with conflicting needs.
b. The same process can then be done verbally as described below.

THE INNER DIALOGUE

Attention: This work can sometimes be disturbing or confusing, and thus, is best done with the help of a professional who is experienced in this type of analysis, dialoguing and psychodrama.

Before moving on to perform the dialogue, it would be beneficial for the individual to fill out the following questionnaire which will help you establish a clearer understanding of which personas you want to reconcile and what their real needs, emotions, and beliefs are.

Persona "A"	Persona "B"
1. Name of persona	1. Name of persona
2. Basic Needs	2. Basic Needs

3. Feelings it has when needs are not met.	3. Feelings it has when needs are not met.
4. Beliefs which create those needs and feelings	4. Beliefs which create those needs and feelings
5. What it would like to express to "B"	5. What it would like to express to "A"
6. What it would like to ask "B"	6. What it would like to ask "A"
7. What it would like to request of "B"	7. What it would like to request of "A"

Having established this information we are now ready to allow these two personas to communicate. As mentioned earlier, this dialogue can be done as a written exercise or verbally in the presence of a facilitator.

In the case that we do it verbally, we will place two chairs, pillows or benches opposite each other. We sit on the one chair and assume one of the two roles. We imagine that the other persona is sitting in the opposite chair or on the opposite pillow. We start the conversation by allowing the first persona to speak to explain to the other persona how he feels, what his needs and desires are, and what his beliefs are which make him feel that way.

We then change positions, now sitting in the other chair, where we then give the opposite side an opportunity to speak about itself, how it feels and what it needs. These two parts will speak back and forth as we get up and change positions whenever we changes roles (it is important to change positions in order to help change mind - set and psychology).

This conversation goes on like any other conversation, as each persona asks questions, changes positions, and then are answered by the other persona. Each persona may accuse, or perhaps express feelings of tenderness and love, or plead and ask for help or even ask deeper questions which help the one part of ourselves understand the other part more deeply and clearly.

The conversation goes on until we have sat in both positions consecutively and have nothing to say from either point of view. This is important, because one side may not have anything more to say, but then when asked a question (when sitting on the other side), another discussion may open, which might last another half-an-hour with many more changes of positions.

Once we have completed this dialogue, we then take a position between the two previous sitting positions and imagine that we are our higher self, or that we are an enlightened spiritual guide. We proceed to give advice to each persona, separately explaining to each what it needs to do in order to live in greater harmony with the other and to proceed more effectively and with less conflict, along the path of spiritual growth or self improvement.

(Note to the facilitators: Throughout this process, the facilitator is there only to facilitate in the case that the subject gets confused, blocked, or off-the-track. The facilitator does not actually speak unless the subject gets stuck, off-the–track, or as some times happens, forgets on behalf of which persona he is speaking.

The facilitator can, if necessary, change the technique after at least 20 minutes have passed, and with the presumption that the subject has exhausted his ability to gain anything more from the exercise by himself. In such a case, the facilitator can turn the exercise into a form of psychodrama in which he plays one of the two personas (say persona "A") which were communicating and the subject plays the other (persona "B"). The facilitator asks him more questions to help him better understand that persona. The facilitator can again change places, asking the subject to identify with persona "A," while he again asks questions which facilitate the subject's understanding of that persona. This can be extremely revealing and helpful).

Whether we perform this exercise verbally or in written form, I am sure that each will find it very useful in resolving conflicts that are often obstacles in our progress.

DIALOGUING WITH OUR EMOTIONS

This may be done with *psychodrama technique* with another person, or as a dialogue as described above. It is a communication between our main personality and the part of ourselves that is controlled by a certain emotion such as fear, hurt, anger, guilt, injustice, bitterness, jealousy, depression etc. We ask that part of ourselves which has the bothersome emotion the following questions (and then we change positions and answer the questions from the point-of-view of that part of ourselves which has these emotions). Note: in the case of the psychodrama, the facilitator plays the role of the individual's "Central Personality" and asks these questions of the subject who identifies exclusively with the part of his self that has the bothersome emotion.

1. What exactly do you feel?

2. What has happened or occasionally happens that makes you feel this way?

3. When did you start to feel this way? When did you start to exist in me?

4. What has happened in our past that makes you feel this way?

5. What do you believe which makes you feel this way?

6. If, at this moment, you stopped feeling this emotion, how would you feel?

7. What exactly do you want:

   a. From the others, and from whom in particular?

   b. From me (the Central Personality)?

   c. From God?

8. If you do not get what you want from the others, what do you imagine will happen?

9. If you cannot get what you want from the other, would you be willing to receive that which you want from me (your own self) or from God?

10. What can I do to help you?

11. With what name would you like me to call you when I need to communicate with you?

In this way, we will begin to understand much more clearly why this part of our self feels the emotion that is bothering us. We will also gain some distance from, and objectivity towards, that part of ourselves, strengthening the witness who is free from that emotion.

CONFLICTS BETWEEN THE SPIRITUAL AND MATERIAL PERSONAS

Because, as we mentioned previously, these conflicts often occur between two groups of personas called the "spiritual" and "material," we are addressing ourselves in more detail to such situations as they are very common among people seeking self-improvement.

The spiritual ego feels the conflict most intensely (if we didn't desire spiritual growth we would not have a conflict) and usually creates feelings of self-rejection, failure, and guilt, when we are unable to satisfy its requirements for it to feel that it is "spiritual" and "worthy." Often, when we do not feel that we are worthy, we also do not feel safe. This occurs when we are programmed that whoever is *not* "good" or worthy in God's eyes is *not safe*, as he does not "deserve" God's love and protection. We might also be programmed to feel we deserve punishment.

These are not good reasons, however, to want to change something in ourselves. These are rather selfish motives. If we want to change because then we will be safe, or others will accept us, we are simply replacing the material ego with the spiritual ego. Nothing has really changed. In some cases, our need to fulfill these spiritual "requirements" for our self-acceptance has more to do with our need to feel that we are **more** spiritual than the others. Thus we simply replace the need for affirmation and superiority on a material level with the same need on the spiritual level.

It is important to realize that our self-worth is permanent and divine. We cannot be worth more or less in God's eyes. We are divine consciousness itself in the process of evolving its ability to express its divinity on the material planes. Our inherent spiritual value is not changed by our actions or spiritual growth. What is changed is our ability to express those values mentally, emotionally, and physically.

Trying to be a better person because we believe that God will love us more, is not the best motive for growth. Desiring to *become a clearer channel for God's plan because we love God and all of His creation* is a better motive. Seeking to purify ourselves so that we can experience that Divine Consciousness in every being and event that we encounter, is a useful motive. Seeking to remove all mental, emotional and physical obstacles so that we can cultivate *pure love, simplicity* and *selflessness*, is also useful.

These motives are free from the games of "who is spiritual and who is not," or "who is more spiritual," or "who is good and who is bad," and "whom God loves and whom God does not love." They are based on the presumption that God is a much higher type of consciousness, and thus is incapable of not loving anyone, no matter what that person might ever do. This seems only logical since God Himself has asked us mere humans to love even our enemies and those who ignore and harm us. Is it possible then that He Himself is incapable of doing this?

This type of thinking also removes us from the game of spiritual pride in which we feel that we are higher, more important, or more favored by God than others. It also frees us from feeling that we are lower, less important, or less favored by God than others.

On the other hand, the material ego in such situations tends to react to the rejection and pressure it receives from the spiritual ego by rebelling and sabotaging the various efforts towards discipline, self-control and self-improvement.

Thus, the more we pressure ourselves, the more our material ego reacts and rebels. In such cases, we experience instability in our spiritual efforts. We are usually, in these cases, playing the roles of parent and child with our own selves. The parent in us rejects the child in us for not being a "good child" and the child then reacts so as to undermine the parents' effort towards control.

In order to move more effectively towards our goal of spiritual transformation, these inner conflicts will have to be dealt with in a more mature manner. Rather than communicating within ourselves as child and parent, it would be more useful to develop a mature adult-to-adult type of conversation or dialogue.

QUESTIONNAIRE FOR "SPIRITUAL" vs. "MATERIAL" CONFLICTS

The following technique is best done with the guidance of a facilitator or as a written exercise.

Our purpose is to allow these two parts of ourselves to have a chance to reflect on what they really want, need, and desire, and then express all of this to the other part. It is best for one to begin with a written analysis. Here are some questions that may help you.

Take for example the Spiritual Ego:

1. What does it feel when it is unable to achieve or maintain a spiritual goal?

2. In which particular situations does it feel that? Give some examples.

3. What does it believe about those situations and particularly about himself that causes him to have the feelings that he mentioned in answer to question 1?

4. Why does he believe those beliefs? Upon what basic beliefs are they founded?

5. What are his needs and desires?

6. What, specifically, does he ask from the Material ego?

7. What can he do in order to have a better relationship with his material ego, and thus, proceed with greater unity and stability?

And we can ask the Material Ego:

1. What does it need and desire in order to feel secure, happy and worthy? Let it make a list of what it needs (objects, persons, situations, behaviors from himself and others etc.).

2. Why does it believe that it needs each thing on the list made in answer to question 1? Let him answer in regard to each answer what it believes will happen if it is not able to fulfill one of those needs or desires.

3. What are the basic beliefs that underlay its dependency on these specific needs and desires?

4. What, specifically, does it ask from the spiritual ego in order to feel more unity with it, i.e. to establish greater cooperation between them and greater happiness for both?

5. What can the material ego do in order to create greater unity and harmony, since they both live in the same body and mind – and must share it?

After answering these questions in written form, we can then do a dialogue between these two parts of ourselves.

TRANSCENDING THE PERSONAS

The eventual goal is to transcend these parts and *experience our whole self,* which encompasses all the personas but is limited or controlled by none. Only then can we be one whole, unified being. This is done mostly through meditation and a simple, moral life.

This can be aided by daily relaxation techniques in which we communicate with these parts of our being in a loving way and educate them with the help of spiritual truths.

A second way is to transcend these parts through daily meditation. This can be studied in detail in the book THE ART OF MEDITATION by the same author. Through meditation, we eventually become the detached witness of all these parts.

Saram

CHAPTER TWENTY FIVE

A CATALOG OF ROLES, BEHAVIORS, REACTIONS AND MECHANISMS CREATED AS A RESULT OF PAST EXPERIENCES, AND THE BELIEFS THAT CREATE THEM AND ARE CREATED BY THEM

In the list below, you may find some parts of yourself which might be experiencing inner or outer conflicts. Of course, you may also find roles not mentioned here.

After each role you will find lists of the following:

a. Possible behaviors associated with that role. Obviously no one person will embody all those behaviors.

b. With which roles this role might conflict internally or externally.

c. A list of possible childhood experiences that might have lead to this the adoption of this role.

d. A list of beliefs that might possibly have lead to the creation of this role, as well as beliefs that are created when one identifies with this role.

Note:
1. Obviously, most persons will manifest a variety of roles and, of course, may not manifest all the beliefs and behaviors listed for each role.

2. There will also be many behaviors and beliefs that we have not mentioned here.

ROLE 1.

THE GOOD, THE RIGHTEOUS, THE SPIRITUAL

Key: I am worthy and secure if I am (or appear to be) righteous, good and spiritual.

A. Some possible behaviors.
1. Tries to appear good or righteous using appropriate deeds, words, and conduct.
2. Suppresses himself and/or others to act 'righteously,' even when he does not feel or believe in what he is doing.
3. Criticizes, rejects or accuses others [and secretly, himself] for mistakes, inconsistencies or "bad behavior."
4. "Advertises" in various ways, the events that show how good, righteous or superior he is.
5. Hides "evil" secrets, perhaps sexual or some other "sin."
6. Plays the role of the savior, the teacher, the counselor, the parent, etc.
7. Could fight and even kill for his "cause."
8. Feels superior to others.
9. He can also play the role of the unjustly treated one.
10. Tends to be fanatical.

B. He may have inner or outer **conflicts** with the roles of the evil one, the rebel, or the indifferent one.

C. Some of the **childhood experiences** that might possibly lead one to this role are those which made the child feel:
1. Injustice, creating the need to never be unjust, and to always be right and correct.
2. Demeaned, criticized, accused, hurt or rejected, creating a need to prove his worth through the role of the righteous, the good, and the just.
3. Guilt, especially in respect to the fear of punishment from God. He then experiences a great need to be perfect and to never allow others see his mistakes. This is often an outward projection that covers his secret "sins."
4.Being compared with others caused him to need to appear perfect

to others, in order to have their acceptance.

5. As a child, he felt ashamed for his parents, or he rejected them.

6. As a child, he experienced some important adult playing the role of the "good, spiritual or righteous one."

Just about all childhood experiences can lead to this role.

D. Many possible combinations of **beliefs** lead to and sustain this role. Some of them are:

1. I will be accepted only if I am right, good, or spiritual.

2. I must do what the others consider right and good in order to have their approval.

3. If I am not good and righteous, God will punish me (He might also punish my children).

4. If I am or appear good, righteous and/or spiritual, I am superior to others.

5. I am worthy only if I am superior.

6. I am no good and I am not worthy as I am; I have to be "good" or at least appear good so that others love me and accept me.

ROLE 2

THE PERFECT, THE CAPABLE, THE STRONG

Key: I am worthy and safe if I am [or appear to be] capable, strong, perfect.

A. Some possible behaviors.

1. Takes over more responsibilities and activities than he is able to handle effectively in a relaxed way (with concentration, love, and without gradually causing a negative effect on his emotional or physical state).

2. He seeks to "advertise" directly and indirectly how much he has done and how perfectly he can do it, i.e. how superior he is, and how worthy he is. He finds it difficult to give responsibilities to others, to trust that they will do something right or that they can solve their own problems.

3. He finds it difficult to allot responsibilities to others or to have faith in their abilities.

4. He finds it difficult to cooperate with others:

a. So as to avoid sharing the results and the recognition.

b. Because the other might make a mistake and ruin the results and

A Catalog of Roles

thus the recognition.

5. Criticizes, rejects and sometimes attacks weakness in others (and subconsciously in himself). Other peoples' mistakes and weaknesses remind him of his own which he cannot accept.

6. He finds it difficult to express his needs, fears or his pains, as they might be construed as weakness.

7. He might laugh when normally he would like to cry.

8. He can disregard the needs of those closest to him, so that he can achieve much, appearing strong and successful to others.

9. He might engage in dubious means in order to succeed.

10. He might confuse power with cruelty and senselessness.

11. He finds it difficult to express his needs or to accept help even when he is ill.

12. He finds it difficult to accept presents. He wants to give always more than he receives, in order to have always the upper hand in the transaction.

13. He finds it difficult to express tenderness, affection and love, because he considers these expressions of weakness.

14. He might get entangled in obsessive thoughts, actions and obsessive various rituals while searching for perfection.

B. He might have an **external or internal conflict** with the roles of the weak, the unable, the lazy, the guilty, the unworthy, the victim, the child, the fearful, the sick, the indifferent, the rebel, the subordinate, and the demeaned.

C. Some of the **childhood experiences** that might possibly lead one to this role might be any of the following:

1. Feeling rejected concerning his abilities.

2. Feeling injustice, pain, demeaned or hurt, because of:

a. Specific weaknesses he had.

b. His weakness in comparison to the power of the adults.

3. Feeling shame or rejection towards a parent and thus, the need to look like and to become a "successful" person.

5. Being compared with others.

6. Being made to feel guilty, that he is not good or he is not worthy.

7. Being abandoned, or feeling that he is alone in the world without support, and thus he would have to be strong in order to survive.

8. He got the message that he was weak, lazy, incapable, and that he would not do anything at all in his life, and that he would not be accepted or secure.

9. He did not receive the affection, the love or the tenderness he

needed so he decided to become "strong," so that he will not *need* it.

10. He experienced sick people who were a burden for the others and decided not to be the same.

11. He experienced that weakness and need led to dependency on, and to oppression by, those he was dependent on. So he decided not to need anyone, so as not to loose his freedom.

12. He came across a significant adult who played this role.

D. Some beliefs possibly leading to this role:

1. I am worthy and secure only if I am strong, capable or perfect.

2. If my weaknesses or mistakes are apparent:

a. Others will reject me, demean me, and ridicule me. I will lose their respect and their love.

b. I will be abandoned.

c. I will be used.

d. They will control me. They will have power over me and I will lose my freedom.

3. Whoever has weaknesses:

a. Is not worthy.

b. Is vulnerable and he will get hurt; he will suffer from others and from life.

4. Life is difficult and hard and there is no protection or support. I must be strong in order to survive.

5. I am the only force in my life.

6. Others are incapable of doing anything right. I cannot trust them. They will ruin the results.

7. My strength, my capability, and my perfection are measured by the results of my efforts and not so much by my motives or my effort itself.

8. One's worth depends upon his capabilities and his achievements.

9. I must be perfect in everything in order to be worthy.

ROLE 3

THE VICTIM, POOR ME, THE ABUSED, THE MARTYR

Key 1. Others created my reality and are to blame for my present situation.

Key 2. Since the abuser is unjust and wrong, the abused is just and right, and therefore, virtuous and good.

Key 3. I do not deserve something better. I cannot have anything better in my life.

A. Some possible behaviors:

1. He does not express his feelings or his needs. Therefore others do not respect them and thus, he gains the right to remain in the role of the victim

2. He often sacrifices himself, even when others do not ask him to, or even do not want him to.

3. He does not allow himself time for rest, enjoyment, recreation, or techniques which might bring him health, vitality, peace, and happiness. Happiness is not "allowed" in this role.

4. He often complains about life's injustices and problems.

5. He finds a lot of reasons why his problems cannot be solved or why he cannot do anything to solve them.

6. He expects others to solve his problems.

7. He is more prone to illness or pain. He may also be able to endure or suffer these pains. These wounds of the "hero, received from the battle of life," make him feel worthy.

8. Occasionally, he is a "silent victim" or a "silent martyr" and he suffers without either expressing his pain in words, or his needs.

9. He usually withdraws when there are conflicts of needs or values; he might remain a silent victim or complain directly or indirectly.

10. Some of the weapons he uses to protect himself are:

a. Sickness, which forces others to pay attention to him and not ask much from him.

b. Sickness, pain and/or unhappiness, for which the others are to blame, and thus they are guilty while he is blameless.

c. Whining and complaining without effective, direct confrontation.

11. Complaining to a third party, about the problems he has with others.

12. He might undermine himself with alcohol, food, cigarettes, medicine, drugs, etc.

13. He might test the love of the people nearest to him with a negative behavior that in the end, pushes them away, and once more this event confirms to him that he is a victim.

B. He might have a **conflict** both **internally or externally** with the roles of the strong, the superior, the bad, the rebel, the parent, the child, the judge, and the liberated.

C. Some important **childhood experiences** that could possibly lead into such a role are:

1. Some form of injustice from the environment (criticism, fear, rejection, punishment, beating, violence, rape, pain, hurt, humiliation, etc.

2. His inability to protect himself.

3. A parent or another important person playing this role.

4. Someone who made the child feel guilty and responsible for others' problems.

5. Guilt through messages from his environment, that he is not worthy of having a good and a happy life.

6. Born female in discriminating countries and being programmed that because she is a woman she does not deserve something better.

7. Being born into a social class that is discriminated against.

8. Not being able to fulfill his needs as a child.

9. Being a child was the only way for him or someone else to have the attention of the others [e.g. through illness or through problems].

10. When as a child he believed that he is responsible for how others are or feel, and that he must sacrifice himself for them.

11. As a child, he believed that he needs the others and without them, he cannot survive or progress. Therefore he must suppress himself in order to have their love and their protection.

12. He was a spoiled child and now, cannot always have what he wants.

D. Beliefs that might lead in such a role:

1. Others are responsible for my reality, my problems, my happiness and my unhappiness, my health and my sickness.

2. I have been unjustly treated by others, life, God.

3. I do not deserve anything better. I cannot have anything better.

4. As long as I am a victim I am right – because the others are unjust. As long as I am a victim then I am right and I am worthy, perhaps even superior.

5. I cannot protect myself from others. If there is a conflict I will get hurt, I will be in pain. It is better to withdraw and to suppress and sacrifice myself.

6. I am responsible for others so I must sacrifice myself for them.

7. I am a subordinate being and I do not have the right to express my needs, my feelings, or my beliefs.

8. If I do not withdraw I will be hurt.

9. I am incapable of facing life alone. I need the others, and for this reason I must suffer injustice so as not to be abandoned.

10. I am guilty and I do not deserve anything better.
12. I am a woman and my role is to sacrifice myself.

ROLE 4

THE WEAK, THE UNABLE, THE SICK,
THE CHILD, THE DEPENDENT, INCAPABLE

Key: I am not able to face the difficulties of life.
Key 2: Life is difficult and dangerous.

A. Some possible behaviors.
1. He tries to find someone to take over the responsibility for his life (possibly someone who plays the role of the parent, the savior, the teacher, the strong, etc.)
2. He becomes lazy as a result of fear.
3. He may become physically paralyzed (mainly in the legs) or emotionally (he cannot work, or sometimes, even to go out of the house).
4. He becomes ill in order not to face life.
5. He avoids finishing school; he does not complete his diploma, so he "cannot" face life.
6. He ruins his chances for success, health, and happiness, by getting addicted to alcohol, cigarettes, overeating, narcotics, etc.
7. He gets trapped in various obsessive habits, thoughts, and rituals engaging his time and his thoughts in order to not be aware of life around him.
8. He creates codependent relationships where he feels that must have the other and often he feels suppressed and abused by him/her.
9. He absorbs himself in various activities with the intention of occupying his mind and his time in order not to face life.
10. He avoids people or seeks company with specific people with whom he feels secure.
11. He praises and flatters others so that they will accept him, and then he can lean on them.
12. He accuses others for his present situation, so that they will feel guilty and take care of him.
13. He often asks for financial support. He finds it difficult to remain in a specific job.
14. He finds it difficult to be punctual and efficient towards

responsibilities, disciplined programs and partnerships, not because he is incapable of doing so, but because his thought-forms will not be valid anymore and he will have to be a responsible person. If he becomes responsible, then there is the danger:
a. That he might fail and then he would feel rejection again.
b. He would need to face life alone, and this is a great "risk and danger" because he doesn't have self-acceptance.

15. He uses his health, his unhappiness or even his life (commits suicide) to "blackmail" the ones he feels "responsible" (usually his family) to take care of him and to take responsibility for him.
16. He underestimates his abilities and his virtues.
17. He does not want to grow up and to have responsibilities.
18. He tests the others' love in various ways.
19. He speaks of how incapable, bad, and unworthy he is and how much he is a burden for others. So whoever is listening to him would tell him the opposite and thus he would gain affirmation.

B. He may have an **internal or external conflict** with the role of the parent, the teacher, authority, the savior, the victim, the powerful, the perfect, the right, and the capable.

C. Some **childhood experiences** leading to similar roles:
1. He did not receive the care, attention, love, and/or affection he needed as a child. Now he receives them through this role.
2. He had a very powerful and successful person as an ideal and he does not believe he can attain that level of achievement.
3. He experienced violence, criticism, accusation, rejection, rape, danger, or comparison with others.
4. He was spoilt and was not allowed to do anything, to confront anything, to take any responsibilities.
5. He was told he was lazy, good for nothing, and that he would not be able to achieve anything in his life.
6. He experienced many illnesses as a child and the thought-form of being weak, and needing protection, was created as a result.
7. He had older siblings responsible for him and he did not cultivate abilities of his own.
8. He was forced to take over a lot of responsibilities as a child. And because he did not enjoy either the freedom of being a child, nor support from another, now he has the need to have this experience. He wants to be a child and to be taken care of.
9. He experienced very strict parents who did not permit him any form of expression and freedom.

10. His parents gave him the message they expected much from him in life, as he is a "special child."

D. Some beliefs that may lead towards these roles:
1. I am unable to face the difficulties of life.
2. I am not able to fulfill my parents' expectations.
3. They will reject me if I try and fail. It is better not to risk it.
4. Life is difficult and dangerous.
5. I need my parents (or my partner, siblings, etc.) in order to feel safe. Without them I am in danger.
6. I am weak, I am not clever or talented. I do not have any qualifications. I am not worthy and I will not be able to succeed.
7. I do not have the discrimination in order to take my own decisions. I need the others to tell me what to do.
8. If I grow up I will have to take responsibility for my life.
a. I will lose my purity. Grown ups are wicked and immoral. God will not love me.
b. I will fail.
c. Others will not take care of me.
d. I will be fatigued, I will be deprived of my easy living.

ROLE 5

THE GUILTY, THE SINNER, THE BAD, THE EVIL ONE

Key 1: I am guilty, I am a sinner, I am no good.
Key 2: I am not worthy of love , acceptance, or help from man or God.
Key 3: I am in danger (I am unprotected, subject to punishment).

A. Some possible ways of conduct:

EFFORT
1. He tries to prove his worth through:
a. Professional and social success.
b. Good deeds and sacrifices towards others.
c. Service towards others.
d. Speaking of his good actions.
e. Says how bad and incapable he is so that others around him will tell him the opposite.
f. Rejects, criticizes, accuses others for their sins and guilt.

SELF-DESTRUCTION

2. He undermines his health, happiness, success and the progress in his relationships:

a. By becoming addicted in food, sweets, alcohol, cigarettes, medicines, sedatives, drugs anything which would "numb" his mind, so as avoid experiencing pain and fear.

b. Breaks his relationships, usually testing the others' love and dedication with negative behavior, in order to push them away and to prove once more that "no one" can love him.

c. Sabotages his successes at the last minute, breaks or tests relationships in various ways.

d. He does not make efforts that might him liberate himself from his problems.

SURRENDERING TO THE ROLE

3. He acts as the "guilty, the bad, the cruel, the sinner, the incapable."

a. He does not take the others' needs into consideration.

b. He becomes "selfish" without feelings for others.

c. He commits crimes (lies, cheats, steals, kills, takes advantage of).

d. Criticizes, accuses, rejects and hurts others.

e. Generally he becomes "bad" out of bitterness, guilt, and self-rejection.

f. He hates "goodness" and fights against it.

4. He takes on a lot more work than he is able to execute in a peaceful manner, and looses his love and also his health in order to prove his worth.

5. He becomes easily upset, stressed and angry. He expects the worst from every situation or problem.

6. He cannot be at peace when others are not happy or satisfied, as he feels it is his fault.

7. Allows others to abuse him.

8. He does not allow time for his personal well-being.

9. Sees everyone as superior, better than him.

10. Lives with the concept of a continuous "must" in his mind. He does a lot of things because he must in order to be "good" and not because he loves doing it, or even wants to do it.

11. He cannot accept criticism at all, or even advice, because this would arouse his already present feelings of self-rejection.

12. He might demand of himself to be perfect in some area of his life (usually cleanliness, tidiness and appearance).

13. He perceives himself as selfish and he rejects himself for that.

A Catalog of Roles

14. He finds it difficult to ask for help, as he does not "deserve" it.

15. He finds it difficult to see, to hear about, or accept his qualities.

16. He is afraid that "punishment" will arrive sometime soon. "Life cannot be beautiful."

17. He is afraid of illness and of death (forms of punishment).

18. He finds it difficult to say "no" or says "no" in an angry way because of the fear of saying "no."

19. He gets angry when he does not receive acceptance from others – then he feels unworthy.

B. He may have an **internal or external conflict** with the roles of the bad, the right, the child, the parent, the capable, the perfect, the weak, the savior, the teacher, and the role of any authority.

C. Some **childhood experiences** which may lead one to these roles are:

1. The child received the message that he is bad, unworthy, guilty or was rejected in various ways:

a. He was told so by their criticism, their accusation, and by their rejection.

b. The parent himself was guilty, not good, rejected.

c. She was a girl, or a child born in a certain social class, religion, or race which was considered subordinate.

d. He was told that has badly "sinned."

e. He was told that God does not pardon, but rather, punishes the guilty.

f. His parents had serious problems and were unable to demonstrate stability and love towards their children, so the child concluded that "I am not worthy – I am bad."

g. The parents did not have time for the child.

h. A parent died and the child took it as an abandonment or as a punishment.

2. The child experienced violence or cruelty. The child came to a conclusion that "I am guilty – the others are right."

3. They caught the child playing with his genitals (alone or with other children) and he was told that he committed a sin, that he was evil.

4. Someone was hurt and the child was told that it was his fault.

5. The child was frequently told about his guilt and about God's punishment.

6. The child was sexually approached/molested and he/she felt guilty, that it was his/her fault.

7. He hated someone for their conduct and finally the other died or

some other calamity befell him. The child feels he is responsible.
8. He was programmed to feel responsible for others in general, and for whatever bad may befall them.

D. Some beliefs that may lead towards these roles:
1. I am guilty, bad, and I am not worthy because:
a. I have sinned.
b. I was not given love and affection by others and this means that I am not worthy.
c. I was told by others that I am not worthy.
d. I was abandoned by others (or they died) which means that I am not worthy (or that they do not love me; or it was God's punishment).
e. I failed to become perfect.
f. I failed to satisfy others.
g. I failed to protect others.
h. I failed to create a reality without problems for the others (then siblings, now children, partners, and parents).
i. I belong to a subordinate sex, race, religion, social class.
j. I am not clever, capable, successful.
k. God does not love me (I was told by my parents, grandparents).
l. Whoever makes mistakes is guilty, a sinner.

3. God does not pardon; he hates and punishes the sinners; my mistakes cannot be pardoned.
4. Whoever makes mistakes does not deserve to have a good time, to have good health, to be happy, successful, and be respected.
5. I am responsible for how others feel and I am guilty if they are not happy and satisfied.
6. I am guilty when others criticize or accuse me or when they complain or are not happy.
7. I am unworthy when others do not trust me.
8. I am unworthy when I do not reach my goals.
9. I am unworthy because:
 a. Eat too much.
 b. Smoke.
 c. Drink alcohol.
 d. Do not work hard enough.
 e. My children have problems.
 f. Others are not satisfied with me.
 g. I don't do what I could do.
 h. Do not help as I much as I could.

i. Have sexual urges.

10. I am unworthy no matter what I do.

11. I do not deserve that others would respect my needs.

12. I will be punished. Something bad will happen to me or to my family.

13. All others are good. I am unworthy.

14. I must do a lot more than others in order to be worthy.

15. When I am criticized or someone raises his voice at me, this means that I am in danger and not worthy.

16. I must be perfect (in cleanliness, tidiness, order, appearance) to deserve love and acceptance.

17. I am selfish.

18. I do not have the right to ask others for help.

19. No one can love me.

20. I do not have the right to say "no."

ROLE 6

THE PARENT THE SAVIOR, THE TEACHER, THE RESPONSIBLE

Key 1: I am responsible for the others' reality.

Key 2: Without me, the others cannot progress, cannot be well.

Key 3: It's my fault if the others are not well.

A. Some possible conducts:

1. He gets worried about others. He becomes stressful about their situations and their problems.

2. He advises them and he tries to control them, he even exerts pressure on them (for "their own good," or prevents them from making a mistake and thus possibly ruining his "results").

3. He criticizes and rejects others when they make mistakes or when they do not follow his directions or orders.

4. He gives advice even to those who do not ask for it.

5. He cannot feel at peace when others have problems. He thinks he has to solve their problems himself.

6. He gets disappointed when others do not follow his advice.

7. He rejects himself for not being able to "save' others, or to solve their problems.

8. He attracts to himself people with problems.

9. He finds it difficult to confess or express his weaknesses, his needs, his fears or his problems. He fears that in doing so, others

will see his faults and lose respect for him.

10. He finds it difficult to express his feelings.

11. He ignores his own problems and he occupies himself with the problems of others.

B. He may have **internal or external conflicts** with the roles of the child, the rebel, the bad, the guilty, the suppressed, the victim, and with other people who also play the role of the teacher, the savior or the parent.

C. Some **childhood experiences** leading to roles such as these are:

1. He experienced someone who played this role in his childhood environment.

2. He was programmed that to be worthy he should:

a. Possess a powerful position.

b. Advise others.

c. Be cleverer than others.

d. Save others.

e. Not have problems.

f. Sacrifice himself for the whole.

3. As a child he experienced pain, injustice, was humiliated because of some weakness, and he decided not to ever experience that role again, so he takes the role of the superior one – the one with no problems.

4. He was programmed to feel responsible for others and for whatever is happening to them. He now continues playing this role as an adult.

5. He felt shame and rejection for one or more of his parents and he thus decided not to become like him/her, but to be superior to them.

6. He experienced abandonment and now he tries to find a way of making himself indispensable to others.

7. He did not experience enough affection, tenderness or love and he is seeking to find these through these roles.

8. He was made to doubt his worth and is searching through these roles to find it.

9. As a child he had to look after a sick person and he is continuing in the same role.

10. He was told that he would not achieve anything in his life and now he is trying to prove them wrong.

11. He had a teacher or a parent who did not play his role well, and

the child decided to play the same role correctly when he grew up.

12. Others were not trustworthy or punctual and he decides to take a power role.

13. He experienced oppression, now using these roles, he feels freer.

D. Some **beliefs** that might sustain these roles are:

1. I am responsible for the others':

a. Health.

b. Happiness.

c. Success.

d. Harmony.

e. Evolution.

f. Security.

g. For whatever is happening to them.

2. If I am not able to create a perfect reality for them, I have failed in my role and I am not worthy.

3. If others are not happy with me, I have therefore failed and I am not worthy.

4. If others do not trust me, I am not worthy.

5. If others do not listen to me, do not obey me, do not follow my advice, then I am incapable in this role, and I am unworthy.

6. If I am no good in my role, I will not be respected, I will be unworthy of their esteem. I will end up alone. I am in danger.

7. If I am not in control of things around me, anything can go wrong. I cannot trust others. If I am not in control, I am in danger.

8. If I show weakness or needs or if I have vices:

a. I will be rejected, I will not be wanted, and I am in danger.

b. My weaknesses will be used as a means to hurt me, I am in danger.

9. I am worthy only if I am in the position of authority – i.e. teacher, savior, parent. Only then can I feel safe and secure.

10. If I am needed (as a teacher, a parent, a savior), I will not be abandoned. I will not be alone.

11. Alone, I am in danger.

12. If I am needed, I will be loved and I will receive what I need from others.

13. In this role I can be in control.

ROLE 7
THE REBEL, THE REVOLUTIONARY,
THE NEGATIVE ONE, THE ANTAGONIST

Key 1. My freedom and justice are in danger.

Key 2: I have to fight for freedom and justice.
Key 3: I need the others.

A. Some possible conducts:

REACTION
1. Does the opposite of:
a. What he is told.
b. What he thinks others want from him.
c. "Must do."
d. . What society asks.
e. . What is "right," "good."

SELF-DESTRUCTION
2. He is destructive to himself.
a. Using various substances inappropriately – food, alcohol , cigarettes, medicine, sedatives, drugs.
b. By having relationships with negative people who, as a result, ruin his happiness.
c. By avoiding success by being inconsistent, reacting negatively, being lazy.
d. By fighting against others.
In these ways he rejects his parents' and society's concept of happiness and "success."
Self-destruction is also a "weapon" he uses to hurt those who have suppressed him and treated him badly.

BATTLE
3. He fights against those whom he considers "bad - evil" people, the "unfair," the "abusers," the "top dogs."
a. Criticizes, accuses, rejects, and wants to change people he thinks represent evil or authority.
b. Behaves aggressively or violently.
c. In every discussion he will find something he doesn't agree with. Whether the subject is important or not, is irrelevant (inwardly he might even agree).
d. Presses others to believe what he believes. He finds it difficult to experience unity with those who have different beliefs or habits.

NON-PARTICIPATION
4. He does not participate in social functions or in whatever he considers a source of injustice such as:

a. Church, religion, spirituality, philosophy.
c. Socially-accepted activities.
d. Socially-accepted dress.
e. Language of the norm.
f. Money.
g. Family activities.

INNER CONFLICT
5. In reality, he is not in conflict with others, but with a part of himself that still:
a. Accepts social, religious, political beliefs.
b. Believes he needs to do or have what the society says to be worthy and secure.
c. Is afraid to be alone without the affirmation and protection of those very ideas he rejects.
d. He rejects the part of himself that resembles others. When he is liberated from these inner conflicts, he will not need to react outwardly anymore.
6. He tests the others' love with a negative behavior.
7. He does not admit being grateful, and pretends not to be.

B. He is in frequent **conflict** with the roles of the righteous, the good, the savior, the teacher, the parent, and authority.

C. Some **childhood experiences** possibly leading to similar roles:
1. Oppression from parents, teachers and others.
2. Injustice, rejection, humiliation, hurt, criticism. Violence towards himself or towards others in his environment.
3. He has lived social injustices, e.g. military occupation, dictatorship, racism.
4. He experienced an adult who played these roles (rebel, revolutionary, etc.).
5. He was told that he was no good, he was incapable, and that he would achieve nothing in his life.
6. He had an ideal he believed he could not "reach" and thus he rejects it.
7. His self-worth was rejected.
8. He was told that he could not make it alone in life.
9. He had to either agree with others or do what they wanted, in order to receive their love.
10. He experienced abandonment and he interpreted it as an

injustice.

11. Sick people in his environment were the cause for his loss of freedom.

12. He/she experienced rape, or was sexually abused.

13. He was frequently told about guilt and the punishment from God.

14. As a child he came in contact with hypocrisy on a large scale.

15. One of the parents was unfaithful to the other.

16. He was a spoiled child and he does not have self-confidence; he feels dependent and reacts negatively towards dependency.

D. Some beliefs able to sustain roles such as these:

1. I am in danger from, parents, teachers, and authority.

2. I might lose my:

a. Freedom.

b. Dignity.

c. My worth.

d. Security.

3. I might be treated unjustly, I might get hurt or humiliated.

4. I am weak, incapable, and vulnerable. I cannot succeed in this society.

a. To be successful.

b. To protect myself.

c. To become happy.

5. I need others, society, and/or family for my security and my happiness.

6. I need the other's approval. I am not worthy; I am insecure without their approval and support.

7. I am not clever. I do not have inner knowledge or strength in order to live my life without others.

8. I am in danger when others do not agree with me because:

a. I might not be right.

b. I need them.

c. They might use control over me and I will get hurt.

9. If I do not react, they might think they are right and I will lose my rights and my strength.

10. If I appear to destroy myself, this will upset them and make them feel guilty.

11. When others agree with me then I am right; then I am worthy and safe.

12. I have to fight for liberty and justice.

13. I am not loved, thus I must protect myself from others.

14. This is a war of control. If I do not fight I will lose my freedom.
15. If I admit that they are right they will use this against me on another occasion.
16. People are hypocrites and underhanded; I cannot trust them.
17. I will never be able to achieve as much as my parent. It is better if I do not participate at all. I should reject the whole success game.
18. I am a girl (woman) and I must protect my rights in a "man's world."
19. I am a victim of racism and I must protect myself.

ROLE 8

THE CLEVER, THE WELL-INFORMED, THE SUPERIOR, THE EXPERT, THE COUNSELOR, THE INTERROGATOR, THE CRITIC

Key 1: Whoever knows best is more worthy.
Key 2: I must appear knowledgeable to be accepted, loved or respected.
Key 3: Then I will be accepted; I will be loved and I will be safe and secure.

A. Some possible behaviors:

1. He talks too much, stating information with the intention of making his knowledge evident. Sometimes directly and at others indirectly through questions or references indicating his "knowledge."
2. He enters quite easily in an "competitive discussion" with the intention of showing others how much he knows (whether the subject is important for him or not is irrelevant).
3. He easily takes opposition views for the sake of an argument.
4. He usually refers to various books, teachers and other sources.
5. He "advises" frequently or orders others.
6. If you do not follow his advise, he gets upset and he even might attack you.
7. He talks abundantly about irrelevant details.
8. He admires people with a vast knowledge or "a quick mind" while he rejects others with limited knowledge and a "slow mind."
9. He is afraid perhaps there are others in the company who would "appear cleverer" and thus he would lose his position, the others' respect and thus, his self-worth.
10. He uses various strategies in order to win battles at home and at work; in this manner he attracts negative emotions from others.

11. He may speak degradingly about others with "less knowledge."

12. He gets bored among a company where he cannot use his brain.

13. He frequently plays the game of "who is right."

14. He tends to be ironic, sarcastic and sometimes even mocks others.

15. He may tend to criticize others and try to tell them how to do things "right."

16. He "knows better" than the others.

B. He gets into a **conflict** with others playing the same role. Also with the powerful, the teachers, the saviors, the parents, the perfect.

C. Some **childhood experiences** leading to these roles:

1. The child received the message that knowledge creates value, superiority, and security.

2. He has been hurt, rejected, and/or demeaned because of a lack of knowledge or lack of swiftness in the mind.

3. He has been hurt or rejected for other reasons (e.g. beauty, physical strength, social characteristics) and he learned to regard his intelligence as his only asset, so he decides that without it he has no value at all.

4. He is ashamed of, or rejects, one of his parents for her/his limited mental capacities and he decides not to ever become like that.

5. He experienced a parent or another important person playing this role.

6. He realized that through intelligence and a quick mind he could avoid work or negative situations.

7. By being clever, he or someone else received the admiration or the attention and love of others.

8. He experienced abandonment and felt lonely, deciding that he must be very clever in order to survive.

9. He has been compared with others:

a. That he was less worthy.

b. He was more worthy.

10. His parents needed badly (for their own survival or security) their child to get an education.

11. They told the child that he is not clever and that he will never do anything in his life.

D. Some possible beliefs able to sustain these roles.

1. My self-worth is measured according to my intelligence.

2. My intelligence is measured by:

a. How it is compared with others.

b. How much information it contains.

c. How swiftly it functions.

d. How correct it is.

e. How much others admire it or show with their behavior their respect for it.

3. I do not know much. I have no self-worth. I will be rejected.

4. I will not be wanted. I will remain alone, and then I will be in danger.

5. I must learn a lot; I must cultivate my mind.

6. I must show others that my mind is sharp so I will be accepted and loved, and then I will be safe and secure.

7. If there is another person more knowledgeable than me, he would be loved more. I must show them that I know more than him. I must belittle him and aggrandize myself.

8. If I have more knowledge than others I can:

a. Control them, use them and rule them.

b. Reject them.

c. Make them need me, and then I will be worthy and secure.

9. I will not be able to be clever enough compared with others. I will reject the whole game. He then abandons this role and plays other ones, e.g. the rebel, the lazy one, the revolutionary, the incapable, the sick etc).

10. I must never accept that the other is right because in this way I will lose my self-worth.

11. Life is difficult and I am alone; I must be clever in order to survive.

12. Only the intelligent receive love, attention and the tenderness they need.

13. I owe it my parents to gain an education, and to become well-known for my education and knowledge.

14. I must show them how much I am worth.

15. I am responsible for others and for myself, so I must be clever.

16. If I am clever; I can protect myself from exploitation and cruelty from others.

17. I do not want to be like my parent(s).

ROLE 9

THE INDIFFERENT, THE IRRESPONSIBLE, THE LIBERATED, THE SNOTTY, THE SENSELESS, THE EVASIVE ONE, THE ALOOF

Key 1. Whoever has responsibilities or does not meet with his obligations toward them is in danger.

Key 2. I will either suffer or fail if I accept responsibilities.

A. Some possible conducts:

1. Avoids responsibilities as much as possible, not due to laziness, but because he doubts his capacities for success.
2. Seems indifferent or insensitive towards matters that are important to others.
3. He lets others solve his problems.
4. He feels oppression and injustice easily.
5. Allows matters to linger until the last minute.
6. He walks out from relationships, jobs and responsibilities when he feels overly pressured.
7. He may criticize or mock people who "take things seriously."
8. He takes on responsibilities or gives promises, but he is conscientious in executing them.
9. Says "yes, you are right, I will change, I will become more responsible" but does nothing about it.
10. He complains that he is being suppressed, and is not allowed creative freedom.
11. He criticizes the system in general.
12. He rejects himself on account of his mistakes, in order to hear the opposite – that it "does not matter," that "it's O.K."
13. He may not speak much. He may not express himself much.

B. There might be a tendency towards **conflicts** with the roles of the teacher, the righteous, the responsible, the savior, the clever, the parent, the powerful, and the efficient.

C. Some possible **childhood experiences** leading to such roles:
1. He experienced rejection, humiliation, hurt, fear, and thus, decided not to have anything to do with the outer world.
2. He had very negative experiences concerning situations of responsibility (e.g. responsibilities towards siblings).
3. Experienced failure in some of his efforts.
4. He was told he was incapable and he will never do anything in his

life.

5. He was compared to others and:

a. He was told he was inferior (he will never make it).

b. He was told he was superior (and he must always be "the best" in order to be worthy).

6. Realized that he had to be very effective in order to be respected and loved – that he is not worthy if he is not efficient and effective.

7. He had the experience of an ideal person in this role.

8. He had the experience of an ideal person playing the role of the strong, the capable, the successful, the perfect, and out of reaction the child abandons and rejects the effort. "I will not be able to make it."

9. He experienced abandonment and he decided that he was incapable so others should take care of him.

10. He did not receive much attention, tenderness and love and so using this role now, others will take care of him.

11. A parent failed somehow.

12. He was a spoiled child and he never learned to do anything for himself and for others.

D. Some beliefs able to sustain roles such as these:

1. I am worthy as long as I achieve a lot of things, as long as I am capable.

2. Having a lot of responsibilities and being able to successfully deal with them, gives one self-worth.

3. "But I am not worthy because I can't, because:"

a. Life is difficult.

b. I am not clever, able, or strong enough.

c. I might fail.

4. If I try and fail, I will be rejected and I will be alone and then I am in danger.

5. It is better if I do not try to play; I am not interested, so I reject this game.

6. If I accept responsibilities, I will exhaust myself and I will suffer. If I do nothing, others will take over.

7. Others are more competent than I am.

8. I reject their neurotic and stressful life.

9. It's better not to play at all, than to play and lose.

10. If I activate myself, they will think that I don't need them; they will not pay any attention to me anymore.

11. Responsibility carries with it criticism from others.

12. Since God punishes our mistakes, I will do nothing so I shall not

make a mistake.

13. I do not want to fail like my parent.

14. I am a spoiled child; I must be taken care of.

ROLE 10
THE GENERAL, THE DICTATOR, THE AGGRESSIVE, THE AGGRESSOR, THE INTIMIDATOR

Key 1. My worth and my security are in danger.

Key 2. I must protect myself and others from the battle of life.

Key 3. Strength is the solution for everything.

A. Some possible behaviors:

1. Shout, accuses, rejects, demeans others when:

a. They make a mistake.

b. They do not function according to his concepts, instructions or orders.

2. He finds it difficult to be democratic in his relationships with others.

3. He is always right and others are wrong.

4. Cultivates fear in order to gain obedience and the cooperation from others.

5. He usually has double standards: for himself and for others.

6. He is usually very sensitive and vulnerable, behind all this toughness.

7. He considers himself superior and he expects others to serve him.

8. He attacks before anyone has the chance to do the same.

B. He has **conflicts** more frequently, both inwardly and/or outwardly with the roles of the child, the guilty, the victim, the fearful, the incapable, the teacher, the parent, and with others playing the same roles as he.

C. Some **childhood experiences** leading to these roles:

1. He experienced someone playing these roles.

2. He himself was a victim of these roles as a child.

3. He experienced injustice and he decided that life is difficult and that he has to protect himself aggressively.

4. He experienced a lot of anger as a child, and this anger is now surging out towards the people closest to him.

5. He was a spoiled child, and now he feels that everyone should serve him.

A Catalog of Roles

6. He was ashamed of one of his parents for being "weak" and for being used, and he has decided that he is going to be tough.

7. He was programmed that God punishes. He might also believe that he is the "hand of God" keeping order in the world.

8. He experienced humiliation, so he considers this role the only security he possesses, so that nothing like this ever happens again.

9. He doubts his self-worth and his mental capacities and he conceals all these with this role, in order to regain his worth.

10. He heard that men are like this.

11. As a woman she might decide that this is the only way to protect herself.

12. He was made to feel bad, sinful, unjust, so he accepts this role; it fits him.

13. He learned that he is responsible for others and he found this role effective in order to be obeyed.

D. Some beliefs able to sustain roles such as these.

1. I am not worthy, I am in danger; my security is in danger.

2. Life and people in general are dangerous, difficult and I will be hurt.

3. I must be tough and aggressive in order to be:

a. Worthy.

b. Superior.

c. Keep them at a distance, so I will not get hurt.

4. I do not want to be "stepped on" like my father (my mother).

5. I am alone in this life. No one cares about me. If I do not take care of myself, nobody will do so.

6. I am the only one who is right. They must listen to me and obey me.

7. No one loves me. I was not given the love and affection I needed. Others must pay for this.

8. Only the powerful, the leader is worthy.

9. I must keep them at a distance so as not to get hurt.

10. Since they consider me to be a bad and unfair person anyway, let it be thus.

11. I am responsible for others. If I do not give orders using a little fear, there's going to be problems. I will not be in a position to be in control.

ROLE 11

THE PARTNER, THE SPOUSE

Key 1: My self-worth depends on how good a partner I am.
Key 2: I must be a good partner in order to be worthy and safe.
A. Some possible behaviors:
1. He tries to receive affirmation concerning her/his self-worth and security through the other in various ways:
a. By receiving tenderness, caressing, affection, embrace, and sex.
b. Receiving positive words of affirmation.
c. Being together.
d. Having exclusivity (the other loves and wants only me).
2. He gets upset and becomes negative when he does not receive the above affirmations.
3. He gets upset when his partner:
a. Is not well, happy, successful.
b. Is not happy with him.
c. Shows an interest – love to others.
d. Shows interest in other activities where he cannot or does not want to participate.
e. Does not agree with him on various matters.
4. Has conflicts with his partner concerning needs and values.
5. Loves and gives special support and affection to the partner.
6. He becomes devoted and gives a lot of energy and time in order to make his partner happy.
7. He does not find any other reason for life except this role; he is in constant fear of losing his partner (and thus lose the only source of security, self-esteem and reason for existence).
8. He might be bored of the role and wish for freedom:
a. He does not participate fully.
b. He is away a lot, and when he is there, the connection is not substantial.
c. He might create parallel relationships.
9. He may play any of the other roles in relation to his partner, e.g. the child, the parent, the dictator, the savior, the rebel, the perfect one, the powerful, the weak, the incapable, the sick, the fearful, the indifferent, the irresponsible, etc.
10. Competes with his partner in relation to who is more right, intelligent, good, powerful, abused, successful, effective, spiritual, etc.
11. Competes for the acceptance, love, and admiration of the children.

B. He would have various **conflicts** with his partner, in respect to other roles he plays in the relationship. This role might clash with other roles he needs to play as a parent, a businessman, a child (of his parents).

1. All childhood experiences construct this role, they can, however, be divided into specific categories:

a. All impressions about close relationships he gained from his parents or others.

b. All the messages he received (from actions or situations):

1. About marriage.

2. About men.

3. About women.

c. All the messages he received about himself.

d. All the messages he received about life.

e. All the messages about when one is worthy and when one is safe and secure.

2. He will react in various ways towards these messages and experiences.

a. Being programmed subconsciously, he would function in a manner similar to that of his parents.

b. It is possible (at least in his first relationships if he has more than one) to attract a partner who would treat him:

    1. In the same way he was treated by one or both his parents.

    2. In the same way one parent treated the other, e.g. replay scenes he experienced as a child in receiving and experiencing to a great extent similar to her/his treatment as before. In many cases, he himself will play the role of the parent towards the other partner (or the children) in the same manner he himself experienced it from his parents.

c. He will react (rejecting the conduct of one of the parents) and he will try not to "repeat" the same mistakes. As long as the rejection exists, he will possibly not be able to liberate himself from this behavior mechanism he rejects.

D. Some **beliefs** able to sustain roles such as these:

1. I am a woman/man (and not an eternal soul without gender)

2. My self-worth depends upon my partner.

a. Whether I have a partner.

b. Whether s/he loves and takes care only of me.

c. Whether s/he gives me what I need.

d. Whether s/he is happy with me.

e. Whether s/he is healthy, happy, successful.
f. Whether others accept and approve of her/him.
3. My security depends upon my partner:
a. Whether s/he loves me exclusively.
b. Whether s/he is strong, stable, and successful.
c. Whether s/he is honest, calm.
d. Whether... other.....
4. A person alone by himself cannot be safe and secure.
5. A person alone is not socially acceptable.

ROLE 12

MAN / WOMAN

Key 1. I am a man/woman.
Key 2. My self-worth is dependent on how affirmed I am in this role.

A. Some possible behaviors:
1. Tries to prove his/her worth:
a. By appearing powerful, indifferent, tough, with no weaknesses.
b. By appearing good, right, perfect.
c. By professional and financial success.
d. By knowledge and mental clarity.
e. By being able to express emotions and needs.
f. By being sexually attractive to or successful with the opposite sex.
g. By having a strong or attractive body.
h. By being aggressive and having a loud voice.
i. By doing a lot of things, being engaged in many activities.
j. By appearing spiritual and pure.
k. By not accepting arguments, acting as a dictator.

2. Tries to win the other's attention (and thus security and self-worth).
a. Through illness.
b. Through weakness, fear or emotional problems.
c. Through sexuality.
d. Through conflict and aggressiveness.
e. Flirting with others.
3. Plays competitive games with people of the same or the opposite sex, as to who is more intelligent, right, good, strong, victim, successful, quick, effective, spiritual, etc.

4. He rejects the parent of the same sex and so he rejects his own sex. Sometime this can lead to homosexuality.

5. Rejects the parent of the opposite sex and thus he has a continuous lack of trust and often is antagonistic to, or rejects, the opposite sex and also his/her partner.

C. Some **experiences** indicating how one would play the role of the man or the woman.

1. All the messages he received through words and behaviors in relation to:

a. When a man is worthy and respected.

b. When a woman worthy and respected.

c. How must a man be.

d. How must a woman be.

e. What is the relationship between them.

2. From which one of the parents he received more love and acceptance.

3. Whether he experienced abandonment by one of the parents.

4. The behavior of one parent towards the other.

5. How he saw his parents behave towards others and how others towards them.

D. Beliefs sustaining the existence of these roles:

1. I am a woman/man.

2. I am safe and secure and I am worthy only through this role.

3. I must have a partner to be worthy and to be safe.

4. A close relationship is the goal of life and the basic meaning of life.

5. Close relationships are difficult and I will possibly get hurt because:

a. The other cannot love me as I am.

b. The other will hurt me.

c. The other will abandon me.

6. I cannot let go in a close relationship because I will get hurt.

7. I am worthy when:

a. My partner loves me exclusively.

b. The opposite sex wants me and admires me.

c. When I am better than others.

d. I am wanted sexually.

8. Women should sacrifice themselves for their husband (to obey him).

9. Men must be more capable and intelligent than their wives.

Support materials

1. Free Audio clips with Lectures and relaxation techniques:
http://www.HolisticHarmony.com/audioclips/index.asp

2. Free Articles on health, happiness, relationships, communication, etc.:
http://www.HolisticHarmony.com/ezines/index.asp

3. Books and ebooks at:
http://www.HolisticHarmony.com/ebookscb/index.asp

4. Learn About Energy Psychology at:
http://www.HolisticHarmony.com/eft/index.asp

5. Become Trained as a Life Coach over the internet at:
http://www.HolisticHarmony.com/introholisticcoach.asp

6. Free Teleclasses and lectures as audio files:
http://www.HolisticHarmony.com/teleclasses/index.asp

7. Free email courses
http://www.HolisticHarmony.com/courses/index.asp

8. Nine New Coaching Tools
http://www.HolisticHarmony.com/coachquestions/index.asp

9. Free Biweekly ezine "Clarity"
http://www.HolisticHarmony.com
* *

More about life coaching at:
http://www.HolisticHarmony.com/introholisticcoach.asp
http://www.HolisticHarmony.com/coachquestions/index.asp
* *

Books and e-books available by Robert Elias Najemy

at http://www.HolisticHarmony.com/ebookscb/index/asp

1. Universal Philosophy

2. The Art of Meditation

3. Contemporary Parables

4. The Mystical Circle of Life

5. Relationships of Conscious Love

6. The Miracles of Love and Wisdom

7. Free to Be Happy with Energy Psychology

8. Saram – The Adventures of a Soul and Insight into the Male Psyche

9. The Psychology of Happiness

10. The Adventures of Petros - Revealing the Truth